SCRUMNASTICS

By Nick Hewyn Holmes

Scrumnastics: *"Harnessing the unique power of the team to unearth and unleash as yet undreamt-of wealth, technology, products and services for the benefit of all."*

ISBN-13: 978-1-9161604-0-8

9 781916 160408

Published by Scrumnastics Press
792, Wilmslow Road, Didsbury.
Manchester. M20 6UG
United Kingdom.

To Sarah, I was going to call my book "How to Manage People and Not Become an Axe Murderer." I hope it works for you. Cheers Nick October '22

Dedication:

For Carol, Sam, Matthew and Sian. Thanks for putting up with your dad while he made this completely bonkers project come to life

My grandfather, Jack Bowen, who was a 'Clerk of Works.' He oversaw the building of Cwmbran New Town in the 1950's and 1960's. He divided all people into just two types: Talkers and Do-ers.

Every night he would bring huge, blue inked, incredibly complicated drawings home with plans for shopping centres, roads, roundabouts, schools, freshwater pipelines, foul water pipelines, gas mains and electricity pylon lines for the new town of Cwmbran.

When I asked him what they were for he would say, "Nick, I have to make these high-fallutin' plans for the pen-pushers, who don't know what they are doing, so that they keep out of the hair of the skilled builders, who actually DO know what they are doing."

That taught me, as a five-year-old, almost everything I ever needed to learn about talkers and do-ers and how you need to treat them differently.

This book is for the do-ers, I hope it helps you do **_more_**.

"When bad men combine, the good must associate; else they will fall one by one, an unpitied sacrifice in a contemptible struggle." - Edmund Burke.

CONTENTS

Contents

Foreword

I have worked with Nick Holmes in several large-scale (to be honest, humongous scale) operations. Usually with the kind of pressure heaped upon him that no-one really deserves or wants.

The way out of a pressure cooker environment is through management, when the pressure is on, the stars shine and correct methods come to the surface, it really is that simple. And handling such pressure using Nick's application method of using Scrum is key to productivity.

No method is fool proof, it is how you apply the system that counts and can you apply and improve productivity instead of just applying a methodology for its own sake.

Nick's use of Scrum and Agile techniques is unique, using the methodology to manage people, tasks, events and the often-encountered surprises of an everyday work cycle and smoothing over and managing the crises before they are even acknowledged as such. What a lot of managers always miss out is the handling of people, well without handling people correctly the rest of it all falls apart.

Agile process are often looked at as widget production techniques, used for "the guys in the back" who are producing something tangible, but people are and always will be the focus of any management methodology, but people just don't know it. Nick does, and his book highlights it.

Nick's book differs from most other Scrum books out there, because it is not just teaching you the processes (called events, formerly ceremonies) and the roles, but showing you how they should be used, who should be involved and why involving the correct people and attributing them to the correct roles produces results, and more importantly how involving the incorrect people does not.

Nick approaches the problems of scrum in a humorous, but accurate and factual way. Ensuring that productivity is the focus of the teaching. Whether your teams are close at hand, or remote, management is the key to ensuring that they are productive at all times. Scrum can achieve this, but scrum used in Nick's manner ensures this.

There is nothing worse than a dry lecture or a dry book or a dry tutorial, Nick's book is the exact opposite – it's meant to be enjoyed and absorbed, there are great stories, all relevant, showing the correct approach to adopting Scrum and making it work, for you, at the optimum.

Read the book, enjoy it, but more than anything else – Apply what you've learned.

Laurie Williams M.Sc., Senior Programme Manager, Agile Alliance Certified Scrum Master, Knowledge Management advocate.

Acknowledgements

An astonishing amount of thanks go to a lot of people who encouraged me to write this book. Chief among them are:

Carol Ann Holmes for simply years of support. You are a star. Thank you with all my heart.

Sam, Matthew, and Sian for putting up with dad while writing this. Actually, now I come to it, for putting up with dad full stop. And Ursula Thomas ('Auntie Urf'), the Mary Poppins of Upper Cwmbran for never not believing in me.

Laurie Williams, (my mate Laurie,) the very finest old-school colleague, Scrum Master, Programme Manager, and Project Manager for laughs, great ideas and keeping me sane whilst working side by side during some of the maddest projects and programmes ever done by anyone. Thanks bro. ("Geoff! Tell Jeanie I love her!")

Peter Lumley, formerly of Thomas Cook Travel, for allowing me to watch him as he led his team for over a decade as I consulted for him whilst I worked for three different companies. His quiet, gentle, and astonishingly and above all, effective manner of team leadership has been an inspiration for my own work as a leader.

Iain Elliot and Ed Mallen for making me laugh like a drain.

Lyn Absolon and 'Ow Bri' Brian Davy, for decades of friendship and raucous laughter. Also for David McCullough. I wish you could have seen this, old friend. Sorry it took so long.

Pastor Robert Parkinson, the finest fisherman of souls I have ever met, and Aileen Doherty, who continued to show faith in me when mine had evaporated.

 A special thank you to the hundreds of people I have trained, coached and mentored over the years. Your input made every one of the courses, and all of this book so much better than it would have otherwise been.

And finally, whatever mistakes there are in here in this book, they are mine and mine alone.

About Nick Hewyn Holmes

"Nick joined a de-motivated team with unclear processes... within 2-3 weeks he had made a huge impact on morale and within 6 weeks had doubled output per person."

Nick Hewyn Holmes

Nick Hewyn Holmes has been doing Scrum since 1995 and running completely remote Scrum teams since 2016. Nick was the EMEA project manager for the first rollout of remote offices for a global company in 1996.

He was programme manager for the £15 million removal of the 40+ million paper driving licences, and MOT 2 (30+ million vehicles annually).

He even uses Scrum to run rock bands. If he can do this for his rock stars, then you know he knows how to get you to run your rock stars.

* * *

Nick has been doing Japanese style management since 1995, where he learned it while consulting at Panasonic Europe. He's been doing Lean and Scrum from that time, and he has been running teams that work remotely on a full-time basis since 2016.

He was an Information Technology Manager by 29, Information Technology Director at 32 and a Managing Director at 35. He has been a managing director ever since.

He has worked offering management consultancy for the Bank Of England, Barclaycard, HSBC, Ministry of Defence, Driver and Vehicle Licencing Agency, Department for Education, Dow Chemical, IBM, Cognos, Astra Pharmaceuticals, Boehringer-Ingelheim, ICI, Christian Salvesen, Royal National Pension Fund For Nurses, Zurich Re, Co-operative Insurance Services, Thomas Cook Travel and Panasonic Europe, amongst others.

Nick was the Europe, Middle East and Africa (EMEA) Project Manager for the EMEA part of the world-wide, and first rollout of remote working sales office service for a Global company in 1996. His territory was every office in every major city between Dublin and Moscow and from Stockholm down to Cairo.

His project he is most proud of is "**the project that never was,**" where he got a retired civil service mandarin to persuade a FTSE company to put up a free to use job site for teachers and schools by suggesting that the Department for Education would do its own service and destroy so their billion-pound business model. (It's at the back of the book).

These days he runs his own teams, and trains, coaches and mentors online teams for clients. He is very expensive.

He has a absurd passion for aluminium-bodied Jaguar V8s and tries his very best not to die horribly when sailing off the coast of the United Kingdom.

He is also the author of the "Leadernomics," and "Scrumnastics" online series of video courses and runs some invitation only business growth clubs for business owners called Leadernomics Elite and

Scrumnastics Elite.

He is currently writing "**Do Not Go Gentle,**" the keto weight loss and kettlebell fitness book for those in their 60's to aspire to be, or want to stay, vigorous and strong and who would rather rewire than retire.

He is also guitarist, singer and songwriter for the finest male-menopause rock band in the world, the Nick Holmes Band.

Testimonials For Nick Hewyn Holmes

1: "The best manager I have ever had." **C Shepherd, Barclays Secured Loan.**

2: "Nick joined a de-motivated team with unclear processes… within 2-3 weeks he had made a huge impact on morale and within 6 weeks had doubled output per person. More importantly, his management legacy means that the high standards continued after he left" - **Infrastructure Portfolio Manager (Grade 6) DVLA.**

3: "Nick has an amazing knack of managing complexity. Drawing on keen analytical and technical skills and first-rate people skills, he has been able to guide us through a Discovery and give us confidence that our direction, although unexpected, was not just legitimate but ground-breaking. He has also generously coached key team members, leaving behind an agile legacy and an enthusiastic team!" **Assistant Director, Pupil Premium Strategy, Department for Education.**

4: "Nick was a great asset to our modernisation work in Department for Education. He initially focussed on leading a ministerial initiative through Discovery phase and early Alpha phase work.

During that time, he pushed hard for user need and developed a route forward which would allow low risk development that allowed Department for Education the best of both worlds; to aim for an end-state solution but build in a number of phases that meant we could look at how industry evolved to our plans.

Following his impact on that area, we retained Nick to help us progress thinking on moving from 'projects in silos' to blending resource and governance across services more readily.

My staff found Nick insightful and knowledgeable, as well as a great coach. He helped me identify leadership challenges and opportunities as a second pair of eyes."   - **Deputy Director, Data**

Modernisation Division, Data Group, Department for Education.

5: "You can give Nick Holmes any business problem and he will always come up with a solution." **Pete Lumley - Thomas Cook Travel**

6: "I can vouch that, as a manager, you're definitely not a psychopath. Some people I've worked with think good management is finding a spark of a problem, let it take hold or even fan the flames and then get everyone to drop everything to man the hoses to put out the fire and then tell everyone how good they are at fixing problems. Not you. You sort it quietly." **N. Griffiths, - Analytics Team, FirstPlus Financial.**

Testimonials For The Book

Testimonials For "Scrumnastics" On Amazon - (4.7 Stars)

Customer reviews

☆☆☆☆☆ 4.7 out of 5 ⟩

4 global ratings

Top reviews from United Kingdom

 John

☆☆☆☆☆ Verified Purchase

A real must for understanding Scrum and agile from a renown leader in the field

Reviewed in the United Kingdom on 9 June 2021

This is less a book of academia (though the author does make multiple and detailed reference to academic works) it is more a manual of how to deliver using agile methodology. Think a 'Haynes' manual for srum and agile delivery. Supporting all the way from the novice, to the practitioner and expert. A how to guide and a reference manual with lots of great tips and techniques for creating and leading high performing teams. The real world examples and the experience of the author are full of colour and give genuine advice on how to achieve. No Agile multi-disciplinary team should be without a copy

* * *

Mike Wilson

★★★★★ Verified Purchase

Much Needed Pragmatic Approach to Scrum

Reviewed in the United Kingdom on 10 June 2021

My personal experience of Agile and Scrum is that the training is often wrapped neatly in theory, theory that works in perfect delivery environments with everyone keen to make it work. This book and the training provided adds realism and gives pragmatic guidance on using Scrum and Agile in the real world. As a Scrum Master, it's reassured me that what I have been doing to get round non-standard challenges is absolutely fine. More importantly it's given me much more in the way of insight into how to develop for the future. Definitely recommend this to Scrum Masters and to anyone else adapting to Agile methodologies.

One person found this helpful

Helpful   Report

 Nigel FN

★★★★☆

Will you be releasing an Audible version?

CHAPTER 1 - OKAY, SO NOW WHAT DO WE DO?

Introduction

"Change Is Not Necessary, Survival Is Not Mandatory."-
William Edwards Deming[1]

This book is five separate manuals on five separate areas of leadership and management. This is a 'How To' book to help you lead and manage better so that you and your teams get more done, quicker, better and with better quality.

How can it possibly help you do that? In three ways. This book aims to:

1. Teach you how to lead people by influencing them rather than trying to impress them. Leadership is a practical craft and a skill - you get better the more you do it. It is not an academic subject. Although there are a squillion academic books on leadership that tell you what leaders do, few of them teach you how to lead. This one does.

2. Rather than scratching around trying to build your own, bespoke method of managing people, it shows you how to implement a proven, effective, agile, world class management system called Scrum. There are more than 12 million people in the world who use Scrum. I think there's a good reason for that, and it's why I became a Certified Scrum Master and Certified Scrum Product Owner.

3. It teaches you how to structure your online video meetings (one meeting, one job). It will help you understand how to make the best of light, sound, backgrounds and technology in your video meetings.

Welcome, Scrumnast!

* * *

---

[1] William Edwards Deming is the finest management guru very few people in the West have ever heard of. However, Toyota, Honda, Panasonic and all the other brilliant Japanese brands have not only heard of him, they have implemented his ideas, too.

My name is Nick Holmes and I run an agile, leadership, management, and project management consultancy called Scrumnastics. We work completely remotely and online.

My teams and I have worked entirely and permanently online since 2016. We had to work out how best to do it before everyone else had to do it. You can learn from our experience without making the mistakes we made as we worked it all out.

A year ago, you would probably have thought this book was worthless. But after the lockdowns? Will everything go back to how it once was? Who knows? Will what we are doing now turn out to be the new normal? I'm not much good at horoscopes so I don't have an answer to those questions. However, I can help you and your team adopt methods to adapt your ways of working no matter what happens, whether you will be office-based, remote-based or some kind of hybrid, you will thrive better than your competition.

It Is Up To Us Now

We are the leaders and managers that we have been waiting for. No-one else is coming. There is no-one else. It's down to us.

It will be people like you and I who will put our economy back together - because we always have, we always do, we always will. It is in our bones. It won't be the politicians that do this. It won't be the bureaucrats. It won't be the technocrats. It will be us.

Because it is ALWAYS us that do that: the people with the desire, grit, stamina and means to get things done working with the people with the skills to do them. This is a book for people of wherewithal[2] like you, and skilled people like the people in your team: practical, pragmatic people who want and need to get things *done*.

Thirdly, this book is for the skilled people who must change into people of wherewithal in order to build, or rebuild, their businesses again. Do what is in this book and you will outcompete all the flashy,

---

[2] People with the grit, stamina, wit, passion, and heft to get things done

showy, but flabby, zombie big logo businesses that look so strong, but really aren't.

Scrumnastics: A Simple Idea

What we do at Scrumnastics is based upon a very simple idea: We bring together the people of capability and the people of skill and ability and put them together in the second oldest structure we humans know: The team. Or, if you prefer the oldest structure, the tribe. That's it.

Of course, calling a group of people a team doesn't actually make them a team and so you need all of the secret sauces in this book to bind them together, so you don't end up with a group of individuals or an ill-disciplined gang, but it relies on the potential of the team.

I don't believe the future belongs to bureaucrats. It will belong to small teams: people of capability, drive and wherewithal, who want things to happen; teaming up with people of skills and ability, who create things and make things happen, and harnessing the power of the team to bring them into being.

There are three things that face today's managers: leadership, management and administration. The beauty of the small tribe is that it largely cuts out most of the administration.

In your competitors' companies, what most managers call management is largely now just a case of administering bureaucracy. Bureaucracy creates an awkward and uncomfortable environment for their people to work in, so they work in an awkward manner. So, if you organise your people in the more natural way that human beings have successfully used for hundreds of generations, they will naturally work better with you, and you will all prosper.

We humans are social, tribal[3] even, and most of us like being in

---

[3] What makes a small-toothed, slow-running, puny, animal like us get to the top of the food chain? 1. The ability to throw a rock at around 60 mph, 2. the

teams. Any methods that work with people's nature, rather than against it, that has echoes of tribes and which forges people into teams is probably onto a winner. Bureaucracy does not do this. It is rules based and creates a completely artificial environment. Besides, it is French, so I really don't think I have to say any more than that.

Where Did The New Bureaucracy Come From?

Two areas: computer systems and the growth of the white-collar department.

1. If you have one or more computer systems in your organisation then you are bureaucratic. It is what computer programmers do: they _love_ encoding rules. If you don't believe me, try to find easy to use Agile project management software.

2. The growth of departments. The HR department, The I.T. Department, the Accounts department. Each one a silo, each one a small kingdom run by a very small king.

In the last chapter of his 1960 book, "The Human Side of Enterprise," Douglas MacGregor posed the question, "what benefits will the advent of the computer and office staff bring to business?" Since 1997, since the introduction of windows-based computing, productivity in the western office has stagnated. Since the 1990s larger companies have cut production jobs at home, and xeroxed them abroad, only to leave a bloated bureaucracy in its wake. We now know the answer to his question: they largely didn't bring any benefits.

The Difference That _We_ Can Make: Become A Great Leader And A Great Manager

But we have an army of skilled people: the knowledge workers. The practical, productive people with skills who make and do things. The

---

ability to sweat, so you don't get heat stroke, unlike your prey and 3. Working together. Working together multiplies the power of 1 and 2.

joiners, the mechanics, the computer programmers and every other skill.

What we need to go with that is great leaders and managers to lead and manage them and their work, and here's our biggest problem: the Harvard Business Review says that only 35% of managers make a positive difference and last longer than six months.

In other words, 65%, or two thirds of managers either make no difference, or make things worse than if they were not there. And then they get fired after six months. That's two thirds of managers. That is an army of uselessness.

If we are to rebuild a better economy, what we need is an army of the 35%. People like you.

Be clear: you do not need an M.B.A. to do this. Leading and managing are not academic subjects: they are practical, social crafts. These crafts are a collection of practical skills that require practice and honing on your part to acquire, not essays. Just as you would not go to university to learn to use a saw, you do not need to go to university to learn to lead and manage.

How Did This Book Come About?

Overnight, on 24th March 2020, the perception of my company went from "Oh, Scrumnastics? Aren't they just those weirdos who work remotely? That's never going catch on, is it?" to "Nick mate! You and your teams work remotely. Can you teach us how to do it? How about today?"

This book came from all the people I taught. Let's start to build it all back[4]. After all, it's only change.

---

[4] I do so love it when politicians use the phrase "Build Back Better." - It's not as though we are planning to "build back worse," is it?

"the essence of management is getting ideas out of the heads of the bosses and into the heads of labour."

- Konosuke Matsushita

That phrase changed the course of my working life. It was 1994, British managers were managing by doing something called "Waterfall." They behaved as though they were in an episode of "Life On Mars[5]:" every single one of them was being a complete and utter Gene Hunt.

I was sent to Panasonic to do a quick data warehouse proof of concept. As I walked into the entrance, this was written on the wall in Japanese and English. It changed my career forever and how I look at everything in business.

Here's the full excerpt:

"We are going to win, and the industrial west is going to lose out; there's not much you can do about it because the reasons for failure are within yourselves. Your firms are built on the Taylor [6]model. Even worse, so are your heads. With your bosses doing the thinking while workers wield the screwdrivers, you're convinced deep down that it is the right way to run a business.

For the essence of management is getting ideas out of the heads of the bosses and into the heads of labour. We are beyond your mindset. Business, we know, is now so complex and difficult, the survival of firms so hazardous in an

---

[5] A BBC TV series

[6] Frederick Winslow Taylor, advocate of Scientific Management, which revolutionised standardisation and industrial production. He published "The Principles Of Scientific Management" in 1909. Sometimes also called "Fordism," after Henry Ford, of the Ford Motor Company.

environment increasingly unpredictable, competitive and fraught with danger, that their continued existence depends on the day-to-day mobilisation of every ounce of intelligence."

- Konosuke Matsushita - founder of Panasonic

The very first time I saw this I thought to myself, "Wow, that is brilliant. If I get the chance, I am going to copy that."

How Does A Geek Get Into Leadership and Management?

In 1994, I was a data architect and business owner when I walked into the foyer of Panasonic Europe for the first time.

A data architect/analyst is a solitary, geeky-technical job, and is *definitely* not a leadership or management role. Like most knowledge workers, I had nothing but contempt for British management. I had hard won skills I had invested time, money and hard work to acquire that made me money. In comparison, they had no skills of any commercial merit.

As the boss of my little business, I went around huge, global companies, slicing and dicing their data and turning it into insights so they could get more clients like their best clients, and fewer like their worst. I did numbers. Posh tens and units. Lots of them.

A lot of this work came through a rather kookie[7] Canadian data warehousing company. Late one Friday afternoon, their manager Steve, called me into his office in Bracknell.

He said, "We need to try something new. Obviously, we can't do this sort of thing with our own staff, so we thought of you. "

"Oh goodie…" I thought.

* * *

---

[7] Almost all information technology and software companies start off kookie. It's only when they get really successful that they turn into the Nazi party.

Steve said, "On Monday you're going to go into a Japanese consumer electronics company. You will be there every day until Friday. You're going to work with a representative of their commercial business who will teach you about their business, and a technical person from their I.T. Department who will get you the data you will need.

It will be your job to make a quick data application that analyses all their customers, all their products and all their sales data, shows them where they're making the most profit and where they are not. They also need a Pareto[8] analysis of that, too.

On Friday you will present your findings to their European board of directors. Best of luck."

Then, with a creepy smile, he finished with, "Oh, by the way, if things don't work out then I'm afraid I won't be able to keep you on after next Friday."

I had a wife, three young children in private school and a mortgage the size of South Wales to keep the payments up on every month. That was one of the longest weekends I have ever had. I had to drive the 160 miles back from Bracknell to Manchester and tell my wife that I might not have too much work for a while after the next week.

Not our best weekend ever.

On the Monday morning, I walked into Panasonic Europe, which was a _very_ different company to your standard British company. It was there I met the very best manager I have ever met in my working life and he changed _what_ I wanted to do with my working life. Like many brilliant Japanese managers, he didn't have an M.B.A. (And _you_ don't need one either).

The very first thing Ikuo did was to hand me a photocopy of an article from the 1985 edition of the Harvard Business Review. It was by

---

[8] Also known as a 80:20 analysis. (80% of _these things_ comes from 20% of _those things_). As in, 80% of your profit probably comes from 20% of your customers, or 20% of your products account for 80% of your profits.

two Japanese management gurus, called Ikujiro Nonaka and Hirotaka Takeuchi, and the article was called "The New Business Paradigm."

Nonaka and Takeuchi. Remember those names, they are important. He told me to read the article and I needed to understand it, because that would be the way we were going to work together for the week. I was to ask him any questions I had.

It was a short, but eye-opening article. Then he took me back to the entrance hall and showed me the quote by Konosuke Matsushita. For the first time in my working life, I understood that management could be a positive tool for change rather than just a rule book for "us" versus "them."

Great management can electrify people. And bad management? It is like you have electrocuted them.

Anyway, we worked like demons all week. By Friday we delivered some customer and product sales insights to the European Board of Directors that they had never had before. The job was a good 'un.

They were impressed enough with me to invite me back for another eight weeks while they got lots more data insights and I soaked up as much as I could about how they manage their businesses at Panasonic.

Panasonic is _different_ to British companies. They do things you have never heard of like:

Their business plan stretches 250 years into the future.

Even though their core business was electronics, they were also the largest bicycle manufacturer in the world at the time.

Three of those stirring sentences from that Konosuke Matsushita quote have stayed with me and have become my watch words ever since.

1. **"Ideas out of the heads of the bosses and into the heads of labour...**
2. **"continued existence depends on the day-to-day mobilisation of**

every ounce of intelligence."
3. "We are beyond your mindset."

And again, I thought, "There's no way anyone can compete with what is in those words, the only thing you can do is copy it. I'm going to copy it in everything I do. And I'm going to find out as much as I can about it."

And so I began reading every management book I could. As I read, the scary thing I found out was that, in Japan, Panasonic aren't even considered to be the very best at management. That prize goes to Toyota. But look how similar this phrase from a Toyota manager is to Konosuke Matsushita's:

"Until management gets their egos out of the way and goes to the whole team and leads them all together ... senior management will continue to miss out on the brain power and extraordinary capabilities of all their employees. At Toyota, we simply place the highest value on our team members and do the best we can to listen to them and incorporate their ideas into our planning process."
Alex Warren, (former Senior Vice President of Toyota Motor Manufacturing - Kentucky plant)

Toyota are serious about their people. As they say at Toyota, *"Because people make our automobiles, nothing gets started until we train and educate our people." - Eiji Toyoda*

We will come back to Toyota throughout the book. Why? Because I think they are the best.

What Did I Read?

Tom Peter's and Robert H. Waterman's **"In Search Of Excellence?"** Yes. Anything by William Edwards Deming? <u>**Yes, and you should too.**</u> Douglas MacGregor's **"The Human Side of Enterprise"**? Many, many times. David Sirota's **"The Enthusiastic Employee - How Companies Profit By Giving Workers What They Want"**? Truly invaluable for a leader.

* * *

Shortly, the kookie Canadian company hit the commercial jackpot and I began project managing global projects for them, including a training programme for hundreds of Dow Chemical sales managers on how to analyse their customer data across all their European, Middle Eastern and African offices.

Suddenly I began working with many of the global companies that were mentioned in "In Search of Excellence," such as Dow Chemical, Dana, HSBC, and Glaxo.

In every great company I visited I asked questions of these real live managers and leaders. Bit by bit I began to know more about leadership and management. Suddenly, I was teaching people with M.B.A.s.

In every one of the great companies, I always saw the same thing. There were lots of people who followed all the procedures but there were also pockets of mavericks. These were the people who didn't follow every procedure, but who created the lifeblood of the company, the new products and services.

In the real world, profits matter. So much so that these huge, global businesses with huge oceans of bureaucratic processes had remote islands in them where these misfits lived.

Who Are You Competing Against?

Most medium-sized and larger companies that you are competing against don't understood this key point. They are on the path to more and more bureaucracy, employing more and more corporate clones and fewer misfits. But companies need misfits, they bring in _tomorrow's_ money.

Why should you care? Because, although bureaucracy beats chaos, it can't compete against more nimble, agile forms of management like we are going to learn. These 'bureaucracies with lipstick on' may, or may not, survive the next five years. But you, Scrumnast, will survive. You will.

Competence Has Always Been Rare. Competent Managers Are Rarer Still. Two Thirds Of All Managers Are So Bad That It Would Be Better If They Were Not There At All

The Harvard Business Review says that two thirds of all leaders and managers are so bad that it would be better if they were not there at all. - Which means we had better make sure we are in the one third who _do_ make a positive difference.

I Must Have Been Doing Something Right

Anyway, for the next three years, whenever I went into a global company to do a data analytics proof of concept, I used the way of working that Ikuo, the manager from Panasonic, had shown me.

Often, by the end of the week's engagement, the senior management would sidle up to me and say something like, "Actually, Nick, we're so overloaded that we can't do anything with the figures because we don't have the capacity. But you could give us greater capacity to do the things we need to do - show us how we can manage projects like you do."

So, for years before Agile management was a thing, I went round the United Kingdom and Europe showing just what a three-, four-, or five-person team could achieve in a week.

This Is How We Worked:

On the Monday we would:

1. Meet and greet each other
2. Agree a bite sized task that we could achieve in a week,
3. Read the Nonaka and Takeuchi article out loud together and a few pages from "In Search of Excellence," by Tom Peters and Robert H. Waterman
4. Do a bit of planning about who would do what

5. Get to work.

6. At the end of the day, we would come back together and show what we had achieved.

For every day after that we would:

1. First thing, have a very short update meeting together to see what went well the day before, plan what to do that day, allocate tasks and share if had anything that was blocking progress. We wrote everything on Post-It notes and stuck them on a small cork board on a table.

2. Get to work

3. At the end of the day we would show what we had achieved.

On the final day we would:

1. Show what we had achieved to some senior management, or directors

2. Agree if it was worth spending any more external time and money on the project or whether they could carry on by themselves

3. Go down the pub to do a debrief on what went well, what could have gone better and whether it had been personally worth it for the people involved. (See the "Thriving Index" section in the book).

We would look at that today and say, "Oh, you mean you were doing Scrum?" But in 1994, Scrum was unknown at the time. This was not as well formulated as Scrum but, scruffy as it was, it still beat what was happening in mainstream management.

But my way of working was missing one *really clever* and essential thing. The thing that Jeff Sutherland and Ken Schwaber, the co-creators of Scrum developed. The events. Four different meetings, each of which had its very own specialised purpose.

I think it is the secret of Scrum's success, and probably the most effective thing in Scrum. They are the reason I use Scrum, and they are the reason you can use Scrum to run a remote, hybrid or office-based team. We will talk about the Events in the Scrumnastics course later on.

I'd love to be able to tell you that when I had eventually returned to the head office of the kookie Canadian company and reported back to them just how successfully we had all worked together, that Steve, the worst manager in the world, said to me, "Wow! That sounds fantastic! We really need to work like that here!"

But of course, he didn't. Steve was one of the sixty-five percent. Like I said, he was a terrible manager - but he made a great Nazi.

Instead, I started to work like this. I still do and I have done for decades. Read this book and you will too, and without paying a consultancy a very large bucket of money.

Sounds Good, But Where Have You Used It?

Over the decades I have used what is in this book to:

Double the work rate of disaffected, demoralised teams inside six weeks without spending a penny.

1.   Led, managed and mentored high performing high-tech technology teams in start-ups.

2.   Led business transformations in a car restoration shop and remanufacturer back into profit.

3. Led Teams in banks.

4. Led wacky alternative eco house building projects.

5.   Project managed arts radio programmes and rock video productions.

And, most challenging of all, led a rock band and the production of three of their five music albums. If I can make it work with wannabe, would-be rock stars, I think you will be able to make it work for *your* rock stars.

* * *

Scrumnastics Is Organised Like This:

1. **"Leadernomics:"** - how to lead. Before you lead a team, you have to know how to lead one person. As soon as you go from anything as modest as a one-man-band and onto a duo, you need to know how to lead, and do it convincingly. Duos are never self-leading. Besides, better led companies prosper, badly led ones rarely do.

Leadership is leadership so this section will be of use whether we go back to work in offices or not.

2. **"Scrumnastics - Guerrilla Management Not Gorilla Management:"** is how to do Agile management, specifically Scrum. Why? As soon as you add a third person to a team, you need to know how to manage the thing you are doing because getting the thing done becomes harder than leading the people. I do not mean doing administration. Great management electrifies your people and inspires them to do great things. Bad management electrocutes them, and they achieve nothing.

Management is management - it will also be of use to you whether we go back to the office full time, or work in some form of a hybrid.

3. **"Scrumnastics ++"**: is about phasing sprints for risk management, and managing and co-ordinating multiple teams, and the path to Lean Management.

Scrumnastics ++ is about advanced Scrum and how to expand it and will also be of use whether you go back to the office or not

4. **"Lights! Sound! Cameras! Action!"**: Using online technologies in the best ways (I know everyone does it, but it is not actually obligatory to have a bookcase behind your head).

This will be of use whether you go back to a hybrid or a home-based system.

Who Knows?

Who knows if these lockdowns will ever return? Or whether we will all go back to work exactly like we did before, or whether we will develop some kind of hybrid approach? We can't know that. But we can prepare ourselves to be prepared for anything, because we have to be. After all, we are the only leaders we have been waiting for. There is no-one else coming along.

But I can tell you that every Chief Executive I know is looking at their office rental budgets with a very hard stare. Many people were used to working from home long before the pandemic, and I did my first project for a global company to migrate salespeople to home working back in 1996.

You need to know how to use online tech and know how to manage remote teams because I don't think they are going away anytime soon.

But the key point that should make you care is that you now know that being a great leader and doing great management is about knowledge, _not_ about your character, or your personal charisma or that indefinable yet magical something that sets you apart from the crowd. It is about your skills, knowledge and using a great set of systems that have already been proved elsewhere and which are very widely used by some of the very best companies around the world.

Welcome to the **Scrumnast Club**. Welcome to the club of the thirty-five percent of leaders and managers who make, and continue to make, a positive difference to their companies, their teams and the world. The world needs you more than ever.

Right, fellow Scrumnasts, let's dig in. I wish you the very best of luck as you become a better leader, a better manager, better at Scrum, Lean Management and a better and better Scrumnast.

Cheers!

Nick Hewyn Holmes   May 2021.

Before we begin, let's end this section with a very old joke that has a bearing on how you should view everything in this book.

Two guys running away from a polar bear:
1st guy: "We'll never outrun the bear!"

2nd guy: "I don't need to outrun the bear. I just have to outrun you."

The moral: You don't have to be brilliant at this to get extraordinary results. You just need to be doing it better than the others. Trust me, I have seen the others, that will not be hard.

Feeling better? Okay, let's begin…

Scrumnastics: Join Us?

If you would like to see more videos on leadership, why not join the Scrumnastics mailing list? I post videos regularly on Youtube, FaceBook and the Locals platform.

Who knows what social platforms we will all be using next year? But if you join the mailing list you can be sure I will email you the latest links to the latest videos on the latest platforms.

You can sign up to the Scrumnastics mailing list at scrumnastics.co.uk (It is always at the bottom of the home page. No, we won't sell your email, and every email has the option to unsubscribe).

Have a real business that you are serious about growing?

Scrumnastics Elite: Open to directors and senior managers with real businesses. Maximum 6 members per club.

COURSE ONE: "LEADERNOMICS" - LEADERS AND LEADERSHIP

"Leadernomics"

"A competent leader can get efficient service from poor troops, while on the contrary an incapable leader can demoralize the best of troops." - General John J. Pershing, U.S. Army

This section does not aim to turn you into another Winston Churchill, but it will try to stop you from becoming another little Hitler. After all, there was only one Winston Churchill, but there are a lot of little Hitlers.

What Is A Good Leader?

They have skills and ways of thinking that you probably don't. But you can learn those things. It is not as though it is genetic. Of course, you will have to practice the skills, and the ways of thinking until you master them, but you can do it. It just takes study, work and practice.

The media would have us believe that leaders are supermen and women, born to be leaders and different to the likes of you and I. But that's just business journalists for you, and most of them couldn't lead a fat kid to a sweet shop. It is nonsense built on stilts. Leaders are normal human beings, just like you and me. In fact, they really are _exactly_ _like_ _you_ _and_ _I_, after all, despite the cliche, most _weren't_ born leaders.

What is a good leader? Someone with the skills, ways of thinking, vision and credibility that persuade people it will be worthwhile following them. Where do the vision and credibility come from? Credibility is part confidence, and that comes from the mastery of the skills and ways of thinking. The vision? There's a section on that later on.

Let's Get Down To It:

First things first: We are the leaders that we have been waiting for.

31

No-one else is coming to save us. There is no-one else. There's only us.

You know that leader that you served under and that you couldn't stand because they were not up to the job? Well, they were only there because you didn't volunteer *first*.

If you don't put yourself forward for leadership then the clowns get the job. And clowns are never funny. These particular clowns wreck lives, teams and companies. In thirty years of consulting, I have seen it a hundred times or more. So, every time you roll your eyes, or sniff eloquently, at the latest, brainless nonsense that came out of their mouth, think on this: they are only there because you weren't courageous enough to put yourself forward to do the job. Step up.

For sure, as we embark on becoming a leader, we will have to do some hard work to hone our skills and transform us. Be careful: once we start, there is no going back. That honing work is like sharpening a blade: it carries on forever. Be sure that this is what you want.

You may be thinking, "But I'm not an 'Alpha' personality type. How can I possibly lead a team?" Don't worry. You can and you will. Because almost everyone can. I have mentored a lot of new leaders over the past 30 years, some of which have definitely started off as what silly journalists call "Beta" type personalities. However, with some training, coaching, and mentoring, and a considerable effort on the part of the trainee, almost all turn into what you would call an "Alpha" personality.

In my experience, there's no such thing[9] as a fixed personality 'type,' there are just different behavioural habits which people move between. Just one thing, though. Once you get into the 'alpha' mindset, it really is a one-way journey, so be careful about what you wish for.

"Leadernomics[10]" is the name of the course I wrote and delivered to

---

[9] I think this only exists in the minds of business journalists.

[10] Whether good or bad, leadership will make a huge difference to your bottom line. Hence "Leadernomics," (like economics but to do with leaders).

more than 200 new, and not so new, senior leaders and business owners. This section of the Scrumnastics book is the distilled essence of that course. If you are really interested, there is also a full-size, online version.

By the end of this Leadernomics section you will be in a position to credibly and confidently lead a small team with your team respecting you as their leader. How? Because you will know more about what people actually want and need from their leaders in order to motivate them to work at their very best, and, as far as it is possible, give that to them.

Don't get discouraged by the words "lead a small team." If you can lead a small team *then you can lead a large team too*. Leading a small team is actually harder than leading a large team. In small groups your people are looking very closely at you, every day. In larger groups, people not only look at you, but they also take their cues from looking at everyone else around you who are also looking at you. Many of those people will be giving lots of positive, non-verbal feedback that everyone will be picking up on. Large groups of people self-reinforce everyone's beliefs. After all, there's a reason why it took so long to see the king had no clothes on.

This Is How They See You - Why Should They Follow You?

You need to understand that the people you are trying to lead are people with hard-won, largely practical skills that they have invested money, time, hard-work and practice to acquire, and which they use to get paid. As a manager, their default view is to look at you as someone with no real skills. Part of your job is to show them that there really are skills to leadership and management, and that you have mastered them. Do that and they will begin to respect you.

They will know that you are some*one* worth following, because you will know how to give them some*thing* worth following. People want a positive return on their efforts: They want to be better off than they were before. Offer them a good chance of being better off than they are at the moment and there is a good chance that they will follow you.

* * *

Just knowing this stuff will make you a better leader than the vast majority of leaders, especially those in Britain.

Sssshhhhhh... Here's A Dirty Little Secret About Leadership. - Don't Tell Anyone.

Leadership is not something that certain, special people are just born to do. Leadership is essentially a craft, or even a trade. Like all craftwork, once you have mastered some fairly simple skills you can only get better and better at it by doing it over and over. We will study the skills as we go but before we do, let's deal with hierarchies.

First of all, there are hierarchies. You may not like it but whether you do or not is immaterial. The only people who will tell you there is no such thing as a hierarchy are those in the middle or at the bottom of a hierarchy. They do this because it makes them feel better.

Obviously, as a leader, you will be at the top of the hierarchy of the group you are leading. Many bad leaders think that you get to the top of a hierarchy by being the strongest, and so strut about, posture, and behave accordingly.

But this is completely and utterly wrong. You actually get to the top of a hierarchy by being the best and most competent at what you do.

Here's a question: Let's pretend you run a really great house building company. It is the very best for miles around. Do you get to be a really good house building company by being excellent at project, time and cost management, knowing where to source the finest materials, seeking out the best crafts people, and running excellent teams, or because you are really strong and good at lifting weights in a gym? It's a trick question, it has nothing to do with gyms.

It is the same with leadership and management. You get to be the best leader and manager by studying, practicing, and mastering skills and then mastering yourself.

* * *

Here's the amazing thing that automatically puts you light years ahead of other leaders and managers: most of them don't bother learning about leadership and management and would rather strut around striking power postures instead.

As Forrest Gump's mother said in the film, "stupid is, as stupid does." But not you, Scrumnast. Not you.

What Makes A Leader A Leader?

Leadership has little to do with being a charismatic and domineering personality or a self-important extravert. It also has very little to do with their job title or their actual seniority either.

When needed, a leader will emerge with no regard to the company organisation chart because they are already there. Leadership stems from a peculiar mix of the right social skills, not formal authority. You do not grab it - your people grant it to you.

A leader is someone who has knowledge of those few skills and behaves in a way that their people look toward for support or direction when they need to. Such leaders are needed, and this is what makes people _want_ to follow them, in good times and bad, towards a vision or set of goals.

But why do people follow them? Among other reasons, because they

1. Know _what_ they are doing - They are competent - not everyone in a position of leadership is.

2. They know _why_ they are doing it - they have a compelling 'reason why.' Again, most leaders and managers don't.

3. They know _where_ they are going - They have a compelling vision of a worthwhile goal that appeals to others.

4. They know _how_ they are going to get there - They know how to successfully organise people, money and things, have mastery at least one form of management and have a working knowledge of others

* * *

5. They know _who_ they can take with them, and what those people want.

In addition, they must also have some old-fashioned character traits like 'presence' and 'heft.'

Old fashioned virtues lend respect. Amongst other traits, leaders must also be emotionally strong and brave, honest, and reliable, behave with integrity and be able to champion their people in front of others.

Get those things right and you have cracked it... I said leadership was simple, I didn't say it was easy.

Here are some words to ponder from an interview of Field Marshall Montgomery, who defeated General Rommel in North Africa during the second World War. He then commanded more than _two million men_ during invasion of Normandy. _Two million men_. Now, that's someone who knows about leadership.

Lord Stephen Taylor: "As you look round the world today, Field Marshall, do you see the need for leadership, still?"

Viscount Montgomery: "Oh, terribly. Terribly. And I see it in industry, I think that many of the problems that go on in the world today are due to the bad leadership on the parts of the people in high places."

But not you, Scrumnast. Not you.

Remember, Thou Art Mortal[11]...

There's something very weird about leadership and management which we need to keep in the back of our minds. It is called the 'power paradox.' The power paradox attracts many to leadership who, although they have the ambition, are completely and utterly unsuited[12] to it. Unfortunately, at the same time it repels those who would be really great at it. I'm guessing that part of the reason you are reading this is because you have been repelled by would-be leaders.

Sadly, their ambitions are seldom an indicator of competence. The heady whiff of status that management offers often appeals to the worst possible candidates. In my experience as a consultant who mentors leaders, the ratio of the good to the bad is truly awful: I'm guessing that for every, one suitable leader, at least ten are unsuitable.

That is why *you* *must* volunteer for leadership. We cannot afford any more clowns.

Here are two quotes to put us in the right frame of mind:

"Authority Has Always Attracted The Lowest Elements In The Human Race. All Through History, Mankind Has Been Bullied By Scum." - P. J. O'Rourke.

"The most improper job of any man, even saints, (who at any rate, were at least unwilling to take it on), is bossing other men. Not one in a million is fit for it, and least of all who seek the opportunity." - J.R.R. Tolkien (author of "The Hobbit," and "Lord Of The Rings.")

See what I mean? That's the power paradox. Let's see what you and I can do to reverse this.

---

[11] Roman generals who had won great victories were awarded a 'triumph,' which was a victory parade through the streets of Rome. As they were being praised by the citizens, they always had a slave who whispered, "Remember thou art mortal," in their ear.

[12] As one of my students once asked me on one of my courses, "Do you mean the 'fist-magnets'?" I thought that was priceless.

First: What Do We Lead? What Do We Manage?

"You manage things; you lead people." - Grace Brewster Murray Hopper[13]

Great words. Got that? Most managers don't know this, but it is fundamental: We use management techniques to manage the things we have to manage such as our stock, our processes and our accounts. Management is planning, measuring, monitoring, co-ordinating, hiring and sacking. We use leadership techniques to lead our teams. Do that right and we will be in a better place than if we do the opposite.

But Which Comes First? Leadership or Management?

Leadership. If you are a one-man band business and you need to take on an assistant, you need to be able to lead them convincingly to help you do your business before you need something that needs managing, like a holiday booking system. That's also why Leadernomics comes before the Scrumnastics part of this book.

What Is Your Strategy For Leadership?

You have two choices: you can either *impose* your authority like a commander does, or you can *entice* them into accepting you and giving you the status of leader. You do this by intriguing them with your vision, your wherewithal, your knowledge and abilities. If you do this, they will choose to *invest* you as their leader.

The first option requires some kind of threat or actual use of force, even if it is only your personality. The second requires a great deal more work on the part of the leader (especially on themselves) but the effect is much longer lasting. Another benefit is that when the time comes for the leader to finish being the leader, it normally results in a much softer landing.

---

[13] Co-inventor of the COBOL programming language and a Commodore in the US Navy - so she would know.

Do You Want To Be A Commander or a Leader?

A commander is different to a leader. A commander belongs to a 'Command and Control' environment, such as the military, the police or the fire service. A commander commands because they have authority, and authority comes from the veiled threat of force, such as, "do this or a) I will shoot you, or b) you will lose your job." The problem with using veiled force is it generates resentment: That is where your people do the bare minimum and only acquiesce to your demands rather than fully accepting the task.

A leader **offers** themselves to the group and the group *__accepts__* them. There is a kind of dialogue or process of negotiation between the leader and the group.

So, broadly, we know there are two ways to lead people:

1. **Commanding**. We've all had this manager. The "Gene Hunt[14]." They shout at and brow beat people, like the typical old 'Theory X[15,] manager they are. The problem with behaving like that is that your people will only *acquiesce* to your demands rather than wholehearted *accepting* them. Why should you care? Well, people who acquiesce aren't as engaged and so don't give you as much effort[16] as people who accept. We will talk about low engagement later on in the book.

They comply with demands by doing the bare minimum rather than over-delivering excellence, and worst of all, being treated badly by your boss breeds resentment. As any enlightened 'Theory Y[17,] manager or leader can tell you, there are many currencies that people

---

[14] The guv'nor in the TV series, "Life On Mars." When I started work, every manager was a complete and utter Gene Hunt.

[15] From Douglas MacGregor's classic management book, "The Human Side Of Enterprise." 1960. Theory X Managers think that people are lazy and come to work for just money.

[16] Personally, I prefer 'effort' to the HR management phrase 'engagement.'

[17] Again, From Douglas MacGregor's classic management book, "The Human Side Of Enterprise." 1960. Theory Y Managers realise that people come to work for more than just money.

SCRUMNASTICS

Nick Holmes B.A. (*Hons.*)
Director

0792 877 2398
nick@scrumnastics.co.uk
www.scrumnastics.co.uk

at work choose to get paid in. Resentment is the most expensive currency there is.

Although it is still very common, this theory X type of leadership has one fundamental drawback: it breeds resentment, and when it comes to resentment there will *always* be a reckoning, and their resentment will be paid back at a time of *their* choosing, not yours.

2. **Leadership As A Craft**: You understand that leadership is partly knowledge of set of skills, as real as the skills of a joiner or bricklayer, and acts as a bargain or agreement between you and your people. A leader says, "I want you to do this. It may be a difficult task but the rewards in increasing your skills, greater competence, job satisfaction and money will greater than the pain of doing it. Afterwards, you will be in a better place than you are now.[18]"

You offer yourself as their leader and, hopefully, after judging whether you have the right stuff, they will accept you. Why should they accept you? Because you really know that leadership is a craft, and you also know that your people will follow you if you find out what they want, and then do your best to give it to them.

But how on earth can you _know_ what your people want?

"The Enthusiastic Employee- - How Companies Profit By Giving Workers What They Want" by David Sirota and Douglas A. Klein.

This is the very best book on people management I know, and it tells you what your people really want. Even better, not many managers have ever heard of it, or read it. I urge you to read it yourself, and then keep it in your very own management library.

---

[18] As a shorthand, we use the phrase, "making the juice worth the squeeze." This is a phrase we use a lot, especially in the 'Thriving Index' part of the Sprint Retrospective. - It means 'does the payback justify the effort?' I have found it is the key to motivating people and knowing how they are doing. Have you ever made own orange juice? It is delicious but what an effort! it takes two bags of oranges to get a big glass and what a mess afterwards.

* * *

Mercer-Sirota, as the company who wrote the book are now called, have been doing all sorts of employee research for seriously huge, global companies like IBM and Starbucks ever since the 1970s. During their work they have learned a thing or two about what employees want, and what they want from their employers.

According to Sirota and Klein, the three factors that are most important to staff are:

1. **Equity**
2. **Achievement**
3. **Camaraderie**

1. Equity:

People want to be treated with a certain fairness at work. That means getting the right recognition and reward for their efforts. They already know that there are no more jobs for life, but they do want to be treated fairly while they are there. One of the little tricks for the Scrumnast manager is to make sure your people move their own work tickets. If they did the job, then let them take the credit. The first lesson for the leader.

2. Achievement:

People want a sense of achievement and pride from their work and also a small measure of control, too. After all, they are spending the very best hours of their day with you. There's a reason why working in monotonous jobs in factories is described as 'soul destroying.' The second lesson for the leader.

3. Camaraderie:

Anyone who has read Douglas MacGregor's "The Human Side Of Enterprise" knows that people don't just come to work for the money. They also come to work for all sorts of reasons, including companionship and to be social too. Work is partly how we validate ourselves. When we meet someone new, the second question we ask them is, "And what do you do?" Human beings are tribal pack animals who thrive when well socialised and do not do well at all when isolated. In fact, some of the oldest punishments we have in all our cultures are about being pushed out from the group: Excommunication, banishment, and being outlawed.

This is the third lesson for the leader to learn and is the hardest one to achieve with remote teams.

As you probably already know, we specialise in managing remote teams. I spend as much time trying to do something to overcome the people in my remote team's sense of isolation as I do on *anything* else. If you are running a remote team do not underestimate just how big a job this is and how much responsibility rests with you as leader to get it right.

An Easy Tip: One of the most successful things I have found is to open *all* the video meetings five minutes early, so that my teams have a space where they can catch up with each other informally before the work starts. This is a simple trick I learned from working with older salesmen in my youth, who spent a great deal of time talking with potential clients about how their families were getting along before doing any hard-nosed commercial negotiations. I also encourage team members to video call each other frequently during the working day if they are working together on a task to minimise this sense of isolation.

Okay, So Now We Know What They Want At Work, But What Do They Want From Us As Leaders?

First of all, most people actually want to be led. Why? Partly because they don't want to lead because their experience tells them the eventual outcome for most leaders is not that great. When leaders get the bum's rush it is not often an elegant end.

* * *

Although they often have the ability to do so, not everyone wants to be a leader at work, and there are as many reasons why that is, as there are people. One of them being that most people want to be liked at work.

Second of all, they may want to be led, but they certainly do not want to be led by anyone who is weak, or incompetent, or without integrity, or directionless, or lacking in vision, or worst of all, uses their status to attempt to sleep with their staff.

Amongst other things, they want their leaders to be strong, ethical, to behave honourably, be of good character, have a convincing vision for the future and have confidence in their competence and their abilities to lead them there. After all, wouldn't you want that?

You may be thinking "Surely he's talking about one of those Alpha type personalities, but I that is not me."

Yes, You Are. In Fact, We All Are.

This needs to be said again. All those alpha, beta, delta gamma, sigma and omega 'personality types' are not really personality types at all. They are simply different behaviours that we all exhibit in different social settings at different times.

Which one you are in any particular situation just depends on the situation. We change how we behave in different social situations.

For example, when I am leading a team or coaching a group online in leadership and management then, in that situation, I will be the alpha because I know more and am more experienced than anyone else, and I am there to mentor. However, in a different social situation I won't be the one who knows more than anyone else. Then it will be extremely unlikely that I will behave as an alpha.

For example, I love to sail yachts and have done for years. However, when I was doing my Day Skipper exam, I was an unqualified skipper, and I was being examined by a qualified skipper. The real skipper was ultimately in charge of the yacht and that made them the alpha. There is no 'faking it until you make it,' self-help nonsense when at sea -

people can die. Even when I was issuing orders to the crew and had the helm, if I had messed up at any time then he would have taken charge and taken over. That made the skipper the alpha. It is the same for all of us: in certain situations, we are alpha, in others we are not.

The Essence of Leadership

- *You <u>Know</u> When You Can Lead - It's In Your Bones*

This is for the skim readers, just in case you skipped the early bits: Leadership is a practical craft, not a gift. You don't get to be a leader by doing an M.B.A. You get better at it just by doing it.

It is not a rare skill. The number of people who can lead a group of people is a *lot* bigger than you would imagine. Outside of work, people are already involved in leadership and management. They are leading clubs and making life changing decisions about themselves and their families every single day without any permission from your H.R. department.

We have all worked for someone who is an awful leader. First of all, we need to make a distinction between a leader and someone in authority. People in authority may not be good leaders.

Second, we need to distinguish between leadership and ownership. Just because the third-generation idiot son of the founder is your boss, it really does not follow they will be a good leader.

The real leaders in any group are the individuals that everyone turns to when it all goes wrong. Often, just after the people who should be in charge have been found to be lacklustre. Again.

True leaders have natural authority and trust in a group, even if they don't appear on the organisation chart. After all, Winston Churchill was Winston Churchill *before* he became Prime Minister of wartime Britain.

Those ambitious, thrusting types sharp elbowing their way to the front all by themselves? They may be the very people that we in the organisation have to watch out for most.

* * *

The Reluctant Leader? Who Are They?

All around us yet are often overlooked. Why can they make good leaders?

1. Because they often see their role of leadership as being part of something bigger than just being about them, which is great for those they lead.

2. They often know themselves quite well: both the good and the bad parts. That allows them to be honest about their weaknesses and so want to continue to develop.

3. Knowing that they are themselves lacking in strengths, often means they are happy to invest in other people's training and development.

4. They don't tend to be pompous and entitled (which is both a really, really good thing and makes a rather wonderful change).

5. They tend to lead with quiet authority, rather than leading by having tantrums and 'terrible twos.'

6. They also tend to be genuine people of substance, rather than people of style and flim-flam.

7. They tend to lack big egos, and so tend to put more trust in evidence than trust their own, or others, eminence or expertise.

8. Above all, because of their experiences of being led badly themselves, what makes them hesitant about putting themselves forward is that they REALLY don't want to be a BAD leader.

There's a long tradition for the reluctant leader. How about George Washington, Moses, Mahatma Gandhi, and Pope Francis? When newly elected, the new Speaker of the House of Commons is dragged reluctantly to the Speaker's chair.

* * *

The Intriguing Leader

Here's a secret that reluctant leaders know in their bones: the secret of leading is not about foisting yourself on them, it is about learning how to get your people to *follow* you.

That requires that you have it within you for people to turn to you with confidence, consider thoughtfully what you are saying and doing, and then commit to invest their time, effort and skills in their putting their future with you.

How do you do that? Partly by intriguing them. You supply your group with a vision of the future that is both evocative for them and worthwhile to *them*. How? By leaving space. The vision must allow them to fill in some of the blanks for themselves. When your people fill in the blanks for themselves, they take your vision, and make it their own by putting their own interpretation onto it. They begin to own it for themselves.

But a vision is not enough. You must inspire them with confidence that you have the wherewithal and heft to defend them from both above, and from the sides. They want and need a champion, not a friend.

Fear, Dread, and Doubt, And The True Leader

If the thought of leading a group of people fills you with dread, then good - You are just the sort of person your people need.

Those nerves in your stomach mean you already have one of the best pre-qualifications there is to become an excellent leader. Those nerves will help to raise your game and your judgement for your people. Good judgement is essential for a great leader.

You may not think so, but ask any actor, comedian or musician:

when you need to perform, your nerves make you do your job better. You just need to accept them.

Not a single day has ever gone by when I have had to begin to lead a new team full of hope and promise, or turn around a gang of disgruntled, dysfunctional, low performers into a group of up-and-at-em high achievers, that I haven't felt 'that feeling' in the pit of my stomach. And just about everyone is the same. So, if you're nervous at the prospect of leadership, don't worry. That's a really good sign.

Here's another thing you should ask of an actor, comedian or musician. Ask them, which is harder to play to, a small audience or a huge audience? Easy answer, right? The big crowd must the harder gig. Wrong, it's actually the small audience.

Big audiences give bigger applause and bigger laughs because of something called social proof.[19] Social proof is when a lot of people look around them at the lots of other people around them and say to themselves "well, they must be good: look at all the other people here. They can't be wrong." The hardest audience to play to is the small audience. It is the same with leading. The hardest group to lead is actually a small group. If you can lead a small group, you can lead a big group.

With the right attitude, knowledge and training, almost everyone [20] can lead.

And there are a lot more leaders in the world than you would think. They are all around us. Just because they aren't leading right now doesn't mean they are not a leader. They may be already leading in all sorts of ways outside of work.

---

[19] This is the original meaning of social proof, not the thing that internet marketers talk about these days.

[20] But not everyone. Especially not those rather 'odd' people in your workplace who think that doing things with spreadsheets and slide software is real work or like real life.

Offering Them Some<u>one</u> Worth Following

True Leaders Have a Vision:

A vision is a 'reason why,' or as Nietzsche would have said, a 'strong why,' they should follow you. It is a plan and also a purpose. A leader has a vision of the future that is better than the vision that everyone else can see. After all, why should anyone follow you if the future you are offering them is worse than the future they think they could achieve without you?

Why is Martin Luther King's "I have a dream," speech still so inspiring? Because he dreamed of a so much better future for his followers, even though knew he would not see it himself. When Doctor King said, "I may not get there with you," he was telling them this future was about them, not him.

Leaders know where they are going and are very confident that it will be a better place than where they have come from when they get there. Their vision is clear, they have thought it through and turned it into words so that it inspires others. It makes enough sense to them that they can make a rational choice and bet on a better future.

The vision must also be a short and snappy thing, saying it all in the fewest words possible.

True Leaders Can Prioritise

Good leaders can do this, and bad leaders can't. But it is a vital ability for any leader. Why? For three reasons:

1. It makes decision making MUCH easier. You have a list. You organise it, top to bottom, in order of importance. Which item will you do first? The top one. Which one will you do second? The second one. When you have run out of money, you will have done the most important things. The end.

* * *

2. The people you are leading need direction. They need to know which thing to do first, what to do second, and so on. It is unfair to ask them to make the decision when it is your decision to make.

3. As a leader you will always have limited resources, and there will always be unlimited demands placed upon them. You may be asked to do everything and more - but you can't. The most vital things is to achieve are the most important things, otherwise you may put your team in danger of achieving nothing. What we are trying to avoid is 'busy work:' that is, activity for the sake of activity. Look around you at your clients and competitors, there are lots of jobs that are wholly consumed with doing busy work. There are very few things as expensive as busy work. But that's okay, because while _they_ are burning resources, _you_ will not be.

Prioritisation is a difficult skill to learn for the new leader or manager. After all, up until becoming a leader or manager, your whole job has been about completing _all_ the tasks you have been given. If you complete them all you get praised - if you don't complete them then you get asked an uncomfortable, "why not?" Suddenly, you have to pick and choose instead of doing everything, and that change in mentality is difficult to square with the history of your entire work life up to now.

Not everyone makes that transition. You can tell those who have not made the change by their anguished howls of, "but it's _all_ important!" Unfortunately, it just isn't. And unfortunately, they are condemned to middle management until they do. But not you, Scrumnast. Not you.

Some Prioritisation Techniques[21]_:_

Prioritising by Value.[22] To do this properly, the first thing you need

---

[21] There are, of course MANY others. These are the ones I tend to use more than any other.

[22] My personal favourite. It seems to put everyone at their ease more than any other technique because it just makes sense to normal people to do the most valuable things first.

is a real idea of the proposed value and cost of each of the items that you intend to make (regardless of whether you are building products or services, having sight of budgets makes _everything_ easier to manage and control).

Secondly, take the list and rank it in order of value.

Thirdly, you need to know how much your team costs to run in total (the 'run rate'), per week or per month.

The run rate for the team, together with the estimated value of the next additional thing, give you a 'decision gate.' What that means is, if the value of the next thing on the list is greater than the team's run rate, then you can go ahead and do it. If the value is lower than the run rate of the team then you don't.

There will come a time when you have completed all the most valuable items, and you have arrived at a 'Minimum Viable Product[23].' But you may still have some budget left. What to do? Should you continue adding bells and whistles, or do you make a value judgement and say, "we're done"? I work with a lot of marketing companies, so their preference is to stop and see if the basic product sells as it is. If it does then carry on. If it doesn't then you give the money back from the budget.

Top Three - What Do You Have To Achieve Today? This is a good method when you are not in a position to know the budget numbers, or when you are in a steady state of work where little is changing.

I once spent three months mentoring a potentially excellent new leader who had been promoted on a "let's see if they sink or swim," basis. He had all the attributes you need to become an excellent leader, apart from his lack of ability to prioritise. This was threatening his ability to swim, and his career.

I had him draw up a to do list with three things for the day that he actually _had_ to achieve. Once he had achieved all three of them, he

---

[23] Imagine you are making ice cream. The Minimum Viable Product (MVP) is a plain vanilla ice cream. No raspberry sauce, no chopped nuts, no sprinkles and no flake. It is some complete stand-alone product that your clients can buy but has no bells or whistles, or any go-faster stripes.'

could draw up another three things but not before. It took a little time for him to get used to it, but once the behaviour became ingrained, he became an excellent, and very rounded leader.

MoSCoW prioritisation: The "MoSCoW" acronym stands for "Must have, Should have, Could have, Won't have." It is an old-school PRINCE2 project manager's technique for prioritising what you are planning to do and what you won't be doing. You take all the attributes that your product could have, and you decide which bucket they will go in. Every product must have certain things, there will be some that it should have, some that it could have and some that it definitely won't have. This technique is still widely used to decide what will be in scope for the development of project, and what will be out of scope.

True Leaders Can Organise

You won't last long as a leader if you rely on your charisma at the expense of your organisation skills. Chaotic leaders do not last long, no matter how charismatic they may be.

In the very next course, called Scrumnastics, we will be learning about a management framework called Scrum. Even if you don't know how to organise a team of people at the moment, then learn this. It will transform your organisational skills, and give you a set of tools that will give you the ability to turn around teams and projects. It will be a lot more effective than that management file that Ferrero and Rocher, your two H.R. Business partners, came up with while being on the outside of two bottles of pinot grigio.

True Leaders Set The Tone

Emotional tone is important. Your positive, confident manner, how you carry yourself and your energy are infectious.

Your team will always take their mood from you. They look to you for all sorts of visual cues and clues to how things are going, especially how they are going outside the team. If you are being positive, then they will be positive.

But if you are nervous, they will be nervous. And nothing slows down the productivity of a team more than nervous agitation, especially if they don't know why you are nervous. Remember, as a leader, you are permanently on display. You must be mindful of your demeanour at all times, but especially when things are not going well. A bad atmosphere is contagious and can run through the team and affect everyone in it in no time at all.

True Leaders Have Good Character - Personal Qualities Of The True Leader:

It helps if the True Leader has, on average, more of the characteristics and attributes that the tribe or group value than the individuals in the tribe or group have at the moment.

You definitely need to be strong, but you don't need to be the strongest in the tribe. After all, you need to let others have some space to excel themselves.

You need energy, but you don't need to be the most energetic.

You need to be smart, but you don't need to be the smartest in the tribe.

You need good judgement, but you don't need to be a judge.

It's who you are in the round that counts most of all.

Above all, you need courage, and you need to tell the truth.

Leaders are decisive. They don't dither or faff about.

Leaders make things right when they have gone wrong. They have the strength to apologise when they realise they have done wrong.

Most of these positive qualities are needed, but all are needed in moderation, especially if they begin to harm the other traits that are more highly prized. For example, you must definitely be enthusiastic and energetic, but if you let your enthusiasms affect your judgement, they will drop you like a stone.

Offering Them Something Worth Following

Offer them a reason why, something worthwhile to invest their time in and follow and something that lends the work a purpose.

Adults need a good reason why to do anything well. A good reason why gives *purpose,* and that is crucial if you want great quality work, done on time and done within budget.

Everyone wants a better future for themselves and their loved ones. It is a simple reason they want to be in a better position than they are at the moment. You need to give them a credible reason why they should believe that following you will make that happen.

You need to give them reasons why they should follow you. You need to have a combination of methods, plans, and confidence that is better than the plan they have in their head. Give them a great way of working. Luckily, you will learn that in the Scrum section of the book.

Integrity: Competency, Character and Commitment

Competency is knowing and showing that you can organise people and things well. This mean that they can be confident that if they work with you, they can achieve a better life than they are enjoying now.

Character: your character is judged by your actions: what you say and what you do. The people that you want to follow you want you to have at least as much integrity as they do. More is better. in the way they go about life. And they have every right to expect that from you. After all, they are investing their future livelihoods with you.

Commitment: Are you a sort of person who will stand steadfast and strong when things go awry? Or are you a fly-by-night character who will disappear at the first obstacle? Will you bind to your people and are you truly committed to the future vision you're offering? Will you balance that with being open to change when the evidence shows you need to change course?

And you need to show that you can do all these things because there are so many bad leaders and managers in the world.

Even when it is done well, leadership and management is the least efficient activity in your organisation, and that little nugget comes from the Harvard Business Review.

What's worse, they also say, "65% of managers add zero or negative net value to the company."

We had better make sure we know how to do it properly, because our teams already know all there is to know about bad leaders.

Toyota and True Leadership

I'm a huge admirer of Toyota and their leadership and management philosophies. These are all bound up in the "Toyota Way," and the "Toyota Production System." Everything you will read in every book on them tells you they are the ultimate in practical, pragmatic, productive people.

One of the many interesting features of Toyota, (and many Japanese companies) is that, unlike companies in the west, they grow their leaders from their own staff rather than buying them in.

Toyota have fourteen management principles. The ninth principle says, "*Grow Leaders Who Thoroughly Understand the Work, Live the*

Philosophy, And Teach It To Others."

There you go. Common sense really. Pick someone you have known all their professional working lives or pay a head-hunter a bucket of money to go and find you someone who may, or may not, change your company for the better. I know which option I would rather pick if I could.

But leadership in Toyota is very different to how we might think of leadership in the west. Here's a quote from Alex Warren, who is a former Senior Vice President of Toyota Motor Manufacturing, at their Kentucky plant:

"Until management gets their egos out of the way and goes to the whole team and leads them all together … senior management will continue to miss out on the brain power and extraordinary capabilities of all their employees. At Toyota, we simply place the highest value on our team members and do the best we can to listen to them and incorporate their ideas into our planning process."

Remember that quotation that I saw on the wall of Panasonic Europe from Konosuke Matsushita? Strikingly similar, aren't they?

What are some of the characteristics of Toyota's management (and other Japanese companies) that we have seen and what makes them so powerful?

They grow their leaders from within, what are the benefits of that?

They don't pay fortunes to head hunters to find them management 'rock stars' who may have a completely different ethos to the company.

That means there is more consistency in sticking with the long-standing company philosophy and they avoid the 'whip sawing' effect of changing focus and direction every few years. Their people know where they are.

Here's an example:

I got into Lean management whilst working at Panasonic Europe in

1995. On about the third week of my work with there, Ikuo, the Japanese manager and I were talking during a work break. I asked him if Japanese managers ever moved between Japanese companies. He simply said, "no."

When I asked him why that was, he said, "My grandfather operated machinery in the Matsushita (Panasonic) factory, my father was an engineer in the Matsushita factory, and I am a manager at Matsushita. My grandson will be a vice president."

Well, if you are working at "Take The Money and Run (2015) Ltd," how does that sound? Naive? Well, hardly. Matsushita has a 250-year business plan and _everyone_ who worked for them knew about it. If you have a business plan that stretches for 250 years, then that gives a worker a certain faith and confidence that they are part of something larger and worthwhile.

Compare that with the life expectancy of a British limited company. Of every company that starts out this year, 80% will be out of business within five years. And that was before the pandemic.

But why can't we have 250-year business plans in Britain? It obviously makes a statement that all your people can commit to. It also leaves the leaders with the idea that they are custodians, not masters of the universe, and that a good part of their duty is to deliver their company to those yet to come in a robust and stable condition.

What's the point of telling you this? Well, leadership is definitely not the same thing everywhere you look, different forms of leadership can bring about very different outcomes and we can learn a lot from them.

Oh, and just in case you're thinking that these are Japanese companies with a long histories of Samurai traditions, and being British, we can't do that kind of thing here, most Japanese management thinking actually emerged from the work of an American called William Edwards Deming, who worked in Japan in the 1950s.

Reluctant Leaders: The Last Overlooked Resource in Organisations.

Human Resources departments have no problem whatsoever identifying the standard 'brand X[24],' ambitious, sharp-elbowed, traditional manager. After all, these charmers tend to self-identify themselves through their ambition, drive and general 'Draco Malfoy[25]'-ism.

But what you may not have heard is that there is a *terrible* attrition rate amongst managers and leaders. Most of them don't last very long at all. Why? Well, and I know I have said this elsewhere, but it is **important.** According to the Harvard Business Review, more than 65% of managers make 'zero or negative contribution' to their organisations. Worse than that, 65% of managers last less than six months before they are 'let go.'

And 'let-go' they are. I have seen it a lot, and it is never a happy day.

Worse, often, it's not only them that gets fired when they get the push. It's normally complete carnage throughout their department too.

It doesn't end there, either. Don't forget that those managers who got fired have no other choice but to go and get a management job somewhere else. *Some* will have used the experience and learned to manage well, but most won't. There's a good living to be had for employment agencies who place bad managers in companies. A sobering thought.

As one of my students told me recently on one of our online management courses, "First, they only promote you onto the management ladder because you are the best in the department at

---

[24] Not quite theory X, but close…
[25] Oh come on, you've read Harry Potter…

your job. But then, they leave you on your own to work everything out for yourself. If you don't, they just get the next person in line."

Which means that there is a never-ending need for **_GOOD_** leadership and management.

Where is it to come from? And where are HR departments looking for it? Not externally. Not any longer. It is not only expensive to search of outside 'talent,' it is a very risky business. Instead, they have begun to look for them internally, inside the organisation. Why? It is cheaper and less risky because they are dealing with known quantities. They even have a name for them now, they call them the 'low-flyers.'

These are the people who have more than just the talent and the ability, but who take the responsibility of leading and managing so seriously that they would rather not do it than be bad at it. It daunts them. Good. The prospect of leading a team is supposed to be daunting. It's the ones who are not daunted by it you should beware of

The daunted? These are the reluctant types.

Ambitious types? Better take note that the good ones are coming to replace you. Reluctantly, but they are coming.

Why Is A Reluctant Leader So Appealing?

Because they often see their role of leadership as being part of something bigger than just being about them, which is both great for those they lead and for the organisation. It's a good bet you haven't bought a psychopath.

They have a certain maturity and often know themselves quite well: both the good and the bad parts.

That allows them to be honest about their weaknesses and so want to continue to develop.

Knowing that they are themselves lacking in strengths, often means they are happy to invest in other people's training and development.

* * *

They don't tend to be stereotypically pompous and entitled (which is a really, really good thing and makes a rather refreshing and wonderful change).

They tend to lead with quiet authority, rather than leading by shouting, screaming, having tantrums and showing they never progressed beyond the "terrible twos."

They also tend to be people of substance, rather than people of style and flim-flam.

They tend to lack big egos, and so tend to put more trust in the evidence before their eyes than trusting their own, or others, expertise and eminence.

Above all, because of their experiences, what makes them hesitant about putting themselves forward is that they REALLY don't want to be is a BAD leader.

There's quite a tradition of the reluctant leader in the wider world: How about George Washington, Moses, Mahatma Gandhi, and Pope Francis? When newly elected, the new Speaker of the House of Commons makes a great show[26] of being dragged reluctantly to the Speaker's chair. If you are reluctant, you're in some great company and there's a good history behind you

---

[26] Okay, I know I am over-egging this, they are never *that* reluctant…

Leadership Sometimes Depends Upon Looking Through The Right End Of The Telescope

Figure 1 When You Have To Lead A Group Of People, It Is A Lot Easier If You Make Sure You Are Looking Through The Right End Of The Telescope...

Look through the wrong end of a telescope and an astonishingly useful tool becomes perfectly useless. It doesn't do its job. It is not that the telescope is broken, it is still working perfectly. It is simply that the user does not know how to use it and anyone who knows about telescopes and sees you looking through the wrong end, will know you are an idiot. Leadership is very similar: for it to work properly you have to know how to use it. That means be familiar with the tool and look throught it from the right way round.

True leaders look through the right end of the telescope. They know that the trick is not to try to lead people, it is to do the right things in the right order so that people want to follow them.

The second trick is that True leaders know that most people want to have someone to follow. Being a leader is hard. Having everyone look to you when things go wrong and you needing to come up with the right answer for them is not easy. It does not appeal to everyone. But then, few people are asked to be leaders, they need to volunteer.

To be sure there are rules that people apply to their leaders, but they are not that hard to live up to.

The Ambitious Leader Versus The Reluctant Leader:

Most ambitious leaders lead from the point of view that, if they charge off into the future, people will follow them because they are convinced their mixture of personal charisma, animal magnetism and dynamism are irresistible. If only.

Of course, this actually works for those rare individuals who *genuinely* possess such talents. Unfortunately, for every single person who truly was born to be a natural leader, there seem to be about twenty or thirty who are just truly convinced they were. The problem is not the true leader, - they will always emerge - it is the thirty deluded ones who think they are true leaders that we have to clear up after.

In comparison, reluctant leaders know a little secret: **people will always want the best future they can get**. Why would they want anything else? If a leader can conjure up a vision of a better and more appealing future for their people than they already have, then people will naturally follow them (as long as they are convinced that that person they are about to follow also has the wherewithal to deliver it).

In other words, they look at leadership through the *right* end of the telescope.

Your People Want A Good Now, But A Better Future

Why is it that people commit completely to certain leaders and are left cold by others?

Why would they leave an almost certain future where they are, and change jobs for an unknown environment?

Why change from what you know to embark on a risky future?

The answer? Self-interest: People want a better future for themselves and their loved ones. Although they like a good 'now,' they are willing to trade a sure not very good now for the promise of a better future.

The same thing goes for voting for governments, life partners, cars and career changes.

So, if we give them a pretty okay now and give them confidence that their future will be even better than that if they stick with you, we can be confident that they will follow us.

It is always worth remembering this every time just before you open your mouth as a manager or leader. They are not following you because of your magnetic personality; they are following you because you are the best game in town.

Which means that you had better be on top of your game, because other games may be available.

Giving Your People A _Now_ Worth Following

How can you _know_ what your people want so that you can give it to them?

You could either ask them directly, or you could read the results of the work of some very clever people whose only job is to ask employees what they really want from their work, who then give the anonymised results back to the client.

That's what I did.

Who would I ask? *The Sirota Institute.* And I have. Why? Because I think they are the best.

The Sirota Institute have been doing employee research for seriously huge global companies such as IBM and Starbucks since the 1970s and they wrote a book.

The book is called *"The Enthusiastic Employee, How Companies Profit By Giving Their Employees What They Want,"* and it is by David Sirota, Louis A. Mishkind, and Michael Irwin Meltzer.

Buy it. Read it. It will make you a better leader.

So, What Do Your People Want? Equity, Achievement, and Camaraderie

We have already spoken about Sirota book's recommendations for treating your staff with Equity, Achievement, and Camaraderie. But the issue is *so* important, and so often overlooked, I think it needs hammering home again and again. So, once again:

Equity:

It turns out people want to be treated with a certain fairness at work.

Who would have thought? Equity to them means getting the right recognition and reward for their efforts. They already know that there are no more jobs for life but they do want to be treated fairly while they are there and working for you. This is the first lesson for the reluctant leader.

Achievement:

Apparently, people want a sense of achievement and pride from their work and also a small measure of control, too. Why not, after all, they are spending the very best hours of their day with you. There's a reason why working in monotonous jobs in factories is described as 'soul destroying.' It often has no purpose for the people doing it, and we all need purpose. This is the second lesson for the reluctant leader.

Camaraderie:

People don't just come to work for the money. They also come to work for the company and to be social. Human beings are tribal pack animals who thrive when well socialised and do not do well when isolated. In fact, some of the oldest punishments are about being pushed out from the group:

Ex-communication, banishment, and being outlawed. This is the third lesson for the reluctant leader and the hardest one to achieve with remote teams. How to instil that feeling that it is great to be in this group?

One of the biggest problems with working with remote teams is fostering that sense of _belonging_. I spend a great deal of my time on getting this this right with my own teams and it pays dividends. In the absence of anyone else to do it, that is our responsibility.

Of course, a lot of this is forgotten knowledge. Actually, we have known much of this ever since Douglas Murray McGregor wrote his classic, and excellent management book "The Human Side Of

Enterprise[27]," which he wrote in 1960.

Sometimes, the secrets of the world are hidden in plain sight.

One of the biggest issues to address in working with remote teams is fostering that sense of belonging to a group. In the absence of anyone else to do it, we have to make it our responsibility. We need to pay special attention[28] to this when we work remotely.

At Scrumnastics, we have added these three ethics to the five Scrum ethics and, to be honest, we have put them _above_ the Scrum ethics because our teams prefer them.

Giving Your People a _Future_ worth Following

How do you give your people a better bet on the future?

You give them a 'postcard of the destination,' - a vision of a better future: a great reason "_why?_"

Why? Because a great 'reason why,' or a 'strong why[29],' lends your quest a _purpose_, and people crave a purpose.

A great, well thought out, reasoned "why we are doing this?" is crucial because, in an often seemingly random world, a sense of

---

[27] "The Human Side Of Enterprise," is another book I urge you to buy and read. It will not only teach you about "Theory X," and "Theory Y" managers, but it will make you a better manager of people.

[28] For that I use the Daily Scrum, to start off the day together, the "Sharpening the Tools," to close the working day together and the Sprint Retrospective, the Sprint debriefing session. Some Scrum Masters think that doing games helps, I do not.

[29] "He who has a why can endure any how." – Frederick Nietzsche

purpose gives your people a reason to commit to, and share in, your dream.

Here's the best 'reason why,' I have ever seen:

"This country should commit itself to achieving the goal, before this decade is out, of landing a man on the moon and returning him safely to earth." John F. Kennedy 1961.

Now that is a cracking reason why, isn't it? I especially like the "and returning him safely to earth" bit. That's what I call really classy.

The most persuasive purposes have the following characteristics of being specific, measurable, assignable (or actionable), realistic and timely. You may know this as the "SMART" acronym.

The fact that President Kennedy's beautiful words also conformed beautifully to the traditional S.M.A.R.T. Management acronym for a goal is probably not a co-incidence.

As you probably already know, S.M.A.R.T. stands for **Specific, Measurable, Assignable, Realistic and Timely.**

1. Specific: " the goal,… of landing a man on the moon and returning him safely to earth."

2. Measurable: Before: We have never been to the moon. After: Oh yes we have. And we can go again.

3. Assignable: Who? "**This nation** should commit itself to …"

4. Realistic: Was it realistic? Well, they achieved it, and they achieved it within a decade. Sometimes, even the most breathtakingly audacious goals can be achieved.

5. Timely: "before this decade is out."

In fact, they did better than that. NASA took three men to the moon and put two men on the moon, and brought all three of them safely back, in July 1969. Heroic.

* * *

The vision of the future is the reason why, Nietzsche's 'strong why,' from all the possible things that the members of your team could possibly do with their time, they should care enough to go with you from where they are now to where you imagine they could be. A shared vision is a transformative thing.

The reason I mention SMART acronym is that when you are stuck for a purpose, SMART gives you a great test for any ideas you may have. If it passes the SMART test, it is very likely that your idea of a purpose will be a winner with your people.

That's the strong why, the reason why.

Giving Your People Some*one* Worth Following

Remember that as a leader, you are not their friend, you are their champion.

You are not there to be David Brent from "The Office." They know that you pretending to be their best mate is simply a manipulative lie, and they will despise you for it. Although they will not show it, they will seethe inside. There will be a reckoning.

The key to being a champion is to have, on average, more of the good personality characteristics that your people admire than they do. They want you to be the person they wish they could be.

It's who you are in the round that counts most of all, but you had better know that you have:

Wherewithal:

No-one wants to follow someone who is floppy and the flaccid for very long. Why would they? Would you?

Instead, you need to show you have that certain 'wherewithal.' That combination of drive, confidence, grit, vision and "Oomph," that they don't, or more likely, can't, show in work. You demonstrating these qualities is what gives them the courage to have faith in you that you will deliver the vision you gave them. This is part of you being their champion.

You also need to realise and be aware just how hard it is to be a subordinate, and, just how hard it is for perfectly capable, mature people to *be* subordinate in work. Outside of work they may lead families, voluntary groups or lead and manage all manner of wonderful things, but in work they have to kowtow to people who they may well have no respect for as people. Be someone they can respect. It will make a difference.

The Ability To Speak Truth To Power:

You do need to be able to serve them as a shield against those from above them. Again, this is part of being their champion.

They need to know that you will be batting for them as individuals and battling for them as a team. I have led many teams composed of the most red-blooded, hairy-chested individuals who make you think "wow, I bet he's afraid of nobody!" Yet, when it comes to talking with a bunch of weedy guys with better suits and higher status, they simply wither when confronted by them.

It's not even limited to physicality. I have led a team of PhD maths wizards who were brighter than the sun, yet they shrivelled in front of a bunch of sharp, shrewd, but ultimately much thicker blokes who had (fake) posh accents.

You need to be smart, but you don't need to be the smartest in the group.

You definitely need to be strong, but you don't need to be the strongest.

But you do need to be strong enough. And have the courage to tell the truth to power. There are too many lily-livered liars masquerading as leaders living among us. Our teams expect better than that and they deserve better from their leaders.

Great leaders are decisive. They may take time to take counsel from their people but when they have come to a decision they implement swiftly. They don't dither or faff about once a decision has to be made.

Great leaders also make things right when they have gone wrong. They also have the strength to apologise when they realise they have done wrong.

Now, Scrumnast, go and be a _great_ leader.

The Physical Aspects Of Leadership: Turns Out Your Grandparents Were Right After All - Shoulders Back, Stand Up Straight: Remember Those Lobsters[30]

A great deal of leadership is knowing how to lead – but a very big part is possessing the *physicality* of leadership.

Why? Because your people are looking at you. Today. Tomorrow. Next week. And they are judging you. What are they judging? Your physical strength. They are judging whether you are still capable of leading them and whether you are still worth following. They will do this every day. You think that heroic thing you did for the team last week will count for something next month? It won't.

We need to have and display that certain status that all leaders have. That certain 'avoirdupois[31],' or heft.

What grants someone that heft? That certain status? How did they get it? How do we get it?

In a word? Serotonin. Serotonin is the hormone that dictates how much status we, chimps, lions, dogs and even lobsters have within a group. The more serotonin in your bloodstream, the higher your status. I wish it were more complicated than that, but unfortunately, it isn't. It is a 350-million-year-old system that is even older than the design of your lungs. And your skin, too.

---

[30] If you don't believe any of this, go and read the first chapter in "12 Rules For Life: An Antidote To Chaos," by Jordan Peterson.
[31] French for 'Feel the weight.'

* * *

You know that (terribly immature) thing where you blast off from the traffic lights and burn off the guy in the rubbish car? Why did you do that? Because you got more serotonin as a result. Get a promotion or a raise a work? You get more serotonin. Get the brush off from that very attractive person who you know is out of your league but, hey, it's been a great day and God loves a try-er, so why not? Less serotonin. Actually, quite a lot less serotonin.

More than that, your brain has a really old, and incredibly clever little bit in it that knows _exactly_ how much serotonin you have. Not only that, it compares the amount of serotonin _you_ have in your bloodstream, with the amount that everyone else has, and _their_ brains are doing the same thing for them at the same time. One of the ways it does this is examining your posture and comparing it with everyone else's.

It's how we all know our rank in life. And ranks change. We can go up and we can go down.

Next time something positive happens to you, just pay attention to how your posture improves. Next time something negative happens, again, pay attention to how you slouch.

Beware of 'status vampires,' the creepy types who get their jollies by making themselves feel good by making other people feel bad. Why do they do it? For a quick hit of serotonin. It's nothing professional, it's entirely personal.

What is the easiest way for you to get more serotonin than anything else? Your posture. The better your posture, the more serotonin you make. Even better, the more serotonin you make the better your posture. It is a virtuous feedback circle.

So your granddad and grandmother were right: Stand up straight, shoulders back so your shoulder blades are touching, then suck your shoulders down into their sockets[32]. Look everyone straight in the eye and talk deeply and slowly. Practice that. In front of a mirror if you must, but practice.

Exercise 1:

No matter what your height, I want you to pull yourself up to your very tallest and then go outside. Remember: shoulders back, chest out, chin tucked in. There is no need to try to look aggressive. Try a hint of a smile on your face. Now, walk down your road and as you pass by a stranger, maintain your most upright posture, stare impassively straight ahead and don't make direct eye contact. Notice out of the corner of your eye what happens about five to seven metres before they pass by you. If you keep do it right, keeping your shoulders back and your head upright, you will notice that as they approach you, they will nod their head slightly. Almost imperceptibly. This means they have acknowledged you as having higher status, even though they don't know who you are. A complete stranger. Serotonin. It's a weird thing. But it works.

Exercise 2:

I want you to become mindful and aware of your own posture throughout the day and how it changes as you interact with different people. When you talk with this person, are you able to maintain a tall and erect posture, or do you feel your shoulders start to pull forward, and your back to slouch? If they do, what happens to the conversation when you catch yourself, put your shoulder blades together, and make yourself as tall as you can? Does the tone of the conversation change?

The Voice Of Command

---

[32] I know it sounds weird but the moment you do it right, you will suddenly feel stronger than you *ever* have before. Go and ask Pavel Tsatsouline about it. He's right.

* * *

There really is no need to do that silly, braying, English public schoolboy, fake deep voice. If you do, please know that everyone you talk to, knows that it is fake. Besides, the next time you speak with someone who has a naturally deeper voice that you, you will _shrivel_ inside.

Just talk as deeply as you naturally can, quietly, and slowly. It will help them listen and help you keep your nerve.

The low voice demonstrates how much testosterone you were exposed to when you were an adolescent (yes, women too). The lower the voice, the more testosterone you made. The more testosterone, the greater the potential harm you can do to someone else. As the saying goes, it's not the dog in the fight, it's the fight in the dog.

Here's an old trick I learned from being a radio producer and presenter and doing radio programmes. - it really helps: Practice speaking deeply and slowly - it will allow your mouth to work slower than your brain. Making your mouth work slower than your brain is _really_ important when speaking in public.

In a radio studio, what you really don't want is for your mouth to be going faster than your brain. If you do, then you get sound gaps, or 'air,' in the sound, and that _really_ freaks out your audience, because it creates a great big doubt in their mind that you know what you are saying and doing.

Similarly, when you are leading your team what you really don't want is your mouth working faster than your brain.   Look at politicians...

Strength And Fitness:

Strength and vitality _matter_ in leadership. Look how many managers do sporty activities. You won't need to be the strongest in your team, but you do need to be robust. After all, you will be required to champion your team at some point.

Many would say it is not my job to tell you to exercise and to watch what you eat, but I am going to anyway. The better you eat the stronger you will be. The physically stronger you are the better leader you will be, especially at the end of the working day. Leaders also need their cognitive strength and there is a link between fitness and cognitive strength. Leaders need to make good decisions at all times of the day. Your team need you to be strong because you are their champion.

Like your mother told you: eat properly and stop eating processed food. When you do start to eat well, you will soon feel fitter and stronger. Even better, make your own food, especially at lunchtime, it will be better than the rubbish you buy from any sandwich shop. Watch the drinking, especially when on your own or at home.

Get fresh air. Every day. Get out at lunchtime and walk for twenty minutes. When you finish work get out and walk for another twenty minutes. Doing those two will make a huge difference to your fitness. Our bodies were shaped by hundreds of thousands of years of activity. We were not designed for office work. Do exercise, especially weights. You don't need a gym membership.

Me? I am a keto carnivore and I do kettlebells but that's just me. I have no idea if the same thing will work for you, but I really think that investing some time and effort in finding some way of eating that works for you is important. Whatever it will eventually be, it's probably safe to say that kebabs, turkey twizzlers, chips, rice, white bread and biscuits are probably not doing you a great deal of good.

Kettlebells offer a fantastic route to fitness, but they are basically cannon balls with handles, so if you find the idea appealing you _must_ learn how to use them properly. The potential for particularly nasty injury is ever present. The best kettlebell person in the world is Pavel Tsatsouline, he has very good books and online courses and also has a fine sense of humour, too.

* * *

Mind Your Language

I really mean it, mind your language. When you want something to happen give clear, direct, crisp instructions using clear, direct, crisp language in an active voice. Say "I want you to…" and not floppy millennial language. "I think it would be a good idea if you…" is pure floppy millennial language and not good enough. - You get the idea.

A lot of new leaders think that being direct is rude, but it isn't. In this day and age, it is actually quite a relief for someone to receive a direct request to do something. The more words you use for a request, the more it can be misinterpreted by the person listening. Do them a favour and get used to using short, crisp instructions that start with "I want you to…"

And don't swear - you are no longer "one of the boys" or "one of the girls." You are a leader; they expect better of you.

One final thing: "Oi! You there at the back? Stand up straight when I'm talking to you!"

The Servant Leader

In the Scrumnastics part of the book, we are going to learn about a method of managing called Scrum. There is a leadership 'accountability' called the Scrum Master. An accountability is Scrum's name for a team role.

Scrum now describes them as being a true leader. But for a long time, the Scrum Master was described as a 'servant leader.' That meant that they did everything from keeping the team and the work running, using the best Scrum traditions, acting as an ambassador for Scrum throughout the organisation, being a 'fixer,' and being an all-round good egg. They served the team by using their valuable skills in order to lead their teams. This description of the role is not new. In your grandparents' time they would have been called the foreman.

Actually, the idea of a servant leader exists outside of Scrum. Captains of sport teams lead by serving as well as shouting, and anyone who has a background in going to church will be very familiar with the idea. Pastors, vicars and priests all act as servant leaders, and it's the same with all sorts of community groups.

There is also a huge body of work in formal management study about what a servant leader does and how every company needs them. Unfortunately, when people hear the term, they tend to just hear the word servant.

As a result, many of the 'self-managed team' frameworks, such as Scrum, and XP etc, have attracted a lot of floppy Herberts [33] who, although they had the necessary qualifications, weren't capable of running an egg and spoon race, never mind leading a team or managing a project. Even worse, a lot of them got jobs as floppy, flaccid 'Agile' coaches and Scrum Masters in floppy, flaccid companies. This has become a problem.

Which is probably why the Scrum 2020 update stopped using the

---

[33] Technical term, obviously.

phrase servant leader and started using the phrase "True Leader," instead of servant leader.

But actually, and occasionally, every leader needs to be a servant leader. It goes with the job.

What Does It Mean To Be A "Servant Leader?"

Here's a practical example of what a Servant Leader does and is. We will use a traditional work team of house builders and their foreman.

Foreman is a very old term for a leader of a team of people with various different skills, such as you would see on a building site. 'Foreman' is short for the foremost man in the group.

You Don't Need To Do "Scrum" To Be A Servant Leader: Bryn's Builders:

The term servant leader is not exclusively part of Scrum. It stands alone and is used in combination with many different management frameworks.

Here's an example where some burly chested builders might use it.

It's halfway through the working day on a building site when the joiner tells the foreman that he is about to run out of screws, and he wants to go and get some more from the building supplies merchant.

The wily foreman knows that if the carpenter goes off site, he is likely to get sidetracked for the rest of the day and it will be unlikely that he will be back on the building site today. This means the team's progress on the house building (that the foreman is ultimately responsible for) will slow down or even stop: Not so good.

Instead, the foreman offers to go and get some from the suppliers, knowing that the carpenter has just enough screws for a few more hours work, which will be enough to keep him going until he returns.

* * *

This means that the carpenter is able to carry on working in the meantime and the team won't fall behind because of any work that they are relying on from the carpenter not getting finished today.

The foreman obviously takes the opportunity to ask everyone else in the team if they need more supplies. They do, and so he offers to get the supplies for the other tradesmen too.

Obviously, some insecure middle manager types, being obsessed with their own status, might see the 'boss' agreeing to run around to the suppliers as demeaning and want nothing to do with it. However, the wily foreman knows that by doing so, he has kept the pace of the work (the velocity, as it is called in Scrum) going today, and, by buying the other supplies, has also removed other potential obstacles (called impediments in Scrum) for tomorrow's work. A side benefit is that the foreman also knows that he is only buying items for his project and not supplying items for someone else's project on the quiet (I told you he was wily). In other words, he has done some judicious budget management at the same time.

In Scrum leadership and management terms, the foreman's actions would be seen as a great success. The foreman (Scrum Master), has removed the immediate problems (impediments), kept the pace (velocity) of the work going, and has also removed potential problems (also impediments), for the other members of the team. Although he is unlikely to be aware of Scrum as a management framework, he has accidentally shown himself to be an excellent and effective Scrum Master.

On the other hand, the foreman _could_ have been so impressed by his own sense of importance that he would have said yes to the carpenter's request for them to go to the shops themselves, but this would have been at the expense of losing the momentum on the project.

Who really won? I think it was the foreman, how about you?

In reality, there are times when every True Leader has to be a servant leader. It is amazing just how many of the very best leaders I have met and served have all said words to the effect of "it is an honour to serve you," to their staff. It doesn't mean they are a dogsbody; it means they serve them with their integrity, their knowledge and their wherewithal.

Rock n' Rollers as Servant Leaders?

On a completely different note, I once saw Bruce Springsteen and the E Street Band in a huge outdoor gig. You can't imagine a scenario that would be less of an example of a servant leader in action.

There were 40,000+ die-hard fans who had gone to see "The Boss," as even his fans call him. Just as they were coming to the end of the concert Bruce told his fans "it is always an honour to serve you." The crowd went wild.

I have no idea whether he was being genuine or not, although his long running reputation would suggest he was. If "The Boss" can be a servant leader, then so can I. How about you, Scrumnast?

Leadership - Extra Resources - W.C.H. Prentice

W.C.H. Prentice, a great leadership thinker, gave us this classic definition of what leadership is, all the way in 1961: *"The Accomplishment of a Goal through the direction of Human Assistants"*

I put his quote for two reasons:

1.   It's a great, concise, practical working definition of what leadership is. We can work with it and we can keep it in the back of our minds.

2.   He was probably the very first person to say that leadership was more than just the result of possessing the physical power to be able to give someone a good kicking or being so much extraordinarily smarter than everybody else around.

W.C.H. Prentice's online article, "**Understanding Leadership**" is tremendous. I urge you to read it. You will learn more about leadership in its seven pages than by reading a bucket of other books on leadership. But it raises its own questions.

Like *how* do we actually direct the human assistants to accomplish the goal?

At this point, most books take some notes from some academics on what leadership is, but Leadership and Management are practical skills, not academic skills.

Instead, I think we are served better by some inspiring quotes from some truly great leaders who, being leaders, can actually tell us what they think leadership is.

Here we go.

"Management is doing things right; leadership is doing the right thing."

—*Peter F. Drucker*

"The supreme quality of leadership is integrity." —*Dwight D. Eisenhower*

"All of the great leaders have had one characteristic in common: it was the willingness to confront unequivocally the major anxiety of their people in their time. This, and not much else, is the essence of leadership." —*John Kenneth Galbraith*

"The task of leadership is not to put greatness into humanity, but to elicit it, for the greatness is already there." —*John Buchan (author of "The 39 Steps")*

"A leader is a person you will follow to a place you would not go by yourself." —*Joel Barker*

"A true leader has the confidence to stand alone, the courage to make tough decisions, and the compassion to listen to the needs of others. He does not set out to be a leader but becomes one by the equality of his actions and the integrity of his intent." —*Douglas MacArthur*

"A leader is best when people barely know he exists. When his work is done, his aim fulfilled, they will say: we did it ourselves." —*Lao Tzu*

"the aim of leadership should be to improve the performance of man and machine, to improve quality, to increase output, and simultaneously to bring pride of workmanship to people. Put in a negative way, the aim of leadership is not merely to find and record failures of men, but to remove the causes of failure: to help people to do a better job with less effort." — *William Edwards Deming.*

"The greatest leader is not necessarily the one who does the greatest things. He is the one that gets the people to do the greatest things." —*Ronald Reagan*

There you go, a bit more inspirational than asking an academic. I am not sure that anyone could add much more to define leadership than these quotations. Did you notice that quiet voice of humility that runs through all of them?

If we aspire to be anything like as good a leader as these were, humility is probably one of the qualities that we need to aspire to. Yet, when you consider the personalities of most leaders that you will actually encounter in business, it's not really humility that typically springs to mind, is it? So, who is right, the ex-leader giant of the free world, or today's chancer in a good suit?

I shall leave the last words to the American historian and classicist, Victor Davis Hansen. Being a Greek and Roman classicist, he's not an optimist on human nature, but he believes that good behaviour can shape your character. For us leaders, I think that is an excellent aspiration.

"Deal in personal trust; your word is your bond; avoid extremes; treat the money you invest for others as something sacred; don't take any more perks than you would wish others to take; don't borrow what you couldn't suddenly pay back; imagine the worst case financial scenario and expect it may well happen; the wealthier you become the more humble you should act." - Victor Davis Hansen.

Leadership Extra Resources 2: Daniel Goleman - Six Styles Of Leadership

I put this in here because a great many M.B.A. courses start off by talking about styles of leadership in their very first term and then set an essay on it so that the students can convince themselves that their, and their lecturer's, complete lack of personal charisma will not be a drawback[34] in being a leader.

Most leaders are not one particular style. They are an amalgam of the styles.

Being academics who couldn't run a whelk stall, the academics who

---

[34] It will be. It really, really will be.

set essays can't fathom that a leader can change their style as is needed, because that is _part of the job_. In fact, most leaders have very little trouble changing between them. Unlike academics…

The Visionary — mobilize people toward a vision. Works best when a clear direction or change is needed. The visionary promotes the most positive climate.

The Coaching — develop people for the future. Works best when helping people and building long-term strength. Again, promotes a positive climate.

The Affiliative — creates emotional bonds and harmony. Works best to heal rifts in teams or motivate people in stressful times. Also a positive climate.

The Democratic — builds consensus through participation. Works best to create consensus or get input. Also a positive climate.

The Pacesetting — expects excellence and self-direction. Works best to get quick results from a highly competent team. This type of leader promotes a negative climate.

The Commanding — demand immediate compliance. Works best in crisis or with problematic people. Again a negative climate.

The most important aspect of these breakdowns is that since each style fits a different situation, a good leader needs to be able to switch between them when the context requires that. A leadership style becomes more of a tool, rather than just a personality trait.

The Finest Leader I Ever Met

The best and finest reluctant leader I have ever had the pleasure of working with is someone called Peter Lumley. Peter worked for Thomas Cook in the days when they made (lots of) money.

Pete headed up the business intelligence and management information division for Thomas Cook. Business Intelligence is what shows you where you are making your money and losing your money.

I knew him because I had taught him and his team how to create a thing called a' data warehouse' and I later designed some of the data cubes that had a few of the snottier technical issues. On and off, I worked with Pete as a consultant for over 12 years.

Pete had a certain knack of handing out tasks to his people that were really finely judged. They always stretched that person a little bit to keep them interested in their job but never so much that they caused them a lot of negative stress. In that way he made sure they thrived.

His small team combined all sorts of computer data from all kinds of different computer systems, none of which wanted to play nice with the others. Everything they succeeded in doing was painful to achieve. They combined data from the world's seventh largest airline, the second largest tour operator in Europe, and the largest retail presence in the UK. They made every piece of software they used scream, and they churned and turned raw data into valuable insights for a bunch of remarkably talentless, ungrateful, largely innumerate senior managers. Who largely ignored it. Which is one of the reasons that Thomas Cook eventually went bust.

One of the systems that Pete's team designed was used when a Fatwa was called on British tourists in Kenya. It was the only system in the UK that could locate every UK tourist and their hotel in Kenya whether they had booked with Thomas Cook or not.

The UK government could not find them and so they turned to Thomas Cook. Or rather, they turned to Pete. His job was to get a list of all of the holiday makers to those special, tough, brave men who you turn to in the dark times: those men who don't do very much but what they do stays done.

Time was of the essence, so it was a good thing that it only took him and his team 20 pretty frantic minutes to get them their list.

Did Peter and his team get a grateful and well deserved 'thank you' from the top management of Thomas Cook? Er, no. The management 'talent' was far too busy taking the credit for themselves to do anything so noble. It was even more cutting when I tell you that, 25 years previously, Pete had lifted the CEO out of obscurity from working in the post room and gave him a job with a future. In other words, it was Pete that had put him on the right path to a brighter future.

Pete's quiet reward was the sure knowledge of a job well done. That he and his team helped in a small way to keep the lives of innocent British tourists safe. Quietly achieving things like that mattered more to Pete than any fake thanks. He was the essence of a reluctant leader.

Like most reluctant leaders, he was passionate about the company, its history and heritage and, above all, the people who worked there no matter how badly the company treated him and his team. Whether doorman or director, Pete knew them all and always had a few brightening words for them all. He was one of the good guys.

Within Thomas Cook Peter Lumley was famous.

He used to joke that if you cut him open, his body would have "Thomas Cook" running all the way through it. Every day his overworked, too small team faced a different, almost insurmountable technical challenge combined with an insufficient budget.

However, Pete inspired, led, enticed and encouraged everyone in his team to overcome each one of the challenges day after day and year after year. I never, ever heard him say a cross word to any of them: the men and women of his team adored him.

He never moaned to anyone about the shabby way that his managers treated him during his career even though it cost him many thousands of pounds in lost pension rights when they outsourced him for eight years and then insourced him back to Thomas Cook when they finally bothered to find out what he did and how valuable his team were to the company.

In his spare time Pete was a Scout Master, so were his wife and daughter. He liked nothing better than quietly organising food and outdoor camping for Scout jamborees, where many hundreds of young people came from all over the world to come together in the big showgrounds of Peterborough. It is customary to smirk knowingly at such things now, but Peter was made of better stuff than that.

Peter was also in charge of the annual scout Gang show for Peterborough. One of the years I was working with him he invited me to come along and see it.

The star turn was a young teenage lad with Down's syndrome who sang the hit song of the show solo. Peter and his team had encouraged and coached him for a whole year.

On the night I went the applause from the crowd and the others in the show when the lad hit the high notes at the end of the song was one of the most moving and genuine things I have ever seen. I used to be a rock musician and I have seen and been to some great gigs: but there wasn't a dry eye in the house that night.

So, thank you, Peter Lumley, for showing me the wisdom and merit of being a reluctant leader and for being the best leader I have ever worked with.

Your inspiration runs through every leadership and management project I have ever done since. You always did the right thing at the right time and always because it was the right thing to do and for no other reward or reason.

You also always did the right thing at the wrong time, even though it always cost you dear. A true reluctant leader and the reason I look for reluctant leaders to succeed me in every team I train, coach and mentor.

* * *

Thank you, Pete.

When Pete retired there were genuine tears of love and sadness from the many, many people that he had worked with and managed over the decades. Pete left a Pete shaped hole in Thomas Cook and somehow it was never the same without him.

When the CEO made Thomas Cook bankrupt there were tears of a very different sort from those whose lives and careers he had ruined.

There are lessons here for all of us to learn.

You may have learned that it is expected that you can tread on the quietly noble, and the humble and get away with it in order to get your way. If so, you may do well in life but you will never be a true leader, reluctant or otherwise. And one day, there will be a reckoning. There is always a reckoning.

Or, you may have been inspired to always treat the people in your care as well as you can and do the right thing by your people, even sometimes when it is to your personal detriment. It's called having an old-fashioned, old school attribute called honour. Having honour means you sleep at night.

And which is more, - you will be a _Scrumnast_, [35] my son.

And How <u>Not</u> To Be A Leader…

In 2006, I was in Cardiff, working as an interim manager as a part of the management team of a subsidiary of a very big British bank.

The Chief Executive Officer was your stereotypical Home Counties,

---

[35] - With very large apologies to Rudyard Kipling's poem, "If"

ex-English public schoolboy: loud, braying voice[36], presumptuous, entitled, bags of unwarranted confidence in his (really quite limited) intellectual abilities and, of course, red braces.

At 10 a.m., every Monday morning, the phones were turned off and three hundred and fifty of his staff trooped up to the big open plan office where he would hold forth for the 55 minutes of the weekly meeting. Individuals were publicly berated and then after that, he told them what a great time he had at the head office in London the previous week, and what a pleasure it was to lead them. What a guy.

He would always finish the meeting by telling an unspeakably filthy joke in front of everyone, including the women. Obviously, they were expected to find this hysterically funny. Oh. How. They. Laughed.

But they made a mental note. And they remembered. There is always a reckoning.

To show just how worldly wise he was, he collectively addressed them in very bad French as "mon brave[37]." Now Cardiff people really believe in education, so whenever he said, "mon brave," the whole room would sigh out a quiet, educated, whispered, correct "mes," after he spoke. Of course, because didn't speak French properly, he didn't understand why three hundred and fifty people were whispering "mes," whenever he said "mon." I have to tell you, three hundred and fifty people whispering under their breath is *loud*.

At the end of the seventh meeting, I passed by the very double of the Welsh singer, Katherine Jenkins. She was one of those young, keen, bright, enthusiastic, woman graduate trainees who are on the way up and in a hurry - I heard her mutter contemptuously under her breath, "that man couldn't manage a bowel movement," and three of her graduate trainee colleagues rolled their eyes in silent agreement. There is always a reckoning. For everything.

In that moment I realised that he had lost command of them. He had

---

[36] See the "Physical Nature of Leadership" section on lobsters
[37] instead of the correct, plural "mes braves."

lost them all. Forever. He assumed that they were his to lead and he could treat them as he liked. But they knew better.

Loyalty is never given, it is *lent*. They had had enough of being treated without respect. He had created a complete disconnection between staff and management, and it was entirely his fault. Once he had broken the connection, they simply tolerated him.

As I looked back towards him, his back-slapping colleagues from the executive committee had gathered around him and were congratulating him on pulling off another great meeting and yet another hilarious joke.

Instead of concentrating on leading their people in their departments, this team of directors were only concerned with back-slapping each other. They had turned in on themselves. There wasn't just a disconnection between staff and management, this was now a chasm - and it was all of their making, not the staff. The staff were just responding to how they were being treated. I have seen it many times in companies where the bosses have convinced themselves they are world class. It often happens just before there is *real* trouble in a company.

Three weeks later he was out. Six months later they were all out.

Banks have a stock of good times managers and a much larger stock of bad times managers that they keep on their books for rainy days, very rainy days, and storms.

When times change, they simply arrange a surprise visit by some very well dressed 'H.R. business partners' from Head Office. They arrive unannounced. The Chief Executive's office door is shut firmly. Suppressed, anguished howls are heard, then a flowery corporate email is sent out to the troops with words like 'pursuing new opportunities,' and a "too good an offer to pass up," and a "we're sure you join us in wishing him well." The Chief Exec then leaves tight-lipped, tight bottomed, and with red-rimmed eyes as they parachute in one of those special kinds of psychopath who wear such very good suits.

* * *

There is always a reckoning. Always.

But I know this will not happen to you, young Scrumnast. Not you. You know better.

You are a Scrumnast.

Summary.

So here we are at the end of the chapter. You may be thinking "why didn't he address the obvious bit about just simply relying on your status and authority as a tool to lead?"

Because status and authority are such very brittle things. Besides, if you use the lessons in this chapter then you won't have to rely on them, you can keep them in reserve. This section is a shortened form of a course I use to teach new leaders and business owners, many of whom already have MBAs. I always ask the MBAs if they found it valuable. They always said yes.

Was it the most exhaustive deep dive into leadership? No, there are whole libraries of books you could read on leadership - but many of them would leave you no wiser about doing the job.

But it was a practical look into _effective_ leadership. We have looked at the True Leader, the Servant Leader, and the Reluctant Leader. You can be all three because you now know not just how to lead, but how to get people to follow you.

Could you apply all the knowledge you now have and go and credibly lead a team today, or a bunch of teams tomorrow, or even build and lead a brilliant company full of brilliant people one day? Yes, Scrumnast, I think you could.

Let's put it another way: could you do a better job of leading a company than the numpty boy from the bank you read about earlier? I think so, Scrumnast. I really think so. Don't you?

* * *

Also remember that unlike you, most CEOs of organisations are not actually leaders anymore. Sadly, they are only very posh administrators.

They file documents at the right time, and make sure certain meetings happen, just like clerks and secretaries.

Always remember there is a reason that the master's level degree in business management is called a Master of Business Administration. It is not called "Masters of Building And Running Meteorically Successful Companies That Generate Astonishingly Useful Products And Services to Humanity And So May Well Be Around In 250 Years, A Bit Like Panasonic and Toyota Plan to".

Now _that_ would be a course worth going on, wouldn't it?

Positive And Cautionary Tales for True Leaders

As we began Leadernomics, I put a footnote about Roman generals, who, after winning a very great victory were awarded a triumph. A triumph was a great public parade where they would be congratulated by all of Rome. However, all through the adulation of the crowds there would be a slave whispering in their ear: "Remember, thou art mortal.[38]"

Even then, sometimes, we need reminding we are mortal, which is why I an putting in J.R.R Tolkien's quotation on his opinion of 'bossing other men.'

"The most improper job of any man, even saints, (who at any rate, were at least unwilling to take it on), is bossing other men. Not one in a million is fit for it, and least of all who seek the opportunity." -J.R.R. Tolkien

---

[38] No, I don't know what happened to the slaves afterwards. But this was Rome, so…

Leadernomics: Join Us?

If you would like to see more videos on leadership, why not join the Scrumnastics mailing list? I post videos regularly on Youtube, FaceBook and the Locals platform.

Who knows what social platforms we will all be using next year? But if you join the mailing list you can be sure I will email you the latest links to the latest videos with on the latest platforms.

You can sign up to the Leadernomics and the Scrumnastics mailing lists at scrumnastics.co.uk (no, we don't sell your email, and every email has an unsubscribe option).

Have a real business that you are serious about growing?

Leadernomics Elite: Open to business owners with real businesses. Maximum 6 members per club.

You can sign up to the Scrumnastics mailing list at scrumnastics.co.uk.

COURSE TWO: SCRUMNASTICS - GUERILLA MANAGEMENT - NOT GORILLA MANAGEMENT

Scrumnastics - Guerrilla Management - Not Gorilla Management.

Management is all about creating order out of chaos, which is the natural state of things. Too much order and nothing happens - your adult children will have very tidy bedrooms once they have left home.

Three types of Order:

There are three kinds of order that we need management for. I am going to give these three things easy to understand terms you will never see a consultancy use, because if you realised how simple they really are, you would never pay them any money. They are:

1. "The Journey - Going From Here to There[39]": We are in a place or a state where we don't want to be, and we want to go to a place or state where we do want to be. In other words a project, or a 'transformation.' It could be that we are trying or making something new, or changing an existing product. That means there will be an element of risk that it may not turn out to be entirely (or even partially,) successful. We need a way of minimising and managing that risk so that we have the very best chance of success. This section of the book is for when you are in this situation. In the I. T. industry we call this 'Dev," (for development).

2. "Keep Calm And Carry On": This is the keeping the lights on work - in the IT industry we call that 'Ops,' or operations. In manufacturing we call it production. This is the normal, day-to-day work that makes a company money right now. All the processes are bedded in, they work just fine, and we don't want too much change

---

[39] We actually call this "From Boo Hoo to Hooray." in other words, this is where we are, which we don't like. Over there is a better place, which we hope we will like better. We need to get from here to there.

here, thank you very much. Although you can use what we are going to use in this section (and I frequently do,) you may feel you would be much better off using something like Kanban, which we will look at briefly later on. Many bureaucrats prefer to use Kanban because in the way they use it, there is less accountability.

3. "Crossing the 'T's' and dotting the 'I's.' ": Record keeping, accounts, governance, HR etc. In other words, bureaucracy. Every organisation has bureaucracy. The trick to success is making sure that you keep it to a bare minimum. You may have heard of "Minimum Viable Product[40]," well, we try to impress "Minimum Viable Bureaucracy," on our clients.

Goldilocks Management

What we want is just enough order that we enjoy good running, but still leave a bit of room for creativity. In other words, a well-balanced midpoint between chaos on the one end of the spectrum and inhumane, spirit-throttling bureaucracy at the other.

Scrum is the most popular of the 'Agile' management frameworks (there are lots of them, although some are quite similar in parts, most are very different. Some aren't even particularly agile).

Scrum is actually part of an even wider family of methods of organising people called 'self-managed teams.' Self-managed teams frameworks are widely used in the more enlightened manufacturing companies, most famously Toyota, which is reckoned to have the best management in the world.

The great thing about Scrum is that it gives you a powerful management framework that's not too big and not too small: Scrum is

---

[40] Minimum Viable Product (MVP,) is the very first bare bones product you release to the market. If you were making ice-cream, you would make a brilliant plain vanilla ice cream with no nuts, no raspberry sauce and no flake. If the market will buy that then they will probably buy the flake etc.

Goldilocks management - it's just right. Almost everyone seems to understand Scrum, because it it makes sense to them, unlike most of the management they have had to endure beforehand.

That's one of the other things about Scrum - unlike many management frameworks you may come across, it isn't actually bonkers[41]. There is a bit of silly jargon in Scrum, but not that much and besides, management wouldn't be management without some daft words in it, would it? More than that, once you have been doing Scrum for a few years, you will find that Scrum is a great springboard into other, larger forms of management, such as the Toyota Production System.

I am a bit of a management nut: I find all the thousands of different ways that human beings have found at getting a group of individuals together and transforming them into a well-oiled and productive team fascinating. The one common thing about them as you study them is that you can be sure that it won't be long before you say "Oh, that's just like Scrum." - That's another reason why I like Scrum, and that's why I recommend it.

Why do I call what we do Scrumnastics instead of Scrum? Well, what we do is all of Scrum AND a few other things as well to help us with managing remote teams better. Conversely, there's quite a lot of companies who do something known as "Scrum-but," which stands for "well, we do Scrum BUT we don't do…(insert one or more crucial parts of Scrum here)". Am I saying that Scrum is not enough? No, the way we work is unique, so we have had to customise Scrum a bit, and 'borrow' some ideas from Toyota, but the core is still Scrum. I will tell you about the custom bits as we go and you can choose to use them or not.

Scrum

There are five interlocking sides to Scrum. These are:

The Who - The Team and their Accountabilities

---

[41] There are lots. This should be a management technical term.

The How - Plan, Do, Study Act - The Events
The When - The Sprint
The What - The Artefacts - the work itself - and the work which shows the planning and progress of the work.
The Why - The Ethics - the reason why it works so well

When you try out Scrum or Scrumnastics, remember to give equal weight to each one of the five sides. You will find it is more effective to do all five in an average way, than it is to try two or three and get perfect at them and then add on others. From what I have seen, this tends not to happen, which means you will probably have to call on someone like me to relaunch it. This is always harder than doing it all from the beginning.

Scrum is what is called an 'improvement framework,' which means you get better at it by doing it. So, it is okay to start off so-so, and keep doing it until you get really great.

Remember, this is about people of capability and wherewithal, who want and *cause* things to happen, teaming up with people of skills and ability, who create things and *make* things happen, then harnessing the ancient power of the team to bring them into being.

As we say in Scrumnastics, "The clients bring the dreams, but we bring the means."

Everything in Scrum is meant to support that.

Scrum: Where Did It Come From?

Although two Japanese Management gurus, Hirotaka Takeuchi and Ikujiro Nonaka, came up with the phrase "Scrum" in management, it was really Jeff Sutherland and Ken Schwaber who took their germ of an idea and developed and perfected Scrum into the robust, management framework during the early 1990s. They announced Scrum publicly in 1995. Sutherland and Schwaber were signatories at the signing of the Agile Manifesto in 2001, which is why Scrum counts as one of the original Agile frameworks.

Hirotaka Takeuchi and Ikujiro Nonaka, first described Scrum in an article they wrote for the Harvard Business Review in 1986 called, "This New Product Development Game." It was this article that Ikuo, the Japanese manager at Panasonic showed me and changed my working life.

"In today's fast-paced, fiercely competitive world of commercial new development, speed and flexibility are essential. Companies are increasingly realizing that the old, sequential approach to developing new products simply won't get the job done. Instead, companies in Japan and the United States are using a holistic method; as in rugby, the ball gets passed within the team as it moves as a unit up the field."

But Scrum really builds on, comes from, and owes a debt to, a richer, older and more mainstream management tradition. More than sixty years before 'Scrum,' or even 'Agile Management' came along, Walter A. Shewhart came up with a method of going from where you are now, to where you want to be, and also be able to control risk, money, people and time.

The basic idea is to learn to walk by taking baby steps: You plan a few short steps, you do the few short steps, you study what you got after the few short steps, and then you take action to see if you could do it better next time round. Repeat.

* * *

Sometimes this is called the Shewhart cycle, sometimes it's called the Deming cycle/Deming circle/Deming wheel, and sometimes plain old "Plan, Do, Study, Act" and sometimes "Plan, Do Check, Act." Whatever, it's always the same thing.

Walter A. Shewhart came up with the idea, but William Edwards Deming popularised it, took it to Japan in the 1950s and the Japanese economic giants paid close attention to it, diligently applied it, and thereby rebuilt their country into an industrial powerhouse.

Why am I telling you this? Well, too many books like this leave you with the idea that Scrum comes from, and belongs in, the Information Technology arena. But it doesn't.

The core of Scrum comes from a much more noble and more intellectually honest tradition: production manufacturing and lean management. - Besides, if it's good enough for Toyota, Panasonic, Yamaha, Honda and the rest to create the Japanese economic miracle of the late twentieth century, it's probably good enough for us, too.

Whatever, it is the bedrock of Scrum, Agile and all the other 'self-managing team' methods of getting things done. It is a four-step cycle which is repeated time and again until you get to where you want to be. The four steps are "**Plan**, **Do**, **Study**, and **Act.**"

The Shewhart/Deming Cycle

1. **Plan** - Plan just enough to take some small steps in the right direction
2. **Do** - Go and do that small step
3. **Study** - Check and see how you did. Did you achieve the plan?
4. **Act** - Reflect on what you did and aim to improve the process

Repeat.

How is this enabled in Scrum? By using the four, specialised, meetings called the Events. These are:

Scrum Event	Shewhart/Deming cycle
The Sprint Planning Session	Plan
The Daily Scrum	Do
The Sprint Review	Study
The Sprint Retrospective	Act

Table: 1

Management theorists will swear blind that they alone came up with the Plan, Do, Study, Act cycle. But they didn't.

If you have ever worked with a tradesman, you will know that is exactly how they work. They plan, they do, they check (known as "offering up") and they make any needed amendments. Every time.

If you have ever sailed on a boat you will immediately spot that Plan, Do, Check, Act is exactly what all sailors always have to do whenever they plot and then navigate a course on their boat to go from here to there. Why? Because no matter which way you intend to steer, the wind will first blow you one way, and then the tide will blow you another, and just as you have made the proper corrections and everything is looking good, all the conditions are bound to change.

In order to make any progress, sailors have to make a plan, sailors have to set out and make progress, but sailors know they always have to check where they are, because where they actually are, and where they should be, are always two different things.

Sailors also mark 'way points,' on their charts, which are points on their chart where they know they need to check where they think they ae and where they actually are. I know it's stretching it a bit, but we could think of these as nautical 'sprints,' following **Plan, Do, Study, Act,** principles.

First, A Bit Of Scrum Theory

Scrum is based on the idea that the evidence of our eyes and real results beat eminent people sounding off and (fake) expertise: In other words, results from the real world beat whatever anyone may think or say.

That is a very subversive idea in some organisations, so you may want to be a bit careful before shouting about it.

That's why I like Scrum - it's a pragmatic practical tool for pragmatic, practical people. I have had to rescue all manner of projects that are in trouble because they were the brainchild of someone at the top of the company, but their flunkeys didn't bother to find out if the market actually wanted it or not first. That kind of failure is expensive, and can be ruinous.

The Scrum message is simple: Do something. Check it works. If it does then refine it, polish it up a bit, and keep doing it. If it doesn't work, then change what you are doing. Or stop.

If you wanted to give this approach a posh title, you would say this is known as *empiricism*. Empiricism[42], also known as empirical process control[43], says that true knowledge only comes from experience, and your decisions should be based on what you see, not on what you hope will be. It is sometimes explained as putting evidence of results

---

[42] There is a whole, wider branch of doing things called 'empirical process control,' and it influences a whole raft of management frameworks.
It has an opposite, called 'defined process control,' which is what happens in factories.
[43] How To Do Empirical Process Control:
1. Start now and learn as you go
2. Things will change - get used to it
3. Take baby steps and check often to limit risk
4. Know that unfortunately, all estimates are about as accurate as horoscopes
(I used to call empirical process control "Ready!, Fire! Aim!")

over the eminence of people calling themselves experts[44].

Lawyers have two phrases for this: **de facto** (in fact), and **de jure** (of the law). In law, (de facto), very often trumps as it should be (de jure).

The other philosophy that drives Scrum is called *Lean*. Lean thinking concentrates on only doing the essentials and reducing waste, whether the waste is in time, resources, or how work flows.

Lean [45] is the response by western companies to emulate what the most successful and influential Japanese production management systems, such as the Toyota Production System, do.

Scrum believes that embarking on anything new is a risky business, so a good way to proceed is to take small, incremental steps, and check on progress as you go.

It believes in producing something called the Minimum Viable Product. That means doing the bare minimum, (but great quality) thing and seeing if there is a demand for that *before* you put any bells and whistles on it.

For example, if you were in the ice-cream business, then the minimum viable product would be a great, plain vanilla ice cream first, before you go for the raspberry ripple with a chocolate flake and chopped nuts version with cookie dough.

This is a lot less risky than going for the 'big one' right from the start. It is also easier to predict success when you are doing a lot of one-at-a-time small changes than when you are doing one or two really big ones.

---

[44] I am not against real experts. I think real experts are brilliant. I am against fake experts. As my mum used to say about fake experts, "an ex is a has-been, and a spurt is a drip under pressure."

[45] If you want to learn more on Lean, (and you If should because it will make you a better manager,) the very best books on this are "The Toyota Way" by Jeffrey K. Liker, "The Machine That Changed The World," By Womack, Jones, and Roos, and also "Lean Thinking: Banish Waste And Create Wealth In Your Corporation," again by Womack and Jones

* * *

It also guards against the very human tendency to 'gild the lily' when making anything.

In order to make sure that everything is checked properly as you work, there are four, transparent, separate, 'events' where progress is checked to allow inspection and adaptation. All of these all happen inside a fixed period of work, called a Sprint.

Scrum is Good For…

"If It Takes A Man With A Shovel Five Hours To Dig A Hole 2 Metres Deep By Three Metres Long And One Metre Wide, How Long Will It Take Five Men To Dig Five Identical Holes?"

In reality, it probably won't. That is the problem.

In the real world, one of them will hit a water pipe, one will have to dig through solid rock, one will break their shovel, one will be completely useless and the lucky one will dig through soft earth giving the project manager an excuse to go and shout at the other four for being lazy and useless.

Which is one very good reason why you should never ask a maths teacher to be your project manager.

The maths teacher's question assumes that the result will always be the same because the question assumes that all the situations will be identical. Many times it does, because that is the nature of simple work: you do something simple here and the thing pops out a little bit later there. But many times, it doesn't happen like that because what you are doing is complex. The nature of complex work is *different,* and *that* is also why your builder will always break your heart.

The real world often offers different situations, such as ground made of granite, buried water pipes or shovels that break. These different situations make the work uncertain, because you can't predict with complete accuracy.

Scrum, or any Agile framework, works best when you are dealing with *complex*[46] work rather than *simple* or *complicated*[47] work.

Simple work is when you do something and you know that the action will always produce the same result, such as someone working in a car factory putting on the wheels on a car. In the factory the mammoth task of making a car will have been broken down into thousands of small steps, so that the environment that jobs are done in are all tightly controlled. The benefit is that you get the same result every time. If you put the hundreds of small, simple steps together and you can build really complicated things, like Swiss watches, cars, or smartphones.

Examples of Complex Work:

When this is the first time you are attempting to do something (perhaps a tech start up, or a new venture, or a build a one-off, dream house).

When this is the first time that the team you are using have built something (perhaps you need them to use unfamiliar or cutting-edge technology).

You want the market to dictate the features of the product (like car manufacturers do with their vast lists of optional extras).

You haven't really defined what the product will do or look like yet but you really need to get started so that you can get a slot from the marketing team (this is much more common than you would think).

When every job is different and you offer a boutique service (perhaps you are a bespoke tailor, or a classic car repair shop, or an online project management consultancy).

* * *

---

[46] Complex work is where you can't know how things will turn out until you do some actual work, like digging holes in the ground.

[47] simple and complicated work are closely linked. Factories build complicated products by combining a lot of simple processes.

So why pick Scrum? Because it limits risk when you are working in an unknowable world.

How Does Scrum Limit Risk? Like This:

1. Define a goal to work towards.

2. Take small, baby steps towards it over a short period (a week, a fortnight, a month).

3. Then you examine what you did.

4. Ask, "was it any good?" If so, do more. If not, stop. Do something else.

5. Look at the goals again to see if what you did was appropriate. Then you look at the way you are organising yourselves to see if you can make improvements

Arithmetic, when used in forecasting is a brilliant tool as long as you have spent the bundles of necessary money so that you can control all the conditions that have an impact upon an outcome. But outside of a factory, where do you have that amount of control?

The most successful environment for controlling conditions is the factory. Factories are extremely expensive, tightly controlled environments optimised for producing things. They might just be the most productive machine we have ever made but even they still can't control everything. Arithmetic forecasting works for most of the time in a factory, but not all the time.

Outside of a factory, using simple arithmetic to forecast anything far into the future is fruitless because so much is beyond your control. Which is unfortunate, considering that how many plans for projects are based upon just upon such simple arithmetic.

On really big projects project managers tend to build immensely complicated plans complete with Gannt charts, spreadsheets and all sorts of doodads. Older, more experienced project managers call those plans 'spreadsheet horoscopes," because they are about as accurate as a horoscope.

The fact is that the longer period you project a forecast or plan, the more inaccurate you are going to be.

A project, any project, is about change. Change, or transformation is about trying to get from where we are now to where we want to be in the future and the future is always an unknown. Every plan we make is forecasting into the unknown. A long term plan only gives the illusion of control.

What we can say is that a plan about what we are going to achieve next week, or the next fortnight, is going to be a lot more accurate than a plan that tells us what we are going to achieve by next year.

When you don't know all the conditions that can affect an outcome and you can't control them you need to work *differently.*

The fact is, most people in the west don't work in factories anymore. Most people do the kind of work where you can't control all the inputs and you may not even be sure that you know what the end result will be.

Scrum and things like it are more suited for projects and work where how you will get to the end goal is a little uncertain. Scrum is great for that kind of **_complex_** work.

For instance, building a dream house out of brand new, state of the art materials like something you see on television is *complex.* Whereas building an executive housing estate from the plans that you have already successfully used to build one elsewhere is just *complicated.*

When you are building the housing estate you already know where most of the problems will arise. You know how big a team you will need, you know what materials you will need and you know roughly how long it will take. Building the estate is surely a complicated job, but it is not complex. Of course, when you build it for the very first time, it will definitely be complex.

* * *

Define a goal and take baby steps towards it, checking at each step against the goal to make sure you are still on track. You also need to examine the way you are organising yourselves as you make it.

Defining Scrum

Scrum is a lightweight management framework, (or management 'scaffolding,') that allows teams of people and whole organisations do things better, faster, quicker, deliver higher quality and do the whole thing a whole lot more enjoyably than any other way I know.

When I say lightweight, please don't think I mean flimsy. Scrum is very robust.

For Scrum to work you need someone called a **Scrum Master**. They have a leadership role for the whole team. They train the individuals in the 'accountabilities,' or roles. They build the individuals into a team, set a Scrum team's working culture and build ways of working where:

1. Someone called a **Product Owner** orders the work needed to build a *complex*[48] product or service and puts it into a kind of list, or plan, called a **Product Backlog**.

2. The **team**[49] take items from the top of that list and their work turns them into things of value. Once completed, these items are called **increments**[50]. All work happens during a fixed length period of work called a **Sprint**.

3. The team and the **stakeholders**[51] look at the things, judge if they are acceptable and worthwhile, and adjust their plans for the next **Sprint**.

4. Repeat the cycle for the next **Sprint**.

* * *

---

[48] A complex product or service is one where you can't know exactly how it will turn out until you're a good way into the building of it. Think of one-off houses, bespoke suits, and custom cars.

[49] People who do the work

[50] An 'Increment' means satisfactorily completed work

[51] Involved outsiders. They don't do the work, but they have some kind of interest.

Scrum is simple. It is also deliberately incomplete. Now, that can drive some people, (especially old-school project managers and people who work with spreadsheets,) to distraction. But Scrum is just a scaffolding. That means it is meant to be a tool that helps you build a building. It is not the building itself and it is not meant to get in the way. The deliberate gaps in Scrum are there for different teams from lots of different companies and industries to fill in for themselves.

You will either find this wonderfully and delightfully liberating, or maddening. This will entirely depend on the type of person you are.

In subsequent chapters, I have put in some techniques so that you can plug the gaps if you need to. We use these ourselves, and so do our clients. We and our clients find them very helpful as a great way to start but, if you find or work out better ways then please use them[52].

---

[52] and if you could share that with us too, that would be great.

THE WHO - TEAMS - THE ACCOUNTABILITIES - KNOWING WHO DOES WHAT -

The Scrum People Structure:

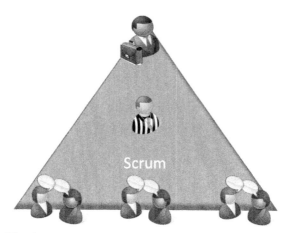

Figure 2 The Scrum People Structure

I have to make clear that this is not an official Scrum picture. It's just something I came up with to explain how a Scrum team looks. You won't see it on any of the official Scrum web pages. it is just the way I introduce Scrum to my clients. I tell them that people in a Scrum team are arranged a bit like a triangle. When I tell my clients that, they just 'get it.' Feel free to use it yourself.

Scrum is 'fractal,' which means that you can use the same basic shape for every level of management, high, medium or low. I use that idea a lot when I am managing multiple teams as you will see in the Scrumnastics ++ section later on.

For now, just think, "Scrum team? It's a bit like a triangle."

At the top is the **Product Owner**, in the middle is the **Scrum Master/** Agile Coach, and along the bottom are the team members, or **developers**.

The Scrum 2020 guide states there is absolutely no hierarchy in Scrum. This is a bit different to what they used to say. If you are all working in a purely internal team with lots of middle managers, this may be the case.

However, in our case, and very probably yours too, our Product Owner is our client, and that means they have control of the budget. When money is involved, there is *always* a hierarchy.

The Scrum Team

…Is the work unit where things are made or done in Scrum.

Why Emphasize The Use Of A Team?

1.   Because a team just works better than any other work unit, especially in comparison to a departmental bureaucracy. Why does it work? This may sound fanciful but indulge me for a moment. I believe there are some common things about a team, any kind of team, whether a sports team, a work team, or any other team that make it so effective.

2. The first reason is that it echoes the oldest of human units, the large family or the tribe. The big difference is that, unlike a tribe or a family, you don't _have_ to be there. You _choose_ to be there, and that makes a difference.

3.   All teams seem to be more successful when they contain people with a mix of different skills. In football, goalkeepers are not known for their side-stepping or sprinting ability, and centre forwards aren't chosen for their ball catching skills. You need the right mix of talent to make it work. How many football clubs would field a team of eleven goalkeepers?

4. They all seem to have an upper working size limit that people just seem to arrive at organically. - Think of a cricket team, and a football team both having eleven players. Why? Did they just come up with the number or did people just come to the conclusion that twelve or more is just chaotic? The only sports teams that have larger than eleven are sports where there are really two sub teams on the field at the same

time, like rugby, where the forwards and backs play completely different roles.

5. Unlike a tribe or a family, everyone in a team _wants_ to be there. - You don't _have_ to play football; the players are there because they _want_ to play football. It is not obligatory.

6. Most people have played in some kind of team by the time they are adults, so they know how teams work. It doesn't matter what the sport is, all team games work in broadly similar ways.

7. Teams have rules that bind them together. This is possibly because, in comparison to families and tribes, the social bonds between team players are weaker so they need a bit of help.

8. No-one in a team has to be related, so there should not be too many age-old enmities, jealousies, and grudges to interfere with its good running.

This is not specific to Scrum. There are lots of different team-based management frameworks. So many that they have their own family name and are called '**self-managed teams**.' They key thing is that they all emphasize the power of the team to get things done.

What Is A Scrum Team Made Up Of?

A team has one **Scrum Master**, one **Product Owner**, and a team of nine or fewer workers. These are officially called **Developers**, but we tend to call Developers the Producers, or the Production Team.

The fewer the people in the team, the more rapid the pace of the work, but the smaller the capability. Although it is possible to have a team of eleven people (including the Product Owner and the Scrum Master), the larger the team, the more difficult it is to manage. Remote, or online teams definitely work better in smaller teams of around six or seven people.

Don't be afraid to split a large team up into two smaller units that will naturally communicate better and probably be more productive. In the

2020 Scrum Guide, it says you need to make sure that if you do split up teams into two, the teams should have the *same* **Product Owner**, the same **Product Backlog** and the same **Product Goal** - because these are how you co-ordinate the work.

Teams are 'cross-functional.' This means that they are made up of all the people with all the skills necessary to complete the job. A housebuilding team would have foundation builders, joiners, roofers, and bricklayers. The job of the team is to achieve the '**Product Goal**.' The Product Goal is a short, pithy phrase which captures the vision for the completed product. In other words, the purpose, reason why, or 'strong why,' it is being built.

There are *no* sub-teams in Scrum. All work is done within the team and no work can be handed off to any sub-team.

Teams are also self-managing, which means that the team as a whole decides amongst themselves what is done, who does what, and how it is done. Obviously, this means that they must be given the clearest possible directions.

The Scrum team is responsible for all the work related to the making of the product in question. The wider organisation are supposed to have enough confidence in the team that they are free to manage their own work.

There are three different job 'Accountabilities[53],' as they are now called in Scrum.

Accountability 1: The Developers

Developers are the workers or the 'do-ers' in Scrum. They are the people of practical skills and ability. There are no individual job titles among developers. Officially, everyone who works is called a developer, no matter what work they do.

* * *

---

[53] If you have any old books on Scrum, an accountability used to be called a role.

Scrum can be applied to all sorts of work in lots of different industries but no matter what the industry, the developers have the following responsibilities:

- Creating a visual plan and a progress update board for the Sprint, which is the Sprint Backlog.
- Ensuring the quality of the product by adhering to the previously agreed 'Definition of Done[54]'.
- Adapting their plan each day toward achieving the Sprint Goal.
- The team as a whole is accountable for the success.

Developer - What's in a name?

Burly and hairy-chested workers in some industries take a great exception to being called 'developers.' I have put Scrum into all sorts of different businesses: chemical, finance, pharmaceuticals, software, video production, classic and vintage car restorers and a builder of dream houses like you see on television. Outside of the software industry, people tend not to like the name at all, in fact the name gets in the way.

We want the do-ers to be as enthusiastic about working in Scrum as possible, so I tend to call workers the production team, or the producers, which they always seem a lot happier with. As far as we are concerned, they are still developers, with all the same responsibilities.

Accountability 2: The Product Owner

The Product Owner is the manager of the product and is responsible

---

[54] The 'Definition of Done' is a miniature contract between the Product Owner and the Team. It says that "This thing is Done when..." The Definition of Done is agreed in the Sprint Planning Session. It stops the team wasting time and money putting in unwanted features, and it stops the Product Owner from playing a fast one and changing the goal posts when an increment has been created. Using Definition of Done creates trust between the Product Owner and the team.

for getting the best bang for the buck from the work of the Scrum Team. They often come from the commercial parts of a business.

They have four primary responsibilities for managing the visual plan for the product or service going to be built (called the **Product Backlog**). This means that:

1. They create, develop, and communicate the Product Goal. The Product Goal is the pithy sentence/vision/'reason why,' the completed product should be built.

2. They create clear, unambiguous, and easily understood items for the Product Backlog.

3. They order the Product Backlog items from top to bottom. The most valuable are put at the top and the least valuable are put at the bottom.

4. They make sure that the Product Backlog is always visible, transparent, and understood by everyone.

Accountability 3: The Scrum Master

Scrum Guide 2020 revised the role of the Scrum Master quite a lot in comparison to earlier versions of Scrum. This is what the Scrum Guide 2020 has to say about the Scrum Master.

> *"The Scrum Master is accountable for the Scrum Team's effectiveness. They do this by enabling the Scrum Team to improve its practices, within the Scrum framework."*

In other words, the Scrum Master helps the team to continually improve as it goes about its work. Continuous improvement is a fairly common theme in all sorts of management frameworks, especially in the Toyota Production System. You may have heard of the Japanese word, 'kaizen,' which is Japanese for 'continually improving.' In Scrum there is one person in the team who has that accountability.

* * *

What is a Team in Scrum?

Scrum gives you the ability to manage one, or multiple teams of people to produce something across fixed units of time called Sprints. These can be a week, a fortnight, or a month long.

What is special about the word team in Scrum?

The team is a working mix of people, each having very different skills to each other. They all come together in order to produce a specific thing or result.

Think of a football team. It *could* have eleven goalkeepers, but it doesn't. It has one goalkeeper, some defenders, some midfielders and the attackers. Each of the skills adds to the total capability of the whole team.

You can have small teams and large teams in Scrum. Small teams tend to work at a more rapid pace than large teams, but obviously do not have their capability. Five-a-side football is played at a much quicker pace than eleven-a-side football.

There are teams and, of course, there are teams. Manchester United play in the Premier League while Didsbury F.C. Play in the Sunday League. They both play football but there's a world of difference between them in depth, breadth, talent, training, and resources.

Many start-ups and new companies actually start off as teams and their success is very often precisely because of the people in the team. This is completely different to how most of those same companies end up after a few years.

As they get bigger and more successful, the norm is to adopt 'functional,' departmental work structures such as the accounts department, sales department, or I.T. Department. Although companies often use phrases like 'Sales Team,' or 'Support Team,' they would not be teams as far as Scrum is concerned. The Sales Team will be made up of salespeople and the Support Team will do be made up of support people. Departments are definitely not teams.

* * *

On the other hand, a group of tradesmen who are going to build a house *would* be a team. Having a group of bricklayers, carpenters, electricians, plumbers etc., would definitely be a good use of the word team as far as Scrum is concerned. Also, in a classic car repair shop, a group made up of different trades such as a car electrician, a welder, a mechanic, a body work specialist, and a spray painter, would also count as the basis for a Scrum team. I have taught Scrum to both, and it worked really well.

Conversely, in a department where people are organised around their job functions, there is a tendency for people to grow to think along very similar lines. Let that carry on and you can start to get group think, or 'silo thinking.' Worse, actual dysfunctional behaviour can emerge where work between departments gets 'chucked over the wall[55].'

So, in their departments, salespeople all grow to think like, and behave like other salespeople. The Accounts department people all grow to think like accounts people and... - you get the idea. These kinds of characteristics are known in Agile circles as "I shaped people[56]."

As we've said, teams are made up of different specialists that work together as a group in order to achieve a given result. The focus is on achieving the product and the team know that they, and they alone, are responsible for its delivery. This is said to develop "T shaped people[57]."

Where does the idea of the department come from? Some say it emerged from government, some from the growth of white-collar staff jobs. Others say that it is a characteristic of a company going

---

[55] For example, in finance companies, I have often seen sales people deliberately batching up sets of 'iffy' deals of questionable quality close to month end, sending them over to the compliance department and moaning that they haven't been cleared immediately.

[56] That is, like a letter "I," their knowledge is deep, but quite narrow

[57] Those who still have great depth of knowledge in their specialism, but also have a wider, but shallower, knowledge of what is going on around them.

bureaucratic. Taiichi Ohno, who did most of the development of the Toyota Way, thought it was much older than that, and that it actually emerged from farming. Who knows? The question is, can you avoid its wastefulness?

I think you can. The reason? Weirdly, two government bureaucracies actually asked me to help them implement Scrum teams for their department. Why? - because they couldn't get their own bureaucracy to work anymore. Their work had come to a halt. Of course, being a government department, they still have all the old, formal organisation charts and all the other paraphernalia. It is just that they politely ignore them and use Scrum instead.

Imagine, two government departments; the most bureaucratic organisations you can think of, have given up on bureaucracy. It makes you think, doesn't it?

Small Teams: Why The Big Guys Want to be Small like you:

Consider the meteoric rise of software companies for a moment. They are an astonishing late 20th and early 21st century phenomena, often originally set up by a bunch of kookie guys and gals who *really* didn't want to wear suits. Instead, they did some really posh typing which *really* paid off.

In much less than a decade, these companies grew from parents' basements and garages into making more money than a lot of countries do.

They have grown so quickly that they can still remember when they started off in their parents' garage or their girlfriend's bedroom, which, for the newest, might have been only four or five years ago.

The founders still remember being in start-up mode team and a time when they got stuff done quickly, got results quickly and they were really having fun. Life was good.

Now many are making so much money that they have run out of buckets to put it in - but they aren't having much in the way of fun. Why?

Well, as any business grows, it starts to pick fewer staff from the kookie classes it started off with and more picks staff from the typing classes (people who do email, spreadsheets and PowerPoint), and also the obstructive classes (governance, HR, accounts, legal). This changes everything.

The constructive/productive classes are people such as programmers, carpenters, plumbers, or anyone else who can actually do things. These are the kind of people Victor Davis Hanson likes to call the 'muscular classes.' In other words, 'do-ers.'

These muscular classes have a different mindset to the typing classes and the obstructive classes. They create. They are refreshing to be around because they want to actually do things, rather than stop people from doing things

As the company grows, the founders quickly find that they are being constrained by exactly the kind of people they wanted to originally escape from: the 'suits.' Except that, apparently, these suits work for them, and not the other way around.

So, enjoy being small while you are small. You are envied by some very rich and successful people.

Because you run in small teams, you can do more than they can. You can respond quicker than they can. And you are more productive than they are. If you really want an eye-opener, take a look at the next section on "Price's Law." Read that and I'll bet you will never want to grow big.

Why else do you think huge software companies and global consultancies farm out so much of their work to small, boutique firms who actually DO things? It is because the boutiques firms can do more things quicker. Never underestimate that. Your agility and nimbleness really are a super power.

Decreasing Staff Engagement (effort) As Teams Get Larger.

Employing a group of individuals to do something is one of the most expensive things you can do in business. Therefore, it is really important to get a grip on how much effort your people are giving you to make sure you don't go broke.

Maximillian Ringelmann

This has been of serious concern for more than a century. In 1913 in Germany, Maximilian Ringelmann was studying what happens to the work rate of the individual as you add people to a team. Did it go up, stay steady, or decrease?

How? He did various social experiments but the one that is remembered is where he took a tug-o-war team and measured each individual on how hard they could pull. Then he put all eight team members on the rope and measured how hard they pulled when together. He found that they only pulled at 50% of the total amount of potential power they could. Obviously, a group can give less return than the individuals that make it up.

This tells us that if we want to harness and unleash the power of the team then we need to do something more than just putting them in a team. We need some kind of framework.

There's worse news...

You have probably heard of Pareto's "80:20" law, which says that 20% of this gives you 80% of that. It is a great rule of thumb used to find, and then focus on, highly profitable niches within a business. Typically, it is done on customers or products to identify the best customers and products, such as the 20% of customers or products who are responsible for 80% of profits. You can also turn it round to do things like find the 20% of customers or products that give 80% of complaints.

Apply this rule of thumb and you can bet that there's a spreadsheet somewhere that proves 80% of work is done by only 20% of your staff…

And even worse…

But very few have heard of an even more scary rule-of-thumb known as "Price's Law." It was devised by Derek John De Solla Price.

Price's Law states that 50% of all work in an environment is done by the square root of the number of people involved. This has huge implications for your competitors.

In other words, the more people work for an organisation, the more 'social loafing,' as it is called, goes on in it. Just have a look at the table below

Price's Law:

Total Number of Employees	50% of all Work is done by…
10	3
50	7
100	10
500	22
1000	31 1/2

Just the quickest glance at it tells you exactly why the big businesses want to be more like the small businesses like you. Employ ten people and 50% is done by three staff and the other 50% is done by the other seven. That's painful enought, but when you employ one thousand people, 50% is done by just thirty-one and a half of your staff while the other 50% is done by the nine hundred and sixty-eight and a half. That's ruinously expensive.

* * *

As a small team advocate, I am so glad I will never have to justify the salaries of the 1,000-employee business to any of my shareholders.

There's an accepted business rule-of-thumb that says the bigger the company, the lower the staff engagement (the amount of effort staff put in). I think we might just have found it.

This is the reason that we advocate scaling (growing) capability by adding small teams. We will examine this in the Scrumnastics ++ section later on.

Simple, Scary, Business Arithmetic.

The biggest cost of any business is the people. Every time. And that's just the headline cost.

Any accountant can tell you, "If it takes a man four hours to dig one hole, how long does it take five men to dig five holes?" You know the answer, right? Well, as we have already seen elsewhere, if you are engaged in complex, or craft type work, you'll be wrong. One will dig in sand, one in granite, one will hit mud, one will be lazy and the last one will break their spade. Outside of factory work, all work estimation gets to be approximate.

But numbers like salary costs? They stay pretty similar, so let's do some simple, scary arithmetic about how much it costs to run a team. We need some numbers.

The **Office Of National Statistics (ONS)**, said that the average UK salary was £36,611 a year in 2019.

But let's say your company is a bit mean, and besides, we want to do easy maths, so it pays about £20,000k for each person in your team. That means a team of 10 people costs £200k a year to run. Anything we are going to build had better make us at least £200k to pay the salaries or we are not going to be around for very long.

But that's too crude to gauge whether a project could be profitable or not, because there's employee 'engagement[58],' to consider. Engagement is normally expressed as the percentage of productive hours you get from an employee. - It is hardly ever a big number. The rule of thumb is: the bigger the company, the smaller the amount of engagement.

Let's say you all work for a large company. You get a rate of 8%

---

[58] It just means the amount of effort your people are willing to put in.

engagement from your staff in your company or organisation. As we have seen from the Price's Law piece, that is actually quite optimistic for a large organisation. That means you are paying £200,000 for £16,000 worth of productive work. That's going to really mess your profit assumptions up and it's not exactly great value for money, is it?

Even worse, you may not even be getting as much as that because one or two in that big group may be so completely unengaged that they are actually pulling you backwards. This is not uncommon in factories[59], for example.

You know that £200,000 a year? Unfortunately, it gets worse. The actual price that your organisation pays for the privilege of employing staff is likely to be almost double that £200,000.

Why? Well, because of things like the Employer's National Insurance contributions, the pension contributions, the payroll costs, I.T. equipment and software and, of course, the considerable costs of your H.R. Business Partners, Ferrero and Rocher. And it is no use saying, "it doesn't affect me because I am not responsible for those numbers." That money still has to be paid.

Add up all the National Insurance, pension, payroll, IT Support and all the rest and that makes your £200k team actually cost your organisation nearer £400k.

And you still only have 8% engagement...

So, 8% of £400k is £32k, which means you are paying out £400k and receiving £32k's worth of effective work in return. You are pouring £368k down the drain. Every year. Ouch. It's probably a good idea to put some effort into getting that rate of engagement up, which is why so many companies are turning to self-managed team frameworks like Scrum.

* * *

---

[59] In the 1980's, before it went into manufacturing partnership with Toyota, General Motors had a car manufacturing facility in California. Some of the workers were deliberately putting glass soda drink bottles in the inside of car doors and then screwing the upholstery over the top of them.

Meanwhile, what about your competitor who has a slightly better rate of engagement than you? Let's say that they aren't particularly good at Scrum or something similar, but they are okay. In fact, they are getting 50% engagement. They are paying exactly the same for staff as your company, but they are paying £400,000 and getting £200,000 worth of value a year from their team.

If their engagement rate is 50% and yours is 8%, they are more than 5 times more productive than you. On every job they do.

If you are both spending £400,000 a year on staff costs, but they are 'only' wasting £200,000 and you are wasting £368,000, how long before they out-compete you?

Well, they are already out-competing you today, so perhaps a better question is, "how long before they put you out of business?"

Small Teams And The "Span Of Control"

Known Since The Early 20th Century, The Span of Control Is The Other Reason Why You Shouldn't Be Managing Really Big Teams (no matter which management framework you are using)

When we looked at Ringelmann's, Pareto's and De Jolla Price's ideas, we had a glimpse at just how inefficient large teams are. Here's another reason you should not have large teams but from the perspective of managing them.

The 'Span Of Control' refers to the number of subordinates a manager can manage properly. The bigger the number, the larger the Span Of Control.

This idea came out of General Sir Ian Hamilton's work in 1922. He was asked to study and then report on the optimum numbers of subordinates a commander should have. Hamilton called this ratio the Span of Control.

"The nearer we approach the supreme head of the whole organization, the more we ought to work towards groups of three; the closer we get to the foot of the whole organization, the more we work towards groups of six." - General Sir Ian Hamilton, "The Soul And Body Of An Army," 1922

So, the lower down you are managing, the more you can have directly under you, but it is still no more than a maximum of six. The higher up you go, the fewer you should have until you narrow down to three.

In civilian life, there is a weird sort of managerial machismo that comes from managing large amounts of staff. Bigger teams get managed by the more senior managers, even when they don't know a good set of management tools.

* * *

Managing a big department certainly confers the manager a higher status than a small team does.

But here's a big bucket of cold water on that idea from Lyndall F. Urwick:

"There is nothing which rots morale more quickly and more completely than poor communication and indecisiveness -- the feeling that those in authority do not know their own minds. And there is no condition which more quickly produces a sense of indecision among subordinates or more effectively hampers communication than being responsible to a superior who has too wide a span of control." - Lyndall F. Urwick

Well, that kind of says it all, doesn't it?

A Ratio Of One To Three, Or One to Six

What does that mean for a Scrum team? We have this strange, split hierarchy in Scrum. Management is carved up between the Product Owner (person in charge of the product and its budget) and the Scrum Master (a team leader/coach/referee/Scrum dungeon master). So we have a product manager and a people manager.

But even then, managing more than six at a time becomes a bit of a chore, especially if they all work remotely. Before they changed the optimum team size to six in Scrum 2020, it used to be said that the optimum size of a Scrum team was eleven. When you were all co-located in a dedicated Scrum office environment with wonderful facilities it definitely *could* be done. But if you were all scattered around the room in a grimy, grim office in Sheffield it was murder. When you are working remotely and you are looking at each other's faces on screens? We have found that six is the optimum and you are really pushing the limit at eight.

Strange, isn't it? Yet again, we have evidence for the optimum ways to work that have been around for nearly a century, yet we have to rediscover them.

Small Teams And The Lamborghini Miura

Small teams can achieve amazing things. For example, the prototype of this beautiful car, the Lamborghini Miura, was made in 1967 - By a team of seven people

The seven people in the team made it in six months. *After work.* In their spare time.

Figure 3 The Lamborghini Miura[60] from 1967 - Built by seven people - Vroom…

Ferruccio Lamborghini, the boss of the company didn't even get to see the finished prototype until he saw it at the Motor Show on the Lamborghini stand.

And the designer, Marcello Gandini, was 22. I know. All that talent. Sickening, isn't it?

---

[60] Photograph kindly supplied by bernswaelz, (and paid for by me).

* * *

For some people (okay, me), this is the most beautiful car ever made. It is an exquisite example of 20th century kinetic industrial art, because it looks as though it is doing a million miles an hour even when stood still. It makes men of a certain age murmur "Vroom…" quietly, under their breath.

But the key point is that it was made by a small team of seven people, each with their own, specific skills. Not seventy. Not seven hundred. Seven. What can a small team accomplish? The Lamborghini Miura, that's what.

The Product Owner

Figure 4 The Product Owner

Product Owners Manages The Product, Not The People

The Product Owner accountability is as the manager of the product or service, which is the 'thing' being made. Unlike a traditional project manager, they are expected to stay with the product *after* it is made.

Although they are in charge of the 'thing[61],' they are not in charge of the team making it. They are the manager product manager, *but they are not the team leader*. That is the Scrum Master. Some Product Owners have a hard time coming to terms with this. Nevertheless, that is a core part of the design of Scrum and a Scrum Master should have enough of a muscular personality to enforce this.

---

[61] could be a product or a service

"Heft"

Truly successful Product Owners have a general air of capability: a mixture of old-fashioned qualities like heft, wherewithal, maturity, grit, stamina and perspective.

These old-fashioned words describe the person with the right combination of status, money, means, grit, drive, vision and passion. Someone who can take a dream, or a germ of an idea of a product all the way from their imagination and drag it, (often kicking and screaming,) into reality.

Why am I using old-fashioned words to describe a new-fangled role in Scrum? Because in the Product Owner, Scrum has taken a very old-fashioned concept, the archetype of the 'gaffer,' and it has buffed it up and brought it into the modern world. The name may be new but what they actually do has been around for many generations.

The Product Owner In Large Companies

In large companies, Product Owners are normally more business focussed than technically focussed. If this is so, this will be a very good thing for your project and eventually, for the product.

Technically focussed Product Owners tend to focus on the details and don't often have a strategic view. They can often get bogged down which means that both the quality and delivery time of the product suffer.

In my experience, having a marriage of a business focussed Product Owner to a technically minded delivery team, is the finest position to be in.

The Product Owner In Small, and Medium, Enterprises

In small and medium sized companies, the Product Owner can be the one single client of the company. In this case it is a good idea for the Scrum Master to train that client to become a great Product Owner as part of the offering by the company. This is a great way to show the client that some action and movement is happening on their project as soon as they sign the contract.

Unlike a traditional Project Manager, a Product Owner will be responsible for the product after it has been delivered and they will continue to live with it. This situation is similar to someone having their own house built. They want it built and quickly, so that you can go away and they and their family can live in it.

The Product Owner Is In Charge Of The Money

The Product Owner should always own the budget for the product. This makes a huge difference in focussing and making sure the product being developed gives the biggest bang for their buck.

Having budgetary control is fundamental to the success of the role and how seriously they will be taken by the team. One of the most common problems I come across in badly performing projects (no matter what project methodology being used) is a lack of budgetary control by a Product Owner (or a traditional project manager).

A development team always have a collective 'nose' that can sniff out Product Owners who can spend on their own say-so, and those that can't. Be under no illusion, almost all of the authority and respect that a Product Owner will ever get from the team will come from their ability to spend money. As one northern team who were having problems with their Product Owner once told me, "We want to speak with the organ grinder, not the organ grinder's monkey." Harsh words, but unfortunately true.

Product Owners are the central point of contact and communication with the Stakeholders. Stakeholders should not be able to contact the individuals in the team.

If the product or service is a commercial product, the Product Owner concentrates on giving the greatest value to the users who will buy and use the product. This is logical. After all, that is where the future revenues will come from.

The Product Owner _owns_ the Product Backlog. The Product Backlog is a plan. It is a continually refined 'Want To Do' . It is a strategic list of the product made up of all the ingredients ranked top to bottom by value. Obviously, if the Product Owner has control over the spend then they have a better idea of what is most important for the team to concentrate on.

Having a good Product Owner gives the project direction, and great direction stops the tendency of a team doing useless 'busy work.' Busy work burns money like nothing else and is something you don't want on your project. Resources are always finite and when the budget is spent, it is spent.

The Product Owner is the only person in the team who can stop a Sprint[62].

The Product Owner chooses to accept and release (and chooses when to release), the various bits of the product. Increments are always complete, "one slice of the pie[63]," additions and improvements that go into a product.

The Product Owner runs and is in charge of the Sprint Review ceremony.

Product Owner's Responsibilities:

The Team supplies the Who, the Where, the When and the How of the building of the product. A good Product Owner will find that everything will go so much better if they not only create a great

---

[62] (there is a separate section on Sprints)

[63] Instead of just ordering the ingredients of the pie, the complete slice would include the processes (such as adding eggs, mixing the ingredients and baking the pie).

What, [64]but also create a good "Why" for the product. A good 'why' is a short, simple and clear vision for their product.

Giving the team a great reason 'why," they should build a great product always makes a big difference to the pace and the quality of product or service being developed. It gives them a reason to build something great.

The Product Owner needs to participate in the Sprint Events:

They must participate in the Sprint Planning, Sprint Review, and the Sprint Retrospective events (more on these later).

They may participate in the Daily Scrum (the more they participate in Daily Scrums, the more successful the project and the product).

The Product Owner works events with the whole Scrum Team and the stakeholders.

They create, maintain, update and revise the Product Backlog as new information or events arise.

Product Owner and the Product Backlog:

They show the team what their priorities are by ranking (and, as time goes by, continually re-ranking) the Product Backlog.

They clearly express the Product Backlog items in simple language, without using any jargon.

Work done in a state of confusion and assumption is wasteful and very expensive. Remember Konosuke Matsushita's words about getting the ideas from out of the heads of management and into the heads of labour[65]? If they are good enough words for Panasonic, I think they will be good enough for us. We want to minimise confusion amongst the team of producers, so they don't go off doing anything

---

[64] A clear set of definitions

[65] I told you that you should have read the Introduction, didn't I?

based on any confused (and so expensive) assumptions.

The Product Owner ensures that the latest version of Product Backlog is visible at all times. With online teams, this is vital to the good running and good team spirit of the team. They also ensure that it is transparent, clear to all, always up to date, prioritised by value and shows the Scrum team what they will be working on in the next Sprint.

Even if the Product Owner delegates these responsibilities to the team, the Product Owner is still totally accountable for them, never the team.

Connects the team to customers (or users). This is often ignored but is a fantastic way of getting what consumers want from a product into the heads of those who are creating it. It is so easy for teams to work in splendid isolation and end up delivering something that no-one wants. The easiest way I know of stopping this is to connect the users (or potential customers) to the builders.

Poor Product Owners...

Can't Prioritise (if you begin to hear "It's all very important!" then they need to be gently taken to one side by the Scrum Master for some training and coaching on prioritisation).

Don't know their own mind or lack that certain 'heft,' in their organisation so that they are not taken seriously by their colleagues. Sometimes projects that are not taken very seriously in the organisation are assigned to inexperienced new managers to see if they sink or swim. It is an expensive experiment but it does happen. Again, training from the Scrum Master can help turn this round.

Acts as little more than an 'order taker' from the stakeholders and never pushes back. I find that a little Scrum training can work wonders with most of this kind of Product Owner. Once they get some faith in the Scrum ways of working they normally exhibit a lot more backbone. Order taking is not management, so you will have to address this.

* * *

Too concerned with high-level, or visionary thinking at the expense of reality. Although vision is a great thing, it needs balancing with a heavy does of reality. Ideas often need grinding out in order to bring them to reality, especially when you're dealing with practically minded highly skilled knowledge workers. This is a clear danger signal for a project.

Lack of clarity in their words and instructions. Ambiguity and assumption almost always lead to calamitously expensive 'busy work.' You may want to try adding the "Sharpening the Tools" event at the end of every day.

Not available when needed. Their job is to direct the outcome. If they are not available to direct, then again, ambiguity and assumption will creep in and things will go wrong.

Uses jargon that the team are not familiar with (especially 'management-ese'). This promotes confusion. My favourite nugget of nonsense was, "I need a champion/challenger, 'A/B' testing scenario," for 'I would like to see two different options.' I find repeating Konosuke Matsushita's "Out of the heads of management and into the heads of labour," mantra very helpful.

Micro manages: Tells the team how to do their job ("I want you to build this kitchen unit out of 200-year-old reclaimed oak and the mortise and tenon joints need to be made with authentic, 200 year-old hand tools and then I want you to use bees wax to…). In my experience, most micro-management stems from a combination of lack of management training and lack of faith in the way of working and the team. Again, some training and coaching can ease this.

Product Owner Practicalities

If you are the Agile Coach/Scrum Master, make sure you continue to train and coach the Product Owner as the project goes along. I find most clients are very keen to be trained, especially if they think they will become a better manager as a result. Tempting them with buzz words like "Agile Management Training Programme," can also go a long way. We try to start our projects with a training and mobilisation sprint for everyone to be involved in the work. We call this, "Sprint - 1."

If the product is for a purely internal purpose within the organisation, the Product Owner should be a representative of the business, rather than a technical person. It is a truism that business-focussed projects tend to be more successful than technically focussed projects[66].

The Product Owner does not do the work directly that is done by the team. The team is self-organising, which means that they define how things are done[67]. Those Product Owners with a tendency to micro-manage need to be reminded of this. Quietly muttering the phrase "micro-management isn't management," quietly in their ear can also work wonders.

Product Owners do not have the power to force the team to work in an unrealistic pace, or tell them how to do their work. This is often the case with new or inexperienced middle managers. I find that this is mostly generated by their fear of failing. Just make sure that they know that you are training them in managing projects, that you are much more experienced than they are, and you are coaching them in ways of working that actually work. If they do try to force an unrealistic pace then the Scrum Master MUST step in and challenge them. That is part of their job. You cannot expect the team to do so.

They exclusively own the Product Backlog. No-one else can own it.

The more work you and the team do in refining and clarifying the items on the Product Backlog list, the better the eventual product will be and the quicker it will be produced. There is a direct link between how much work the Product Owner puts into the Product Backlog and

---

[66] When was the last time you heard the words, "Oh how brilliant, yet another exciting, successful initiative from the I.T. department!"?

[67] Personally, I have always thought it a better idea to get the carpenter to cut the wood, rather than me

how successful a product will be.

Many projects run into problems because the Product Backlog is too vague, has not been prioritised, has not had enough refinement work done on it, or falls into a state where the Product Owner starts to ignore doing the work needed on it. This work really needs to be done continuously or you will find that you will waste a great deal of time that you don't really have when you get to the Sprint Planning session.

The refinement is needed because the items need to be transformed from the initially vague, dreamy, or ambiguous wish lists into concrete requests for work that practical knowledge workers can bring into being. This takes time but it is worth it because in the end it saves everyone money.

There is a worked example (with lots of pictures) on how to actually do a Product Backlog in the "Artefacts" section in the book.

Words for the Wise Scrumnast:

Although it may seem obvious to you to have a Product Owner, nonetheless, lots of companies (including some REALLY expensive global consultancies who really should know better) don't bother. Then they complain how Scrum doesn't work for them when they get into real trouble in the project.

It is a bit like doing a jigsaw puzzle with some missing pieces in it: it takes loads of work but only delivers lots of frustration.

The following is a real conversation I had with some representatives of a global I.T. consultancy. They called me in because the project was more than two million pounds over budget, fourteen months late, and what had been delivered had been loathed by the client, which was a high street name in banking and finance. Forgive me for not mentioning their name but they will have far more spiteful lawyers than I will ever be able to afford.

Anyway, they were doing multi-million-pound 'Agile' project for a major British financial institution.

They really should have known better…

* * *

Me: "How many Product Owners from the client's business do you have in total?"

Them: "We don't have any Product Owners from the client's business."

Me: "How's that working for you?"

Them: "Not very well. What do you suggest we do?"

Me: "Errmmmm,… Ask your client to appoint some Product Owners?"

Them: "Huh. You're not very good, are you?"

Me: "You're welcome, - don't mention it. - Oh, you didn't."

…Remember at the start of the book that I told you that you don't have to be that good to do this well? - Now do you believe me?

Accountability 1: The Product Owner in the Scrum Team

If the Product Owner has never had any prior Agile, Scrum or management training, then our aim, as the wider Scrum Team, is to train them and help shape the Product Owner into a confident, decisive, clear thinking, prioritising manager for our project because this will make our job easier.

We want them to be able to use Scrum effectively, stand up for what they believe in, and fight their corner for resources. The role responsibility for training and coaching the Product Owner is the Scrum Master, but the others in the team also have a supporting role to play, too.

We do this with a mixture of encouragement, training, coaching and support. And also, when they are trained, by holding them to account, especially on their Product Backlog work.

One of the greatest skills a Product Owner must have is the ability to prioritise. Prioritisation is a rare natural talent among normal people but having a budget to spend can work wonders. However, by training them and relentlessly repeating the point that if they prioritise, it will make their project run better, cheaper and quicker, you can appeal to their better self-interest.

Every project, and every management event, will run into problems if the Product Owner (actually, any manager,) can't prioritise. You need to make this clear to them right at the beginning, not at the middle or end of the project. Because by then their money will be spent and it will be too late.

The team take their priorities from the Product Owner, so if the Product Owner can't prioritise, they won't know what to do first. That can be very expensive because simple, trivial tasks ('busy work') may end up being done before hard to do work that is more important. You are probably going to get sick of me saying that busy work is expensive, but it really, really is.

Where The Product Owner Appears In The Hierarchy:

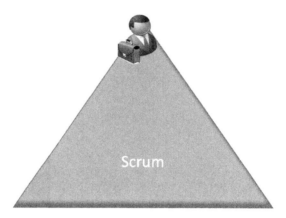

Figure 5 The Product Owner In The Triangle

They are at the very tip of the triangle, and, in a similar way to a traditional project manager, they are the focal point for everything to do with the success of the product and the stakeholders. All external communication goes to them and comes from them.

However, although they are in charge of the building of the product or service, they are not leading or in charge of the team. When the team say no to a demand by the Product Owner, that should be an end to it.

A Product Owner may not browbeat, 'doorstep[68],' bully or micro-manage anyone in the team. This sort of behaviour is normally the sign of a weak or badly trained middle manager going nowhere in life or

---

[68] Where a manager stands just behind their ear as they are sat at their desk while getting on with their work.

their career. It is up to the Scrum Master to take them to one side to train and coach the Product Owner.

A good Scrum Master sometimes occasionally needs to be quite hefty in defending the team against bad behaviour by weak or poor product managers. That's leadership for you. A weak, weak-willed or floppy Scrum Master is neither use nor ornament to any of the Scrum team.

Product Owner Responsibilities:

The Product Backlog:

All of the Product Owner's work starts with the "What," of what needs to be produced. Most of them start out as a crude 'to-do' list. However, a Product Backlog should end up as a visual plan.

It is quite okay for a Product Backlog to start out as a crude list. The important thing is thing is not to let it stay like that. The value a Product Backlog gives is in the transformation of often initially crude ideas into refined and worked out work requests. (There is a 'how-to' on how we do Product Backlogs later on, please feel free to use it).

Properly defining what is to be built is key to the success of every project, whether you are using some form of Agile[69] or more traditional project management.

The Product Backlog is created and <u>owned by</u> the Product Owner alone, but the team can, and should, help the Product Owner to refine their ideas and help to make them practical and 'do'-able. - There is a separate section in the book with a worked example how to do a Product Backlog.

To paraphrase Konusuke Matsushita, we say, "The Product Owner brings the dreams, the team brings the means." The magic arrives because of the polishing and refining of the ideas by the whole team,

---

[69] such as Scrum

not the writing of lists.

Every item that the Product Owner thinks is needed to create the product should be captured and put on this list (and they will probably put a few more on besides).

A great Product Backlog can often be a messy thing at times. - That's fine. Success is often cooked up in a messy kitchen. You can always tidy it up later.

The ideas and items should appear top to bottom, ranked by value. The Product Owner puts the most valuable items at the top, less important towards the bottom. They and the team continually finesse, refine and update it throughout the life of the creation of the product. New items are often added to the Product Backlog as time goes by.

Wise Words For Scrumnasts:

After you have done a few Sprints, you will soon recognise that **Product Backlog Refinement** is easily overlooked. Worse, it is one of the most often ignored things in a badly run project. It is one of the first things I look at in any project I have to turn round.

If the Product Owner does not spend time on refining their Product Backlog *with the team*, then your project will either run into the sand or, because of the absence of definition or priorities, the team will start to do 'busy work.' As you can imagine, useless, busy work can devour a project budget quicker than anything.

Because refining the backlog can easily become neglected, especially when working online, I developed another ceremony called, "Sharpening the Tools" which we added to our way of doing things at Scrumnastics. Again, there is a section on "Sharpening The Tools," later on.

To be completely clear, Sharpening the Tools is not an official part of Scrum and it is completely up to you to use it or not. But I think the benefits are too big to ignore and my team think it's valuable.

* * *

Sharpening the Tools dedicates a small period (15 minutes) at the end of each working day for the Product Owner and the team to work on Product Backlog refinement. This ensures that it will get done.

The second benefit is that we use "Sharpening the Tools" to close the working day. If you go to remote working, you will discover that some of the team tend to work a lot longer than the hours you are actually paying for. This is not fair, and you know it.

Unfairness breeds resentment, resentment breeds anger, and anger breeds 'go-slows' and, eventually, sabotage. Resentment is expensive and counter productive. It is also unsustainable long term and may lead to a team member burning out. Now you may have a traditional project manager viewpoint and say, "They are only a resource. I'll just get a replacement and mend it that way." But you won't mend it that way. The rest of the team will permanently look at you in a different and unfavourable light. Burn out is not only incredibly disruptive for the team, it ruins the 'velocity of work[70]' for weeks and is also very expensive.

The third benefit is that my team start the day together and they now end the day together and so it adds to the building a sense of community.

The fourth benefit is that my teams also have to do incredibly creative and imaginative work for our clients. That requires adequate rest and recuperation time every night. Tired, work out brains do not produce inspired, creative work.

I also happen to know that while they are enjoying their leisure time, their subconscious minds are mulling over work, considering options, letting ideas gently percolate into better solutions.

Guess who wins?

---

[70] This is agile-speak for the work rate.

The Product Goal (And the Product Owner's Vision Statement)

"He who has a 'why' to live for, can bear almost any how." - Friedrich Nietzsche.

The Product Goal And The Product Owner's Vision Statement: A Reason Why.

As well as their Product Backlog responsibilities, the Product Owner, or any leader, should be able to come up with a reason 'why' the product should be built. This is sometimes called the 'vision statement,' by consultancies. The reason you do a vision statement is to give the people who are building it a better sense of purpose and meaning, because we all work better when we have purpose and meaning.

Why Bother With That?

Knowledge workers love to have a good reason why they should do something. They already have the skills, and they use and hone them every day. A good 'reason why' gives them an extra reason to use their hard-earned skills and helps to make their work seem more worthwhile. They feel that they are doing more than just earning their money. They feel are creating something that matters, and that's probably why they got into learning that skill in the first place. Creating a Product Goal really makes a difference to the quality of the work you will receive.

The Best Reason Why:

"This nation should commit itself to achieving the goal, before this decade is out, of landing a man on the moon and returning him

safely to earth."[71]

A breath-taking goal and a cracking 'reason why.' Inspiring, isn't it? I especially like the "and returning him safely to earth" bit. That's much classier than "put a man on the moon, and then sod it." Classy.

That President Kennedy's beautiful words also conform beautifully to the traditional S.M.A.R.T. Management acronym for a goal is not a co-incidence. Incidentally, S.M.A.R.T. stands for **Specific, Measurable, Assignable, Realistic and Timely.**

- **Specific:** "the goal,... of landing a man on the moon and returning him safely to earth."

- **Measurable:** *Before* -We have never been to the moon. *After* - Oh yes we have. And we can go again.

- **Assignable:** Who? "**This nation** should commit itself to ..."

- **Realistic:** Was it realistic? Well, they achieved it, and they achieved it within a decade. Sometimes, even the most breathtakingly audacious goals can be achieved.

- **Timely:** "before this decade is out."

In fact, they did better than that. NASA took three men to the moon, put two men on the moon, and brought all three of them safely back, in July 1969. Heroic.

The vision statement is the reason why (Nietzsche's 'strong why'), from all the things your team could possibly do with their time, they would rather work with you. It should make them care enough to go from where they are now to where you imagine they could be. After all, we are trying to generate a transformation here.

Now that we have that wonderful President J.F. Kennedy statement in our minds, at some point you will probably have to coach a Product

---

[71] - John F. Kennedy 1961.

Owner to do one for the Product you are building.

Some Tips For Developing Your Product Goal/Vision Statement/Purpose:

Make sure that the vision statement is short and pithy. It really makes a difference to the impact that it has on people's minds.

We don't need an essay. Short and sweet should be your watch words here. As a rule of thumb, more than eight words in the sentence will probably make it boring (unless you are a really, really, really, really good advertising copyrighter). Simplicity really works.

Above all, _please_ avoid long boring, anodyne, 20th century corporate managerial speak. Thankfully, those days are behind us. After all, we are speaking to grown-ups here. Give them some inspiring words to be proud of. When it is all over we want them to be able to tell their kids "I helped to build that."

Knowledge workers really do feel that. They _want_ to be proud of their work. I still remember my grandfather, who was a clerk of works (building construction supervisor), taking me to see newly finished skyscrapers surrounded by the men who built them. The pride amongst them was tangible. It was real. They would never work _in_ those buildings, but they could show their families they had worked _on_ them as they pointed to them with pride.

Give Your People Something They Can Have Pride In.

If I am training a Product Owner, I tend to use Peter Drucker[72]'s description of how Marks and Spencer built their business:

"To subvert the British Class structure of nineteenth century England by making available to working and lower-middle-class customers upper-class goods in superior quality but at a price the customer could afford."

---

[72] Probably the best known management guru of the 20th century

* * *

If a new Product Owner is having problems coming up with a statement, then I always suggest they start with "To subvert...?" I find even the most strait-laced corporate person or bureaucrat loves the thought of being a little subversive, just sometimes.

Try it yourself.

My favourite is to suggest to a civil servant that they could start their vison statement with "subvert the norms of bureaucracy and galvanise their colleagues to..."

Just for the briefest moment, their little eyes light up. And shine.

How To Recognise A Poorly Performing Product Owner, And Why Product Owners Need Training.

"If you think Training is expensive, try ignorance." - Peter Drucker

If you train and coach them properly, the vast majority of Product Owners are actually pretty enthusiastic about using Scrum. Of course, if you don't train them and expect them to be any good then you will be disappointed. Most are quick to see that Scrum helps them do their job of getting the biggest bang for their product.

However, that's not true for all of them. Unfortunately, there are some that won't be trained.

Here are just some of the poorly performing stereotypes of Product Owner that I, and some of my fellow Agile coaches have come across. I sincerely hope that you don't.

I put these here for you because training has become a bit of a dirty word recently. I am a huge fan of training because good, timely training saves everyone time and money. Running a team is one of the most expensive parts of any business, so I think it makes sense to make it as efficient as possible, so you and they get the most for the money.

The 'Floppy' Product Owner:

Has no real authority or respect within the organisation and is treated by stakeholders as a taker of orders. This rarely ends well: in my experience, great Product Owners are never wallflowers. They all have a certain combination of 'gumption' and 'heft' in their personalities. Product Owners are not much use to a project if they have to spend most of their time quietly grizzling in a safe space praying not to be triggered.

The 'Can't Prioritise' Product Owner:

- "It's ALL important!" This mostly happens when the Product Owner is either new or just weak (see 'floppy,' above). There is no getting around the fact that great productivity in any endeavour is largely due to prioritisation. It is as simple as that. If you want a project that ends up like a messy blancmange, don't prioritise.

This inability to prioritise normally happens when the Product Owner is under so much pressure from their stakeholders that they feel they can't push back. You can help them in this by training the new Product Owner and supporting them too. You can also have a quiet word and a coffee with the stakeholders (and you should) as well as train *them*. However, a weak Product Owner needs a really heavy dose of hand holding and upward management by both the Scrum Master and the Team (similar to the Floppy Product Owner).

The "No Money" Product Owner:

This one has no budgetary responsibility. A great deal of the authority and respect that the team give to the Product Owner is derived from them knowing that the Product Owner has their money in his or her pocket. Having the money, or budget and the ability to spend it just elicits respect. It just does. However, teams frequently find it difficult to give any respect to someone who can only say no but can't say yes. In Manchester there is a phrase, "we need to talk with the organ grinder, not the organ grinder's monkey." Like most things Mancunian, it's harsh. But it's true.

The "I'm Not Technical, So I'll Leave It To You Guys," Product Owner.

This is often used as a camouflage by a teflon-shouldered middle management type to get out of their responsibilities as a Product Owner. What is the answer? Tell them that they

- don't have to be technical
- it is better that they aren't
- their role is to give the businesses' point of view in order to give balance to the technical point of view that they will get from the team.
- They are ALWAYS accountable for the everything to do with the Product, and this cannot be delegated.

The 'Dreamer' Product Owner.

Only concentrates on the high-level vision and hands off all the detail work to the team. As you might imagine, these projects lack proper direction and may end up being 'technically driven,' with a lot of busy work 'gilding the lilies' rather than delivering a tightly defined and tightly executed minimum viable product.

The 'Ambiguous' Product Owner.

Reluctant to give direction so the team has to figure things out for themselves. this ends up with a technically driven, rather than a business-driven product. This also opens up a project for abuses by the team, such as putting in uncalled for expensive features that cost a fortune to build but are never actually used by the people who actually buy the thing.

The 'Absent, Never There" Product Owner.

This seldom turns out well unless you can get more time with them. I have had many calls from consultancies who are working with a semi-detached Product Owner and want a workaround. But there isn't one. There is no magic solution. The only solution is that you need to get more time and commitment from the Product Owner, otherwise, everything will end up in screaming recrimination towards the end. I tend to tell the Product Owner that this is a real likelihood unless they commit more time.

The "Micro-Manager" Product Owner.

* * *

Unfortunately, this is very common. First of all, micro-managing is not managing, it's really just a posh term for meddling. If you have gone to the trouble of assembling a team of specialised and expert and _expensive_ knowledge workers who can do things that you can't do, although you can give clear direction, it makes very little sense to try to tell them how to do their jobs. Product Owners should concentrate on prioritising their list of items and then work, and rework, and grind out those ideas until they become clear and understandable to those who will bring them into reality.

'No Product Owner At All.' ("We Don't Believe In Product Owners Here...")

I really have come across this more times than makes any commercial sense, and bizarrely, often from big name consultancies who say they are Agile who really should know better.

Successful Scrum relies on a marriage between the technical ability of the team and the business ability of the Product Owner. If you don't get this marriage right, then you will simply get a lot of 'busy work.' If you want to burn your budget and end up with very little for your money, then this is what you (and they) do.

Accountability 2: The Scrum Master

Figure 6 The Scrum Master

The Scrum Master Is The Team Leader - They Have The Central Role In Scrum.

They are the Leader of the team. They are responsible for all training, so are the person who trains and coaches the Product Owner. They are the also the person who initiates and maintains order and discipline in Scrum. They are the Scrum Coach, and the expert on all Scrum procedures.

* * *

In other words, they lead the people and the Product Owner manages the product.

There is normally quite a lot of opposition to this idea from traditional departmental managers. After all, in traditional management, the manager manages both their people and their work, so splitting their role can seem both threatening and wasteful to them.

Of course, the two types of work environment are completely different: Departmental work is about doing the same work over and over, whereas you use Scrum to try to develop something completely new, which means the risk profile between the two is completely different.

Why do you need a Scrum Master? Because being a subordinate (a member of the team) is difficult and the team members need a buttress and an intermediary between them and the Product Owner. The team members may have extremely high levels of skill but, in comparison to the Product Owner, they will have a lower status. Sometimes they will need a leader to intercede on their behalf.

Knowing that is important because if the Product Owner insists on them doing something wasteful, expensive, or even plain stupid, they will probably acquiesce and do it. But there will be consequences if they do. We do not want waste, unnecessary expense or stupidity to jeopardise our project. That's why they need a champion, and that is part of the Scrum Master's job.

This role focusses on leading. That means a combination of enthusing, empowering, encouraging and defending team members and, in doing so, developing a great morale and team spirit, or 'esprit de corps.' Over time, this develops a powerful 'can do' spirit and momentum.

Within the team itself, the Scrum Master makes sure that everyone is an equal and no-one in the team has low status. Because when that happens, all sorts of undesired, delinquent behaviour can erupt within the team and it can descend into becoming a gang. You really don't want that. I have had to turn around four gangs in my career - There are much easier ways of earning a living.

If the good Scrum Master's efforts are successful then over time their behaviour will become more and more mature, rather than becoming more and more infantile.

Some Agile coaches think that their people need to play agile games in order to build team spirit. We do not play games. We are at work, not play. Besides, good luck with getting a hairy-chested, time-served, 'robust,' non-millennial, muscular worker to take time out to play with some building bricks. Please video the results and send them to me.

Although Scrum Master is a relatively new title, many decades ago, your grandfather and grandmother would have recognised this role but they would have used a different name for it: The foreman.

Of course, some of the things that the Scrum Master does today would never have been done by the foreman but there are still a lot of similarities. The very best Scrum Masters of today are much more enlightened than foremen of old. Sometimes they need to behave in the same way that a lot of the very best foremen ever did. Both jobs are about making sure that the team can deliver what they need to do.

Question: Who do you get to tie this all together when your team is online?

Answer: The Scrum Master.

As well as their traditional responsibilities, we found the secret of success in going online with a Scrum team is to add a new specific, responsibility to the Scrum Master. The Scrum Master becomes the chairperson for _all_ the Scrum Events, even the Sprint Review, (although we hand over the chair role to the Product Owner once their review is underway).

What Does That Mean?

1. That means they are on the video call before anyone else

2. They are the person who admits people to the meeting 'room.'

3. They open the meetings five minutes before the allotted time so that people can catch the mood of the meeting.

4. They maintain meeting discipline by insisting that all questions and comments go through the chair (in other words, them).

This means you need a Scrum Master with _even more heft_ than a normal Scrum Master has.

You can't use the Product Owner, because they are often not available as they are normally tied to the business or may even be the client.

You can't use any of the developers because they all have exactly the same status level as each other, and a chairperson needs a higher status than them to pull the role off.

The only role left in Scrum is the Scrum Master, and they are in a particularly good position to step into the role. After all, they are already responsible for the good running and good order of Scrum in the team.

The Scrum Master is both the Product Owner's advisor and the leader of the Team.

They should at least know all the rules of Scrum but also other ways of Agile working, such as kanban. Some knowledge of 'Lean Management' is also always very helpful.

A certified Scrum Master is the only member of the team who has to pass an examination.

What Else Do They Do?

1. Help the Product Owner refine work.

2. Know all the Scrum rules.

* * *

3. Act like a foreman/team captain/coach/referee.

4. Own the workflow and removes any impediments to work.

5. Own the team's productivity and morale.

6. Should have a wide knowledge of different Agile frameworks.

The Scrum Master Who Didn't Know He Was A Scrum Master.

The very best Scrum Master I ever met didn't even *know* he was a Scrum Master. In fact, if I had called him a Scrum Master, he would have (probably,) given me a thick ear.

His name was Geoff, and he owned a car repair body shop in the north of England. When I say body shop his shop actually remanufactured eye-wateringly expensive exotic Italian and British motor cars that their dopey, Premier Division football playing owners had crashed.

Geoff's shop typically took a completely brand-new body and chassis and put brand new, and the only the very best, tip-top parts from the wrecked car back into it. Then they lovingly remanufactured the car, painted it and shined it until it was gleaming and possibly even better than when it was new. Two months later and "Presto!" the young footballer would be given back the keys and allowed out to see if they could win a Charles Darwin Natural Selection award second time around.

Geoff's team worshipped him. Geoff's shop was a great place to work. They did great work on interesting projects.

* * *

He paid them well and he was fair. He made sure all the equipment in the shop was always the very best, really well maintained and safe. If there was ever a rush on then he would pay double overtime, buy them all food to eat and get his daughter to ring all their wives or girlfriends to apologise, and go buy and deliver some flowers, chocolates and a good bottle of wine to say sorry for spoiling their plans. If any of them had a problem at home to do with their kids, wives or snotty neighbours, Geoff would always help out.

Once, Geoff's feckless, useless son had been working on his old, rusty, smelly, 1960's 'bag-of-spanners' British MG Midget sports car which he had left on top of a 2-metre-high car ramp right next to an exquisite, newly-repaired, burnt orange Lamborghini that was all ready to go back to its footballist owner that very afternoon. As so frequently happens around useless people, a freak accident occurred, and the son's bag-of-spanners car leaped off the ramp and into the lap of the Lamborghini.

It was ruined. So was the Lamborghini. So was Geoff's business.

Except... it wasn't. His team of time-served, skilled men rallied round. Because it was Geoff.

Apologies were made to the footballer (who fainted when he learned the news, poor lamb). Telephone calls were made to some of the finest metal workers and body formers in England (all of them ex-Rolls Royce coach builders). And after they had finally stopped laughing out loud, they picked themselves up off the floor and employed their mysterious arts and arcane skills in which hairy, barrel-chested men with fingers like pig's tits, used words like 'doily,' without a trace of embarrassment. The car was remanufactured.

In two weeks. For nothing.

Nobody in the team charged Geoff a penny. None of the ex-Rolls-Royce coach builders did either.

What is the point of the story? Simply that the aspiration of being a great Scrum Master is not achieved by just knowing all the various Scrum techniques or doing all the various bits in it. You don't get to be a great Scrum Master by paying over a grand to go on a two-day course where you get to play with building bricks and 3M Post-It Notes.

You get to be a great Scrum Master by aspiring to be the kind of servant leader who builds up so much social capital with your team over so many years that if disaster should ever strike, they will have your back.

The Scrum Master - Notes for Scrumnasts

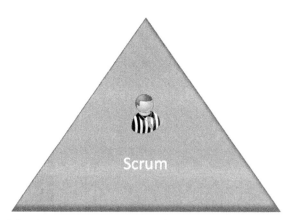

Figure 7 The Scrum Master - Notes for Scrumnasts

A Scrum Master is the specialist who knows not only how to work in Scrum but should really be aware of a very wide range of different management frameworks, and not just Agile ones. After all, Scrum is a very good toolkit, but different jobs may need different tools.

Unfortunately, expertise alone is just not enough. Sadly, there are lots of ineffective, floppy, drippy, qualified Scrum Masters who wouldn't say boo to a goose. To be effective, Scrum Masters need a strong personality, courage and they also need 'heft,' in their character.

What Do They Do?

The Scrum Master is concerned with the good running of the team of productive or knowledge workers. When push comes to shove, they are the ones who defend the team and also sort out disagreements within it.

A good Scrum Master overcomes and takes away the problems that interfere with work of the team. Even better, they should have the emotional IQ to be able to see any potential problems and sort them out before they become problems. They are also the type of person who can sort things out and get things done when everyone says, "we just can't get through this problem."

In the old days, before Scrum, we might have called them the foreman. In the armed forces, we have might called them the Sergeant, and on a ship they might be the first mate. In a sports team, they would be the captain.

Different words, similar role.

Where Do You Find Them?

It is strange but great Scrum Masters rarely figure highly on the formal management organisation chart when in large companies. They are not managerialists. Nevertheless, they will be around in your organisation. They are the people with the quiet, natural authority and they are the people that employees turn to informally when the behaviour of those on the formal management ladder has been found wanting yet again. The good ones are never creepy or brown nosing. The bad ones are.

The best ones seem to prefer people to status. Their standing comes from being valued by the people around them rather than where they are on an organisation chart.

This is why you need to co-opt them on side in your team if you are a Product Owner, a senior manager or the business owner. If you do that then you will have much greater natural authority within the team.

After all, knowledge workers know perfectly well that they need a champion so if you pick someone they already acknowledge as a champion then you are off to a good start.

Although Scrum Masters don't have a great deal of formal authority in Scrum, the best don't actually need any. That is probably because they possess enough natural authority in themselves. It springs from who they are, what they have done for others in the past, and how they carry themselves. They have a great deal of social capital. People just naturally look to them[73].

Who Do You Not Want?

As I said above, there are a lot of floppy, drippy millennials who are certified Scrum Masters. They are a waste of time. They will pose a risk to the success of your project. You can, and must, do better than that.

If you want to bring someone in that you haven't worked with in the past, then you really need to do more than look at their Agile qualifications. Unfortunately, in my experience this can count for very little. Interview them a number of times in various settings. Watch how they treat others in these settings, especially how they treat the 'unimportant' and low status people. Of course, employment agencies will hate this, but your company is much too important to risk getting a bad Scrum Master.

One of the jobs of a Scrum Master is to make sure that everyone in a team is treated with respect - especially the weakest members in the team. Do not underestimate the strength of character needed to re-

---

[73] Think Nigel Green (Colour-Sergeant Bourne) in "Zulu."

establish a healthy work culture - especially if the surrounding culture is toxic. You want them to manage a team, not an unruly gang, so their ability to talk to everyone and treat them equally is important.

Weak middle managers (and we both know there are lots of them) tend to loathe good Scrum Masters. I think they are jealous of their strong character, natural heft and that they have their own opinions. That is their problem, not yours. But do be aware that good Scrum Masters are sometimes the victims of Chinese whispers from the mean spirited, the spiteful and the useless.

But not you, Scrumnast. Not you.

You already know that good people have opinions and good people managers need heft. Do not confuse their penchant for the truth with cynicism. There is an old military saying that says, "the best soldiers moan the most." It is worth remembering. Good Scrum Managers cannot afford to be floppy because the people they lead will look to them for strength during possible dark times.

In larger, 'staff heavy[74],' bureaucratic companies, they are able to deflate the intended effect of the latest Head Office directive in under a second with nothing more than a well-timed, eloquent sniff. The people who look to them will take their lead from this.

However, strong, experienced, confident, senior managers and business owners will always make a real effort to get them on side because, despite what your latest PowerPoint organisation chart may show, they are the natural leaders of groups of people.

Tying together the people in the formal management structure with those on the informal management structure has always paid dividends in my teams. They work better, faster and in a more relaxed manner.

Having good, natural leaders on your team trumps having to email

---

[74] As opposed to production-heavy, or management-heavy, or the worst of all, consultant-heavy.

some stranger on the latest organisation chart to whom they apparently owe some allegiance because a dotted line says so.

When companies have lots of huge, slow, bureaucratic procedures to do anything THEY are the person that everyone asks for help when there is a rush on to get something out of the door.

In larger companies, you can normally find them being informally asked for advice by their colleagues in the kitchen or at the water cooler.

Words to the wise: It is far, far easier (and more successful) to train someone with this 'fixer' personality type to become a Scrum Master than to try and encourage a floppy Scrum Master to grow a pair. Good luck with that.

The Scrum Master: A Crib Sheet.

Figure 8 The Scrum Master - part leader, part trainer, part referee

Ethics:

Enforces the five core Scrum working ethics within the team. These are:

- Focus
- Commitment
- Openness
- Respect
- Courage

* * *

They also maintain the three Scrum pillars[75] of

- Transparency
- Inspection
- Adaptation

Knowledge:

As you might expect, the Scrum Master is the Scrum specialist in the team. They should know all the rules of Scrum which means they can teach and coach both the Product Owner and the Team on the best ways to work in Scrum.

They should also be aware of other Agile, Lean or Self-Managing team frameworks and have a general interest in management. After all, although I think Scrum is brilliant, it is not the only tool in the box. I do use other tools as well and so should your Scrum Master.

A certified Scrum Master is the only member of the team who has to pass an examination to get their qualification[76].

Character:

The most important character traits they need are old-fashioned

---

[75] These are also the 'pillars of empiricism,' which is posh-speak for a way of using evidence to base your decisions on rather than getting some posh bloke to tell you what to do.

[76] Weirdly, I and some of my other Scrum Master colleagues find that those that get 100% are always just a bit too evangelical to be useful and helpful. It's not a bad rule of thumb to interview a few Scrum Masters who did not get 100% and ask them why. Most will honestly tell you that there was one question on the exam that, although they knew they should have answered a certain way, they could not bring themselves to do so (Yes. I got 97.1%, now you come to ask…)

moral fibre, courage and backbone, otherwise known as 'heft.' They need to have the inner strength to push-back on unreasonable demands from the Product Owner or anyone else in the business. Especially if they get too pushy or unrealistic in their demands on the team. They need this quality in order to be to earn respect from the team. They need a robust, and sometimes muscular personality, ideally, without resorting to mindless violence, however tempting (trust me, this can be so much harder than it sounds at times).

They are the 'True Leader' of the team. We will speak more on what this term means later.

Although it is not part of classic Scrum, when we do a project, the Scrum Master is often the person who hires and fires individuals in the team. If you are running a small business which runs teams then you may be doing that too.

To Sum Up:

The Scrum Master:

Sets up and facilitates all the events and makes sure they are run as per Scrum.org

Maintains good Scrum Discipline for all members of the team at all times

Pushes back against ANY unacceptable behaviour, from any direction

Is a naturally good 'fixer.'

In an online environment, is the chairperson for ALL the events.

What does the term "Servant Leader" actually mean?

Although since Scrum 2020, the Scrum Master is no longer described as a servant leader, there are, and always will be, many occasions when a leader serves their team.

To be a good servant leader requires that you are secure in yourself. Snowflakes do not prosper as Scrum Masters.

In a bygone age, your grandparents would have called the Scrum Master a foreman

Here's a practical, outside-of-Scrum example of Servant Leadership using a traditional work team of house builders and their foreman.

'Bryn's Builders'

Bryn's Builders is a bunch of very competent trades people led by the gnarly and burliest chested of them all, Bryn. Bryn's Builders specialise in building beautiful trophy houses for successful men of a certain age, to make their trophy wives, and their trophy children and even their trophy bank manager happy and comfortable.

Halfway through a working day, the on-site carpenter tells the foreman that he will shortly run out of screws, so he wants to go off-site now and get some more from the building supplies merchant.

The wily foreman knows that if the carpenter goes off site, he is likely to get side-tracked for the rest of the day and it will be unlikely that he will return to the site today. This means the team's progress on the house building (that the foreman is responsible for) will slow down or even stop: Not so good.

Instead, the foreman offers to go and get some from the suppliers, knowing that the carpenter has enough screws for a few more hours work, which will be enough to keep him going until he returns with the screws.

This means that the carpenter is able to carry on working in the meantime and the team won't fall behind because of any work that they are relying on from the carpenter not getting finished today.

* * *

The foreman obviously takes the opportunity to ask everyone else in the team if they need more supplies. They do, and so he offers to get the supplies for the other tradesmen too.

Obviously, some weaker managers, who are obsessed with their own status, might see the 'boss' agreeing to run around to the suppliers as demeaning. However, the wily foreman knows that by doing so, he has kept the pace of the work (the velocity, as it is called in Scrum) going today, and, by buying the other supplies, has also removed other potential obstacles (called impediments in Scrum) for tomorrow's work. A side benefit is that the foreman also knows that he is only buying items for his project and not supplying items for someone else's project on the quiet (I told you he was wily). In other words, he has done some judicious budget management at the same time.

In Scrum terms, the foreman (Scrum Master), has removed the immediate problems (impediments), kept the pace (velocity) of the work going, and has also removed potential problems (also impediments), for the other members of the team. Although he is unlikely to be aware of Scrum as a management framework, he has accidentally shown himself to be an excellent Scrum Master.

On the other hand, the foreman could have been so impressed by his own sense of importance that he would have said yes to the carpenter's request to go to the shops themself, but this would have been at the expense of losing the momentum on the project.

Scrum Master Working With The Product Owner

The Scrum Master often does some initial training of the Product Owner and then continues to coach them throughout their time together. They do this both in the role itself and also in working with the Product Owner in the refining of the Product Backlog, the Sprint Planning Session, The Daily Scrum, the Sprint Review and the Sprint Retrospective.

Scrum Masters are the go-between between the two sides of the whole team, as they stand between the Product Owner and the team itself.

The Scrum Master makes sure that during every Sprint that there is complete understanding between the team and the Product Owner. Why? Let's refer back to Konosuke Matsushita and Panasonic one more time: We need to get the ideas *"out of the heads of management and into the heads of the labour"* with maximum clarity and the minimum of confusion. Confusion is expensive, clarity is cheap but hard to achieve and takes time to arrive at. I believe it is cheaper to get everyone to revisit a planning session than it is to let a team work under false assumptions for a whole Sprint. Working under false assumptions plays havoc with productivity. Things go a lot more successfully, and a lot quicker, if everyone truly knows what's going on and any and all assumptions are driven out.

Ensures that the goals, the scope, and the vision of the product's world are understood by everyone on the Scrum Team. It is easier for a team to produce truly great work if they have a reason why they should produce truly great work that is more inspiring than "because I pay you[77]."

The Scrum Master coaches all members of the team in effective techniques for Product Backlog creation, refinement and management.

They train and facilitate the Scrum events. They give a clear lead to begin with, and then, as everyone in the team becomes familiar, move from training and handholding and on to empowering and coaching both the individuals and the team.

---

[77] You would not believe the number of times I have heard this line from weak, ineffectual middle managers.

Accountability 3. The Developers (The Team Members)

Figure 9 the Developers/Team Members/Production Team/ Producers

The people who do the work in a Scrum team are technically called Developers.

The point is that the team is a cross-functional, multidisciplinary team, drawn from a wide variety of specialisms, just like a football or a cricket team has a wide range of different skills.

A Scrum team should have _all_ the job specialisms needed in it to complete the task.

There are no individual job titles in a Scrum Team.

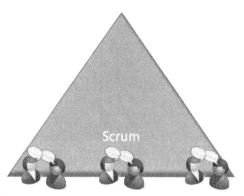

Figure 10 The Team

Who Are The Team?

The Team are the highly skilled, productive, multi-skilled collective unit of knowledge workers, technicians, or trades people. They are the workers. They are concerned with using their various skills to to do the work and complete all the individual tasks that go into completing and delivering the product.

Teams are permanent.[78] Unlike traditional project management, people are not swapped in and out of teams as needed. Teams are composed of people with all the skills needed to complete the job. There is no handing over work to other groups so when certain, seldom needed skills are lacking, if possible, the people in the team will attempt to do them to the best of their ability.

If you are assembling a Team, you are looking for people who can work collaboratively, and who are willing to learn new skills on top of their specialism.

You always have to bear in mind that some people are team players and some just aren't. There are just those who like to play team games and those that just like to play tennis. In my experience it is often

---

[78] Teams are permanent but the individuals are not necessarily. Manchester United are a permanent team but it has been a long, long time since Sir Bobby Charlton, Nobby Stiles MBE, and George Best have played for them.

better to have a competent team player than a best-in-the-industry rock star who doesn't play nicely with anyone else.

One of the attributes you want to promote amongst the people in your teams is the desire to broaden their skills. This is known as changing from "I" shaped people, who have the traditional deep, but narrow skillset into "T" shaped people who share the same deep knowledge of their primary skill but are keen to broaden their skillset.

Office workers often think that the term "knowledge workers" only describes them but they are wrong. The term is much wider than that. It also means trades people like carpenters, plumbers, mechanics, electricians too.

Why Does Scrum Work So Well With Teams?

Some of the reasons it works so well with knowledge workers is that everyone in the team:

- Know that someone has the money to pay them[79]. - the Product Owner

- They know who to go and ask if they have a problem and they have someone whose job it is to solve that problem[80] - the Scrum Master.

- All the meetings that leech time away from their working time are short and kept to a minimum. Knowledge workers like to work rather than talk for the simple reason that they get paid to work rather than talk[81]

A team needs to contain all or most of the necessary different skills

---

[79] NEVER underestimate that power

[80] This stops them fretting about distractions so they can concentrate and focus on the task in hand

[81] Unlike managers, who get paid to talk more than do. Many managers forget this.

needed to successfully build the particular product. In the jargon, this is known as being a 'multi-disciplinary' team.

For example, if you were running a football team, then it makes sense to make sure that you have all the different individual skills needed to win a game. You need a goalkeeper, defenders, midfielders and the attackers. Fielding a football team made up of eleven goalies would be silly. But at work we often see 'eleven goalies' departments organised around functions such as sales, HR, governance, accounts, etc.

However, when it comes to businesses, many medium and large companies have a mental block about getting this right when it comes to Agile. It is probably because they are so used to organising themselves into 'silo' departments such as accounts, sales, or service that they can't see any other way of organisation.

Everyone in the Team has equivalent status. There are no bosses in the team itself. The most junior member has the same status in the team as the most senior and the team is responsible as a whole for the work produced.

The team is led by the Scrum Master.

On Teams And Their Estimation Skills

Knowledge workers and craftspeople: no matter how skilful and experienced they are, the nature of their work means every time they approach a new job the results are _very hard_ to predict. This is the same reason why builders are so hopeless at giving estimates for work and will always break your heart.

Here's a real-life example. For a short while I managed the Information Technology hardware modernisation team for the Driver Vehicle Licence Agency in Swansea.

The DVLA have one of the largest computer server farms and I.T. 'real estates' in Europe. And every last electronic box needs to be changed every three or four years. The job is immense. It is so immense that you need a special method of estimating how long a job will take. This is called "Delphic estimation."

What happens in Delphic estimation is that when you need an estimate for how long it will take to replace the 'string and the tin,' (the black boxes and the bunch of wires attached) one of my team would go and ask the I.T. expert (the bloke who did it last time around) who would say, "Er…, half a day?"

No matter how many times that expert had done that job he would always be wrong. It wasn't incompetence. The reason? Because that new black box and wires with the same brand name as the old black box and wires is completely different on the inside. Inside the two black boxes, the old one looks like your grandmother's tv and its replacement is a fully functioning computer server with more computing power than an Apollo moonshot.

Once the poor guy starts the job, he finds that he's not just replacing like for like but actually implementing a brand new, untried, untested, piece of new technology that might work, or might not. The only similarities are that the box is the same size and colour.

* * *

No matter how many times they have measured it, craftsmen and tradesmen often use the phrase "offering up" their work to see if it actually fits first time. Very few things will do so without some serious finagling and a really big bucket of swearing.

Of course, this drives people who work with numbers but haven't got a clue how things actually work, like accountants, bureaucrats and technocrats[82], absolutely bonkers. They think the world is like the posh tens and units they work with every day. But it isn't.

Scrum works really well with knowledge workers, but it is not popular with bureaucrats and technocrats. There is something about how Scrum actually measures real achievement that seems to unnerve them. I think there is something in the "it wasn't working/I did something/now it is working[83]" process that makes them feel inadequate. Being in the presence of competency has that effect on certain people.

---

[82] a technocrat is a bureaucrat with a Master's degree in Human Geography and an Apple MacBook Pro.

[83] Or empiricism, if you want to be posh.

Knowing Who Does What: The People: The Team, The Hierarchy And Their Accountabilities

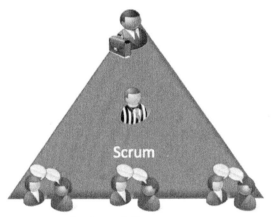

Figure 11 Knowing Who Does What

The People: Knowing Who Does What – The Three Accountabilities:

The Product Owner, The Scrum Master and the Team.

Traditionally, people who work in a department work for one leader/manager who is responsible for the people, discipline, the work, the budgets, risk, the administration and everything else in their area. When you are doing departmentally based work this makes sense because your people are organised into similar work areas such as accounts, sales, HR, or what have you, and everyone has the same skills.

* * *

However, Scrum is different. It is like a sports team. It organises people into teams made up of individuals with different skills. A Scrum team is made up of people with all the different, individual skills needed to make or build something. Scrum teams don't really do just accounts, or just sales, or just HR. They build complete cars, or complete houses, or complete software, or a complete anything.

So, in a Scrum team, there is a lot more need for both leadership and management and that's why it is split in two into someone who leads the team, and someone who manages the creation of the product. The people who are doing the productive work know that if they have a product question, they talk to the Product Owner. If they have a work or people issue, they talk to the Scrum Master. As leader[84], the Scrum Master defends the team against any potentially toxic behaviour from the manager of the product, or the wider organisation.

As you may already know, there is a classic management term called 'the span of control' which stands for the ratio of people to management. The classic ratio is 1:6[85] when you are at the lower levels and 1:3[86] for the higher levels. Scrum teams can be larger than this (though never larger than eleven[87]) and the fact that management is split into two areas helps when working with this larger team size.

The whole Scrum team is made up of three different types of accountabilities, or roles, a bit like actors in a play or a film.

The Team:

The first role is for the 'do-ers,' who are the productive/skilled

---

[84] actually, servant leader

[85] One manager and six subordinates.

[86] One manager and three subordinates.

[87] Don't think that all teams should be eleven. Smaller teams generally move a lot quicker, and burn a lot less money too. By the time you get to eight, nine, and ten people, adding another person can really give you diminishing returns, while considerably expanding leadership and management effort.

people in a Scrum team. In days gone by we might have called these people the workers. In Scrum, we call these people the team. The team are the people who get stuff done. In the above triangle diagram, they would be the people on the bottom line of the triangle.

The Scrum Master:

The Scrum Master role primarily looks after the team as a servant leader, makes sure there is nothing slowing them down or stopping them from working and leads discussions of finding better ways of working. They are also responsible for the good running of Scrum as a framework for the whole team, including the Product Owner, and also training and coaching.

The Product Owner:

The Product Owner focuses on the thing being made and the money being spent. They manage the creation of the product. Having the power to spend money is really important for a Product Owner. Those that don't have a budget that they control rarely do well.

Why the need for a Scrum Master?

A Scrum team needs quite a bit to initially mobilise it in order to work successfully. Scrum requires a fair amount of initial training, ongoing training and coaching for both the team and the Product Owner. In other words, leadership.

You also have to recognise that there is an inevitable and constant tension between a manager and the rest of the group. The manager has the desire[88] to get something created, they have high status and also the wherewithal to pay.

The team are socially subordinate: they have the necessary skills, but they are in need of the money. That puts them at a disadvantage. It is hard being subordinate in work, especially when, outside of work, you

---

[88] sometimes a fanatical desire

are successfully dealing and managing all the things that you need to do in order to live as a successful adult. Then at 8:30am, you suddenly have to ditch all that to have to listen to someone who you might not trust to even sit the right way round on a toilet seat. Sometimes you need a referee, or a layer of protection.

An Example Scrum Team

Below is a simple picture of a Scrum team. I always use a triangle to show a complete Scrum team. Within it, the top person is the Product Owner, the middle person is the Scrum Master and along the bottom line is the Team of knowledge workers.

What is a knowledge worker? Anyone who knows how to do something you don't, and you need to pay them to get them to do it. In other words, _any_ skilled people. Everybody from computer programmers to mechanics to electricians to carpenters. Scrum works really well with knowledge workers.

The triangle is not an official Scrum thing but is just a quick shorthand that I came up with when talking to clients about their teams. I find it helps to strengthen the idea that a team is a clearly defined unit, in a client's head.

I also use it when I need to create, organise, mobilise or grow a team or create multiple teams. We will go into why it helps later in the book.

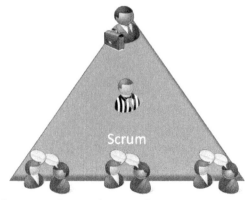

Figure 12 The Scrum hierarchy and the triangle

* * *

We now know that there is a simple hierarchy in Scrum made up of:

The Product Owner: Manages the creation of the product and has the money. They are the point of contact for any external people such as stakeholders, or governance.

The Scrum Master: Leads and looks after the team. They are the point of contact for the team if they have any problems.

The Team: The people who do the work. There are no individual job titles in the team. All are Team members, or Producers (or if you are making software, developers).

The Production Team/
Producers/Developers Crib
Sheet:

Figure 13 The Team crib sheet

In Scrum, the people who do the work in a Scrum team are officially called Developers

This is a great name if you are actually developing software, but if you are in front of a bunch of hard drinking house builders or hard drinking car repair tradesmen it can raise an eyebrow or two. Most groups in any industry respond well to the term Scrum team, or Production Team. We actually call them Producers. If you are going for your Scrum Master exam, don't forget to call them Developers.

A Scrum team has all the job skills inside it to complete the task. Sometimes that means you end up with some unusual combinations. That's fine.

A team is a bit like a football team: each member of the football team is a specialist, so there is a goalkeeper, a striker, a bunch of defenders, midfielders and attackers. It would be very odd if a football team turned out with 11 goalkeepers and it would probably not be very successful.

There are no individual job titles in a Scrum Team. Everyone has the role of Producer or Developer or a part of the Production Team

Scrum Teams Are Composed Of Knowledge Workers

The people who make up a team are knowledge workers. Knowledge workers are those practical, productive people who know how to do things that you don't know how to, do or can't do.

They would like some of your money in return.

They have invested time, money and effort in acquiring these practical, productive skills and want a return on their investment in those skills by being paid. That is their gig and that is what motivates them: Getting paid. Spreadsheets don't motivate them. Nor do PowerPoint slideshows. These are members of the muscular classes. They are not members of the typing classes.

They know that the more they work, the better they are paid. The more their work is interrupted, the less they will get paid. They are largely not interested, or impressed by, management work and especially not interested in doing it. In fact, most feel a mild contempt for it because they don't see it as real work[89].

The reason that knowledge workers like Scrum is that, although there are four different meetings, they can see that each meeting does a real, productive job. That means they don't have a lot of their time wasted in going to long, boring, meaningless, unproductive meetings. They can spend more time doing their work instead.

1. They know that the **Sprint Planning** meeting is where the work for the upcoming work cycle is examined, defined and agreed between all the parties (which means their time will not be wasted).

2. They know that the only daily meeting they have to attend is the **Daily Scrum**, which is the one where they update teammates on their progress, highlight any upcoming problems, and plan what they will do for today. Even better, it can only be a maximum of 15

---

[89] If you doubt this, think of the British army and ask yourself why the Other Ranks, (like sergeants and corporals,) will all tell you they work for a living, unlike the officers. That's part of the reason why they call them "Ruperts."

minutes long. And they can get back to work. No email, no PowerPoint, no Excel spreadsheets and no pratting around on Slack.

3. They know that the **Sprint Review** is the meeting held by the Product Owner and all the progress made during this Sprint is examined. As long as the Product Owner invites them, the Stakeholders can come along to the Sprint Review so that they can also see progress and perhaps get their agreement for more work to be done in subsequent Sprints.

4. And they don't mind doing the **Sprint Retrospective** meeting, where they can air their frustrations at slow, clumsy ways of doing things, suggest better ways, be listened to, and have their team's 'temperature' taken. In the old days, this could be done in the pub and was especially popular if the Scrum Master was paying.

The Stakeholders

Who And What Is A Stakeholder?

A Stakeholder is anyone who is outside of the working team who has a vested interest in the successful roll out of the product.

Stakeholders often have different and even conflicting demands to each other. It is the Product Owner's job *alone* to reconcile these.

For example, if you were building a house, your mortgage company manager would want it done on, or under, budget. However, the council's planning department might want the house built in a way that is in keeping with other houses nearby, which may make it end up a lot more expensive.

The group of stakeholders that the Product Owner has to take notice of is really wide, such as family members, the mortgage company, the planning department and the various utility companies (such as electricity, water supply and plumbing). All of them have a stake.

Not many of these interests have much in common with any of the other stakeholders' interests. Also, some interests are more important than the others at various points in the project, but their views need to be noted and it would be bad management to ignore them.

The Stakeholders are a core and necessary part of any project, including Scrum. But they are not part of the team in Scrum.

Stakeholders interact directly **only** with the Product Owner *and not with individual members of the team*. This ensures a single point of communication for the product being created.

The Product Owner uses the ***Sprint Review***, where the Product Owner can invite any stakeholders that need to attend so that they can view the progress which the Product Owner can demonstrate to them.

Delivery Managers

This is a totally made-up role promoted by the gormless people who work for job agencies and accepted by people who haven't got a clue but should know better.

I know why the 'role' is so popular: ignorance on the part of the agency/consultancy, and cheapness on behalf of the client.

The cheap and nasty client thinks that they are getting two for the price of one by combining the leadership and management roles.

The agencies/consultancies just want the client's money. They are also very familiar with the term 'embedded cost.' What that means is that you provide a team that come pretty close to delivering by the time the budget runs out but didn't quite get there. In order to get the thing finished, the client has to cough up around 40-50% more budget. It's an old and heartless trick.

Although you may see the Delivery Manager job title frequently, there is no such role in Scrum. Or Agile, actually. It is basically just an old-school project manager with the word 'Delivery' in front of the job title instead of 'Project.'

Just to recap: the reason that the leadership and management roles are split in Scrum, (and a lot of other management frameworks, too) is that we lead people, and we manage things. The responsibilities are split. That's it. That works.

That's why we have football captains and football managers, and your grandparents had foremen and gaffers. We lead people, we manage things.

When we give the leadership and management to one person it very often doesn't work. That is why everyone (including the U.K. Government) has abandoned the old project management frameworks like Waterfall and PRINCE2 where you have one project/programme/portfolio manager.

* * *

Look, I get it, you think that you can save money by saving on one job role. Unfortunately, you won't save money - I have been there. Remember one thing: you are paying for a team. And there aren't many things in business as expensive as running a team, so you had better make sure it runs as efficiently as possible, so that it delivers as early as possible.

If you have ten people in your team and it takes the Product Owner and the Scrum Master six weeks to deliver the thing you want, that's a bargain. In comparison, with a Delivery manager running the same team it will take them longer to deliver the thing. What if it takes them ten weeks? Or twelve?

It's your money, Scrumnast.

THE HOW - THE EVENTS

What Are The Events?

"Meetings are a great trap. They are indispensable when you don't want to do anything."- John Kenneth Galbraith – Economist.

Meetings. Do they fill you with dread? They do for me. Actually, they do for most effective and productive people.

When I was a programme manager for one of those global IT consultancies at the DVLA[90], even the bureaucrats tried to get out of going to meetings. When bureaucrats try to get out of meetings, I think that speaks volumes.

There has to be a better way of communicating, and I think that Scrum has found it by using a very simple but effective idea: instead of using lots of general purpose meetings where anyone can talk about anything, they use a specific meeting for a specific job.

We might need a meeting for planning, one for updating everyone on progress as we go, one for demonstrating how things have gone, and one to debrief and see if we can find better ways of doing things next time.

These Scrum people really do seem to know what they are doing, don't they? Actually, this idea comes from an old-school management guru who too few people remember these days. He was called William Edwards Deming, and in the 1950s, he really influenced most of the Japanese companies like Toyota, Honda, and Panasonic.

One of his many fine management ideas is the "Plan, Do, Check, Act" cycle, which states:

1. Plan the next thing you intend to do
2. Go and do it

---

[90] Remember when you had to have a paper driving licence to go with your card licence? I made it go away. MOT amendments for MOT2? Yep, me too. Online Payments for fines? Guilty as charged.

3. See how it went

4. See if you can improve it for next time you do it.

How these are enforced in Scrum is through the meetings, or events. We are kind of using the same template for success that Toyota, Honda, Panasonic and all the other really successful Japanese companies use, we can have confidence that we are in good company from a management point of view.

In Scrum, meetings are called "**Events**."

There are four of them, each with its own individual purpose, and each Sprint must always have _all_ of them.

Figure 14 the Sprint

All of the Scrum events can be done online, and this is the chief asset you have in order to manage fully remote and online, in-office, and any hybrid teams you may have.

The events are:

* * *

1. The Sprint Planning Session
2. The Daily Scrum
3. The Sprint Review
4. The Sprint Retrospective

Planning, and only planning, happens in the Sprint Planning Session (and in no other meeting)

Daily work updates by the team happen in the Daily Scrum (and nowhere else)

The latest work is demonstrated in the Sprint Review (and nowhere else)

Improvements to ways of working are explored in the Sprint retrospective (and nowhere else)

For my teams, I have added a fifth event, called "Sharpening the Tools." It is not recognised by Scrum, so you don't have to do it. But we have found it very useful. Scrum has nothing to say on doing additional events, it just says that you must do the four core events.

We use Sharpening the Tools to define a specific time for the Product Owner and the team to refine the Product Backlog and also to close the working day.

Remember, my teams work remotely, so we felt we needed a meeting to come together as a team and officially close the working day together.

I have worked both with Sharpening the Tools and without it, and all my teams always prefer to have it, but you will have to make your own mind up about it.

I find most Product Owners are also very enthusiastic and relieved to have it because they find it is a good thing to have a specific time in their working day actually allocated to refining their ideas for their product.

* * *

Meetings And The Production Team:

Okay, you have to sell the idea of all these separate meetings to your team. Meetings have become the bane of the working lives of most knowledge workers, producers, and technicians. Who can blame a new team, who have never worked with Scrum before, groaning audibly when they first learn that there are so many meetings in Scrum that they have to be involved with?

So, we have two problems to overcome:

1. Meetings don't have the greatest reputation anymore.

2. These people in the teams are do-ers. They get paid for what they produce, not going to meetings, and you have just introduced a bunch of time-wasting meetings.

It is very important to reassure the team of producers that, although it looks like there are a lot of meetings, each has its own purpose and most of them are meant to help them, rather than help the management. All of them are limited in length. The Daily Scrum is their own meeting where they can report their progress to each other and to management. Aside from these meetings, their work time is their own.

When I tell my teams that their day is their own, their eyes light up because they realise, they don't have play to "email tag" anymore, or get door-stepped by appalling middle managers who think that multi-tasking[91] is a real thing, or that micro-management[92] is a legitimate management tool and also that it works.

Although it is counter-intuitive, it turns out having four, different, specialised, short, meetings, each with its own purpose ends up being

---

[91] it isn't a real thing. Human beings can't multi-task. Computers can't multi-task, either. They just 'time-slice' unbelievably quickly which looks like multi-tasking, but isn't. So there you go, there is no such thing as multi-tasking, apart from when you attempt to do lots of things simultaneously: _all badly._

[92] Micro-management is not a legitimate management tool. It is simply the mark of a rubbish manager. And no, it doesn't work either, so _stop doing it._

a lot more productive than having a lot of those ad-hoc, formless, time-wasting business meetings with an agenda stretchier than an elastic band.

The Scrum Events

The Events[93] are four meetings and each one does one, specific job. They are where Scrum follows the "Plan, Do, Check, Act" cycle popularised by Walter Shewhart and William Edwards Deming and followed by many Japanese manufacturers.

What does Plan - Do - Check - Act stand for?

Plan - A little bit of planning. Think about where you are now, where you need to be and what you need to do to get there

Do - Go and do the thing you have planned

Check (sometimes referred to as 'study') - Measure how you have done

Act - Review how you have done and take actions from the lessons you have learned.

Let's see how the Events map onto Shewhart's and Deming's Plan, Do, Check, Act cycle. The four events are:

Sprint Planning –

A planning session for the work to be done in the Sprint about to start. It is attended by the Product Owner, the Scrum Master and the team. Scrum teams may use various planning techniques such as 'T-shirt sizing' or 'planning poker.' We use planning poker, and there's more about that later on.

Daily Scrum –

A strictly time-bound, 15-minute daily meeting. Only the Scrum team have speaking rights at the meeting, although anyone may attend

---

[93] These used to be called ceremonies.

as an observer (without the right to speak) as long as they are invited. In our online teams, we do the Daily Scrum as the first thing in the working day and we use it as a team signal that we have started the working day.

Sprint Review –

This is where the results of the latest Sprint are demonstrated. In a way, it is a governance meeting. It is sometimes known as the "Show and Tell" meeting.

Sprint Retrospective –

Something like a cross between a debriefing session and a 'wash up' meeting where the work and ideas about how to improve the ways of working are discussed. Some teams also record the 'Thriving Index' which captures how the team are feeling at the end of this Sprint

Sharpening the Tools –

Not a core Scrum ceremony but something extra we do at Scrumnastics because we found we needed it when we began to work online. It's entirely up to you whether you use it or not. Before you make up your mind, let me tell you the five reasons we use it.

1: I needed a way of bringing the team together to formally shut down the working day because, with online teams, you tend to get a lot of people over working their hours. This is not as great as you may think - I run a consultancy so I need fresh, creative and bright people being fresh, creative and bright; not shattered, slogging, dull people turning in lacklustre work. For that to happen, I need them to give me a great 8 hours of work but to have 16 hours away from work. Because of the kind of people they are, I know that ideas are percolating away in their minds in those 16 hours and, when I see them the next day, those ideas will be great.

2. Most Product Owners are very time poor, but they can normally spare 15 - 20 minutes at the end of the day to give us their latest

thoughts on upcoming work. Client priorities can change at very short notice, so it is good to have a heads up.

3. It also gives a dedicated time for refining items on the Product Backlog. Product Backlog refinement is vital to good quality work. It also aids communication between the team and the Product Owner and avoids nasty surprises in the sprint planning session.

4. It also gives the team and the Product Owner some time to mull over some of the items that are planned for the next sprint so that they are not a surprise when it comes to the sprint planning session.

5. It also lends the team a sense of perspective. If Scrum has a weakness, it is that focussing on the work to be done in the current sprint can sometimes make everything feel a little frantic. It's good for team morale and the rhythm of the work to have 15-20 minutes at the end of the day where you raise your head and look at what is coming up and also what part the current work you are doing is playing in the big picture.

1: The Sprint Planning Event

"Plans are worthless, but planning is everything." - General Dwight D. Eisenhower

"Everyone has a plan until they get punched in the face." - Mike Tyson

The Sprint Planning Meeting

A meeting where the work that is meant to go into the new Sprint is estimated

When? At the beginning of the new Sprint

This is Goldilocks planning: not too little, not too much, *just right*

Figure 15 The Sprint Planning Meeting

This meeting is held to plan the work to be done in this Sprint. Not the next two Sprints, not the next three Sprints. This coming Sprint.

The plan for the work is a collaborative effort arrived at by the ***entire Scrum Team***. That also means the Product Owner and the Scrum Master (who should know quite a few different planning techniques, especially 'planning poker[94]' and 'T-shirt planning[95]').

The Scrum Master facilitates the Sprint Planning session. Meaning they make sure the event actually happens, that everyone attends (especially the Product Owner), and that everyone understands why and how it is going to happen.

* * *

---

[94] individuals size up a potential job using relative rather than absolute numbers (0,1,2,3,5,8,13,21,34,55,89, and infinity)

[95] Is this job a Small, Medium, Large, Extra-Large, or Humungous one?

Timings

Until the November 2020 Scrum update, there was a set time limit on how long a planning event should be. Although scrum.org has now largely taken these timings away, they are handy rules of thumb, especially when you are starting out. We still use them. These were:

- Two hours maximum for a one-week Sprint

- Four hours maximum for a two-week Sprint.

- Eight hours maximum for a month-long Sprint

These are maximum lengths. Of course, they can be shorter (ours normally are). The Scrum Master is responsible for making sure that the timings are kept to.

We use video for just about all our communication, including planning. Any kind of planning is intense and requires a lot of mental energy from everyone, even in the days when we all used to work face to face with each other. Doing the same thing using video makes it even more of a stretch.

Therefore, we make sure that there is at least a ten-minute break at fifty-five minutes for a two-hour meeting. If anyone calls for an extra break, then that is automatically granted. After all, fresher minds do better planning.

Planning is intense and can be very wearing on people. I would rather have extra breaks and fresh minds than a team miss or misunderstand a crucial point simply because they were too mentally worn to spot it. My advice is not to force planning work because *any* reworking that has to be done as a result of misunderstandings will often prove to be expensive.

As I said above, as a rule of thumb, if we are working on two-week Sprints then we break at fifty-five minutes for a ten-minute break. We also have a twenty-five minute break for food, at the end of the second hour. The final session can only be thirty minutes long. We do not have a fourth hour. If the team do run out of work during a Sprint, then we have agreed to run another short Sprint Planning session later on in the Sprint (but we have never actually had to do this).

As of the November 2020 update, the Sprint Planning session is supposed to be divided into three parts that are called topics:

Topic One: *Why is this Sprint Valuable?*

It is a more useful question than you might at first think. Running a team can be a considerable expense. Therefore, one of the questions that the Product Owner has to ask themselves is, "Will the intended work pay back more than the cost of running the team?" If it won't then they should not go ahead with the Sprint.

The Product Owner gives their thoughts on what best could be done to increase the value and usefulness of the product in this Sprint. The whole team then spend a short time creating a Sprint Goal that captures this idea. This has to be done by the end of the Sprint Planning Session.

Topic Two: (which is split into two parts)

Part One: *What can be produced and achieved?*

As we say, "the Product Owner Brings the Dreams, the Team bring the means." I call this the "chasm of negotiation." This is the Product Owner's dreams meet the hard wall of reality. Neither side will get their own way completely.

Part One is negotiated by the whole team (It is _vital_ that the Product Owner attends this part of the Sprint Planning session).

Sprint Planning Session Part One: What can be done in this Sprint?

What happens in the meeting?

* * *

1.   The Product Owner gives a review of what has been actually achieved in the project so far (five to ten minutes, maximum).

2.   The Product Owner should show the completely current and up-to-date Product Backlog (we use the Sharpening the Tools ceremony to make sure that everyone in the team and the Product Owner is working with the latest version of the Product Backlog) (five minutes - shown on Trello on Zoom but everyone can also access Trello separately).

3.   A rough idea of the past productivity and performance of the team (velocity report - probably done by the Scrum Master - one minute).

4. A realistic idea of the amount of work that can be achieved in this coming Sprint (Are any of the team on holidays?).

The Product Owner _must_ have a very good idea of what they want to achieve this Sprint. Their Product Backlog should already be ranked by value, and they always want to prioritise getting the most valuable items done. (See the specific section later in the book called "**Doing a Product Backlog in Trello").** It doesn't have to be that detailed, but they do need to have thought about what the upcoming Sprint should achieve, because it will shape the direction of the Sprint.

The Product Owner presents their prioritised Product Backlog. The top items off the Product Backlog will be up for inclusion in the upcoming Sprint, but only the team can decide on how much work is realistically achievable and how much can be included in the Sprint. Of course, if you are using Sharpening the Tools then everyone will be much better informed than normal and so this can be very short.

The Entire Scrum Team works together in trying to really understand all the work required so that there is no confusion and no assumptions.

The production team forecasts the items that it believes it can deliver and the whole Scrum Team comes up with an objective, for the Sprint Goal. We name the Sprint after this Sprint Goal.

* * *

It may seem wasteful to spend time on coming up with the Sprint Goal, but a good Sprint Goal helps the team to come up with much more creative solutions than they otherwise would and also stops them from getting tangled up in the weeds when doing really detailed work. It also gives a short term 'reason why' for the Sprint, which is always helpful.

Sprint Planning Session Part Two: How Will The Work Be Done?

Remember Konosuke Matsushita's quote[96]? This is where the dreams from inside the head of the person with the wherewithal, get transferred into the real world by the practical heads of the practical people.

There is always a negotiation in how much work can be done by the team.

The Product Owner will almost always want to overload the team with work. However, if the team genuinely think that they have reached maximum capacity for the Sprint then the Product Owner must accept this as true. If they don't, then the Scrum Master must intervene on the team's behalf. After all, if they run out of work during the Sprint then they can always ask the Product Owner for more.

We are now in the land of making estimates. Mike Cohn's book, "Agile Estimating and Planning," is probably the best book on this and is well worth buying.

Words For The Wise Scrumnast:

It is typical for everyone involved to want to deliver a time-based estimate for upcoming work.

---

[96] *"For the essence of management is getting ideas out of the heads of the bosses and into the heads of labour. We are beyond your mindset. Business, we know, is now so complex and difficult, the survival of firms so hazardous in an environment increasingly unpredictable, competitive and fraught with danger, that their continued existence depends on the day-to-day mobilisation of every ounce of intelligence."*

* * *

Here is the rule of thumb that I use for time-based estimates that I am indebted to, and borrowed from, my valued Scrum Master colleague, Laurie Williams. He calls this the "NASA gate[97]"

The NASA gate:	
1. Have we done this before?	[Yes/No]
2. If so, have we done it recently?	[Yes/No]

(If you have done the work recently then any estimates may well be accurate. If you haven't, then, unfortunately, any estimate will have little basis in reality).

For example, If I am a Product Owner and I say, "This is the Sprint where I need to get the secret underground man cave built," Bryn's[98] team of builders will know that they need to do the following:

- Dig a very big hole (4 days - luckily, Bryn has two diggers, and he and his his mate, Charlie, can both operate them)
- Dig a 50-metre-long road sized channel from the very big hole to the secluded back road (3 days - probably Charlie)
- Put a load of hard core down on the floor with steel rebar for foundations (1.5 days Dai and Euan)
- Pour in concrete floor (1 day to pour, 2 days to set - Bryn to organise the concrete people)
- Install steel shuttering for walls (2 days - Bryn and Charlie with diggers)
- Install external and internal steel walls (2 days, full team)
- Install and weld steel panels on roof (1.5 days - full team)
- Cover whole structure with earth (2 days Bryn and Charlie - diggers)
- Put turf on top of the earth (3 days - full team)

* * *

---

[97] Laurie has worked with NASA

[98] "Bryn's Builders Ltd," are my mythical team of seen-it-all, done-it-all, hard-to-impress, time-served tradesmen that can do any building job, on-time, and on-budget. Like I said: mythical.

It all looks reasonable, accurate and plausible, doesn't it? Unfortunately, it isn't. Human beings are terrible at forecasting precisely how long something will take. For the same reason that we are terrible at doing horoscopes: We don't know what the future holds. No-one does and no-one ever has. All these estimates will be wildly optimistic.

Why? Well, in Agile lore, it is said that people are not good at estimating in absolute terms (such as where someone says "five hours," or "forty days," etc).

Personally, I think the reason is simpler. I think it is because unless we work in a factory, anything we estimate is _always_ an unknown. The problem with unknowns is that you don't know how long a task will take until you have done it. You can guess, but that is all you are doing. That is the nature of complex work, or craft work. Complex work will always end up turning out differently, every time.

The human race has a special name for people who swear blind they know what will happen in the future. We call them astrologers.

What can we do instead?

'Relative Sizing' For Estimation:

This is a great solution for when work gets complex (such as when you are trying to do something you have never done before).

It turns out that although people are terrible at absolute sizing, people are pretty good at relative sizing. For example, picture a car. Now picture a single decker bus. Just for fun, how many times bigger is the bus than the car? Three times bigger? Five times bigger? More? I bet you can come up with a pretty good idea. We are pretty good at that kind of estimation. Now tell me how much the bus and the car weigh in tons and kilogrammes. We have no idea, do we?

* * *

You can turn that human ability to be able to do a rough and ready relative estimate to your team's advantage.

This is what we do: we take any one of the simpler, smaller tasks in front of you and ask the team, "How big do you think that task is? If it was a number, would it be a 1, 2, 3, 5, 8, 13, 21, 34, 55, 100 [99] or bigger?"

Let us say that the team all say it is a 2. Now in everyone's mind, that task is anchored at 2. Everything else is now smaller than 2, equal to 2, or bigger than 2.

Now pick another, seemingly bigger task. How hard will that task be to do? Get the team to vote by picking one of the numbers above. Because you have anchored the simple task at 2, you have constructed a reference point to gauge the size of all the other tasks. If the team comes up with a range of numbers, ask the team members who come up with either end of the extremes to tell the team why they think it was so hard or so simple. Then vote again.

Repeat this process until someone in the team thinks that they won't be able to do any more items in the upcoming Sprint.

Now add up all the numbers that everyone has voted on. The total is the number of points that this team thinks it can achieve in a Sprint. I know it sounds loose and unmanaged, - and a bit chaotic. But it works.

This planning technique is called Planning Poker and, although it is nothing to do with Scrum itself, is a widely recognised method of planning that actually works, especially when you are dealing with complex work[100]. We do a lot of complex work so we use it all the time.

---

[99] These look quite like the Fibonacci numbers, but they aren't. They are there to aid the relative sizing.
[100] Where you don't know how work will turn out until you have actually started to do it.

2: The Daily Scrum

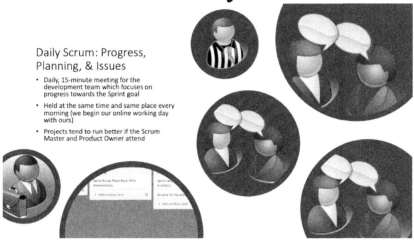

Daily Scrum: Progress, Planning, & Issues

- Daily, 15-minute meeting for the development team which focuses on progress towards the Sprint goal
- Held at the same time and same place every morning (we begin our online working day with ours)
- Projects tend to run better if the Scrum Master and Product Owner attend

Figure 16 The Daily Scrum - Who attends

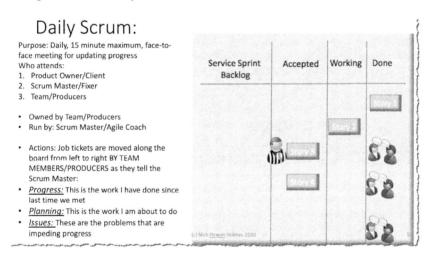

Daily Scrum:

Purpose: Daily, 15 minute maximum, face-to-face meeting for updating progress
Who attends:
1. Product Owner/Client
2. Scrum Master/Fixer
3. Team/Producers

- Owned by Team/Producers
- Run by: Scrum Master/Agile Coach

- Actions: Job tickets are moved along the board from left to right BY TEAM MEMBERS/PRODUCERS as they tell the Scrum Master:
- *Progress:* This is the work I have done since last time we met
- *Planning:* This is the work I am about to do
- *Issues:* These are the problems that are impeding progress

Service Sprint Backlog	Accepted	Working	Done
			Story 1
		Story 2	
	Story 3		
	Story 4		

(c) Nick Hewyn Holmes 2020

Figure 17 The Daily Scrum: A progress update Event (meeting)

In Scrum, we call this meeting the Daily Scrum. Many people call it the 'Stand Up' meeting but actually, that is what it is called in XP, which is a completely different management framework.

The Daily Scrum is the project's daily catch up, update, planning and problem-solving session that happens at the beginning of the business day. Scrum.org stipulate that the Daily Scrum is limited to 15 minutes maximum. In our case, we mostly get this done in around 11 or 12 minutes. It is a matter of pride to our teams that we never go beyond 15 minutes.

What Happens:

Each of the team takes it in turns to answer the following three statements:

1. "What I worked on yesterday in order to help the team achieve the Sprint Goal."

2. "What I am working on today in order to help the team achieve the Sprint Goal.

3. "These are the issues/problems/blockers I have and need help with overcoming." (With help from the Scrum Master.)

As they speak, the individuals move their work tickets through the particular work stage, whether it is "**Accepted**," "**Working**," "**Done**," or "**Done, Done**." - That's it.

Now you may be thinking, "hang on, I know a bit about Scrum. What happened to all those 'What I did yesterday,' 'What I'm doing today,' and 'These are my impediments,' speeches?"

Well, that's what we used to officially say before Scrum 2020, and it was great as a set of training wheels for the first four or five sprints while everyone was getting used to Scrum.

But by the time you had been doing this for some time (like when you go to Sprint 126,) using the statements all felt a bit contrived and artificial. By then, everyone knew exactly what to say and they knew the reasons why they said it.

If it is a good team, Daily Scrums would tend to naturally evolve over time into rather quiet affairs, where the team members would move their work tickets, and that would be about it for the meeting, aside from telling the Scrum Master whether they had any problems or impediments.

I think that one of the hidden benefits of the Daily Scrum is social pressure: everyone has to pass the 'truth test' every day, as judged by their peers. After all, it is easy for a social climber to try and pull the wool over the boss's eyes, but it is a great deal harder to brazen it out and attempt to convince your peers you have done something when they know you really haven't.

The Daily Scrum is also a good way of getting interaction between the team, and also to focus the team's minds on the Sprint Goal in everything they do.

Remember, only members of the team, the Product Owner and the Scrum Master may speak at the Daily Scrum.

For example, observers *may* attend but not *speak*. If there are observers, they can often get caught up in the enthusiasm of the moment, and attempt to speak. You will find the meeting goes better if the Scrum Master announces that only the team has speaking rights at the beginning of the Daily Scrum, otherwise you will find it very difficult to finish within your fifteen minutes.

In old-school Scrum speak, the reason given for only the team having speaking rights is explained by the age-old agile story of pigs and chickens[101].

The pigs' and chickens' story may be gruesome, but it is true that you often need to stop spectators from speaking. They don't do it from mischief, they just genuinely get caught up in the excitement of working in Scrum.

---

[101] When you are making bacon and eggs, the pigs (the people doing the work) have a lot more skin in the game than the chickens (everyone else).

The Car Park:

Optionally, once we have formally closed the Daily Scrum ceremony, if needed, we tag on an additional, separate meeting which we call the 'car park.' (Or the 'parking lot' if you're an American).

The car park meeting is for individuals, not for the whole team. It is there for brief discussions on things that only involve two or three of the team, or where someone needs a point of clarification from the Product Owner for something that is coming up soon.

The car park is not part of formal Scrum therefore attendance is entirely voluntary. After all, the members of the team have work to do and they need to get on with it.

Wise Words For Scrumnasts:

Handy hints on how to run a great Daily Scrum:

We begin our working day with the Daily Scrum. Video is mandatory, phoning in is not allowed. This gets rid of the temptation for remote people to turn up for work in their pyjamas or their onesies. After all, this is work. The Scrum Master starts the video conference 5-10 minutes prior to the fomal start, so that individuals can enjoy a bit of non-work catching up talk with each other. The Daily Scrum ALWAYS starts on time.

The Scrum Master should always get the team members to move their own work tickets on the Sprint Backlog, rather than the Scrum Master doing it. It is a small thing, but it pays really big benefits.

Doing this gives you two things:

1. **Peer Pressure:** You properly harness the power of peer pressure within the team. It is pretty easy to 'fib' to the boss, but it is much harder to do that in front of your colleagues and try and look them in the eyes. If one of the team moves a ticket from "Working," to "Done" when it really isn't done, then the colleagues will make it

clear to them in a non-verbal way. If you are using video, you can really see their reactions because you can see all their faces on screen.

2.   **Heightened Status within the group**: That satisfaction of demonstrating the completion of a job to your peers is a great feeling. Moving that ticket and announcing that the job is done to your colleagues really finishes off the task.

Conversely, one of the ways _not_ to reap the benefits of the Daily Scrum is for the Scrum Master to move the tickets for the participants. This seems to take away just that little bit of payoff of job satisfaction for a job well done to the person who actually did it. It is one thing to do a job, but it is quite another to announce the completion of a job to your colleagues. Let them have their kudos: let them move their work tickets.

A Daily Scrum - A Worked Example

A Practical: A Worked Example Of A Set Of Daily Scrums:

This is a worked example for the **Daily Scrum** event, which interacts with a progress and update planner called the **Sprint Backlog**. The **Sprint Backlog** is used in Scrum to record the progress of the work during the current work period, or **Sprint,** as we call it in Scrum. Later on in the book there is also a separate worked example that focuses on how a team works with the **Sprint Backlog**.

The **Daily Scrum** is the meeting that updates the progress of the work on the **Sprint Backlog**. It is a short[102], daily progress meeting where the whole team can see how things are going in the current **Sprint**.

There are normally two kinds of tasks done by a team:

1. Those that can meet a level of quality that is pre-determined by the team.

2. Those that need to meet some outside standards and need to be verified.

We will deal wih both here. We will also deal with what to do if you unexpectedly finish the planned tasks early in the Sprint.

This is our scenario: Imagine you are part of a Scrum team on day one of a Sprint. You have just finished the **Sprint Planning** event. During this event the whole team (the **Product Owner,** the **Scrum Master,** and the developer **Team**) agreed amongst themselves the jobs

---

[102] Scrum says this should be no longer than 15 minutes. Once the team get into the swing of doing Daily Scrums, it normally drops to about 9 - 12 minutes. We work entirely remotely from each other and we begin our working day with the Daily Scrum event.

that are going to be completed by the end of the Sprint.

During the **Sprint Planning** event, each of the jobs were given an agreed definition of what makes them completed and finished. In other words, each job has been given some acceptance criteria built into it. In Scrum this is called the '**Definition of Done**," and forms the contract between the dev." and the Product Owner. As long as the piece of work meets the acceptance criteria, the job is considered "Done." Each individual "**Definition of Done**" is attached to each job's job card and follows the words "**Done When**:".

In preparation for the first **Daily Scrum** in this Sprint, all the jobs have been written up onto the **Sprint Backlog** board and and put in the "**Accepted**" column, to show that they have been accepted by the team as jobs to be done in this Sprint..

When they looked at the jobs, the team decided to split the work up between them. One part of the team will work on one task and the other part of the team will work on a second task.

Day One:

What happens: If you are working remotely, it is probably a good idea to open the event five to ten minutes before the scheduled time to allow everyone to join in a relaxed manner. We use video for all meetings and no-one joins with audio only. The meeting is opened by the Scrum Master, who acts as chairperson for the event.

Day One:

On **Day One**, prior to the first Daily Scrum, our Sprint Backlog looks something like this:

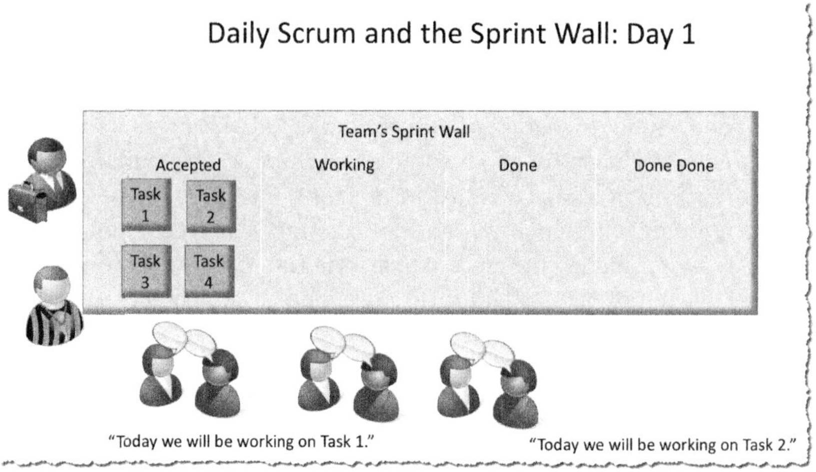

Daily Scrum and the Sprint Wall: Day 1

Figure 18 Day 1: The Product Owner, the Scrum Master and the Team and the tasks.

During the Daily Scrum, the team announce what they will be working on for the day. Notice that it is the team that make the decision, not the Scrum Master and not the Product Owner. In this case they will move the job cards for **Task One** and **Task Two** from the **Accepted** column onto the **Working** column to show that they are now working on them.

The job cards/work tickets are only moved during the **Daily Scrum** and _at no other time_. This means that at the beginning of the Daily Scrum for Day Two of the Sprint, everyone sees the status of the work as at the end of the previous day's Daily Scrum.

So, at the beginning of Day Two, the Spring Backlog looks like this:

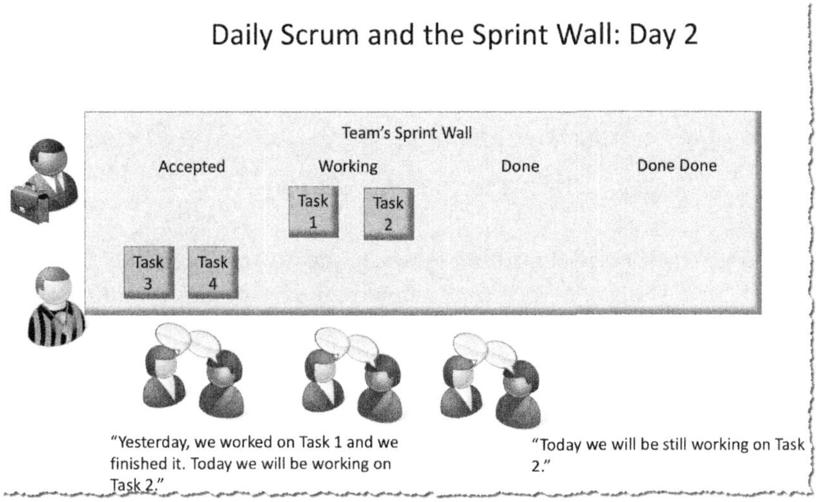

Daily Scrum and the Sprint Wall: Day 2

Figure 19 Beginning Of The Daily Scrum On Day Two.

The Day Two Daily Scrum:

As we said above, on Day Two, the whole team sees the status of the Sprint backlog as it was at the end of yesterday's Daily Scrum

The developer team are going to state what they did yesterday to meet the team's **Sprint Goal**, and what they intend to do today in order to meet the team's Sprint Goal.

First of all, they announce to the whole team that they finished **Task One** yesterday, that it meets the "**Definition Of Done**" standards previously agreed with the Product Owner, which means it is ready to be put into the **Done** column.

However, **Task Two** has not been completed yet. The team need to decide what to do. The team could do one of two things: they could either join together in order to finish **Task Two**, or, if Task Two is almost finished, they could choose let half the team finish it and get the other half to start a new task.

They discuss amongst themselves which is the best plan, and they quickly choose to let half the team finish Task Two and the other half the team will move on to the next task.

How Did Everyone Know That Task One Was Finished To An Acceptable Standard?

During the **Sprint Planning** session the team asked the **Product Owner** for a short sentence that defined successful completion for the job so they would know when they were finished. This short sentence is known as the "**Definition of Done**."

This tells the team exactly what the thing has to be able to do in order to be finished. No more and no less. This gives clarity to the people doing the job, stops any unfortunate "But I thought you meant,…" words, and so is both a great time-saver, and stops workers from being tempted to 'gild the lily.' The Definition of Done was written by the Product Owner on the bottom of the job card by the Product Owner, before the work was accepted into the Sprint. Actually, with us it is a condition of being able to be accepted into a Sprint.

Remember Konosuke Matsushita's of Panasonic's "out of the heads of management and into the heads of labour" phrase? This is one of the ways that idea works in Scrum. Let's carry on.

The part of the team that were working on **Task One** are now ready to begin working on **Task Three**, so they move the **Task Three** job card from the "**Accepted**" column and onto the "**Working**" column.

The other part of the team is still working on **Task Two**, so they simply announce to all of the attendees of the Daily Scrum that they are still working on Task Two.

How The Sprint Board Looks At The End Of The Daily Scrum For Day Two:

* * *

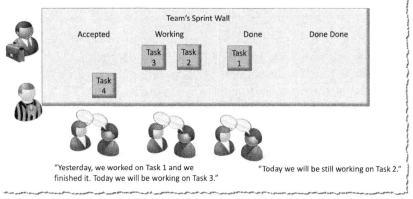

Figure 20 Sprint Backlog For End Of Day Two - Beginning Of Day Three.

Daily Scrum For Day Three:

Again, as ever, the Sprint Backlog board looks unchanged from how it was left at the end of yesterday's Daily Scrum.

Today the two parts of the team announce that:

1. The part of the team that began **Task Three** yesterday will still be working on it today.

2. The other part of the team has now completed **Task Two**.

However, let's imagine that the work on **Task Two** needs some kind of extra check, or some kind of external certification before it can be signed off as completed. This might be because it has to meet safety standards, as it would if it was to do with electricity or gas supply. For this circumstance, we would take advantage of the "**Done Done**" column on the Sprint Backlog.

Because this safety certificate is conditional on a successful inspection, the team move it to the "**Done**" column but not the "**Done, Done**" column - (because the work might not be judged as acceptable, and might have to be redone).

If **Task Two** does become certified, the team can then move it on to the "**Done, Done**," column as you can see in the picture below.

However, if the work has to be done again then the work card would be moved back into the "**Working**" column and the work would be redone if there was enough time left in the Sprint. Otherwise, it would probably be included in the next Sprint's backlog.

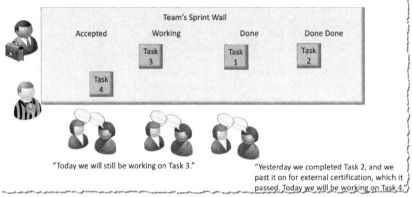

"Today we will still be working on Task 3."

"Yesterday we completed Task 2, and we past it on for external certification, which it passed. Today we will be working on Task 4."

Figure 21Sprint Backlog For End of Day Three - Beginning Of Day Four.

Daily Scrum For Day Four:

As the team begins the Daily Scrum on **Day Four**, the Sprint Backlog shows **Task One** has been completed and is marked as **Done**.

Task Two has passed inspection and is now certified so is in the "**Done Done**" column.

The Sprint Backlog also shows that part of the team is still working on **Task Three.** The only unstarted task is Task 4, which is the only task left to do.

So for today's Daily Scrum, one half of the team announce that they wil continue on **Task Three** (which they hope to finish today), and the other half of the team will start working on **Task Four**.

* * *

As you can see, there are now no longer any Tasks in the "**Accepted**" column. All the tasks are either being worked on or are completed in one way or another.

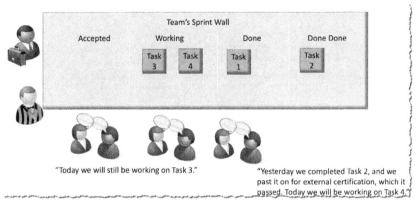

Figure 22 Sprint Backlog For End of Daily Scrum for Day Four And Beginning Of Day Five.

Daily Scrum For Day Five:

In today's Daily Scrum, the team announces two things:

1. They have run out of some of the materials that they need to finish **Task Three**, so they need to bring this to the Scrum Master's attention for the Scrum Master to resolve the problem. **Task Three** stays at the "**Working**" status.

2. The other half of the team have now finished **Task Four.** However, just like **Task Two**, it also needs some kind of check (this time they need to check acceptability with the client,) before it can be moved to the **Done Done** column.

Once the Daily Scrum finishes, the Scrum Master goes away to try and resolve the materials problem.

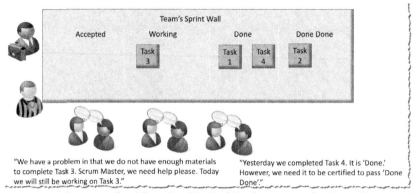

Figure 23 Sprint Backlog For End of Daily Scrum for Day Five And Beginning Of Day Six

Being the ace 'fixer' that they are, the Scrum Master obtains the all the necessary materials a little later that day and gets them into the hands of the team so they can continue work.

Daily Scrum For Day Six:

During today's Daily Scrum, the team are able to announce that all the planned tasks for this Sprint are now complete as either Done, or Done Done.

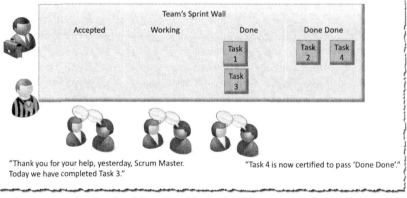

Figure 24 Sprint Backlog For End of Daily Scrum for Day Six And Beginning Of Day Seven

* * *

The Team have now finished all the planned tasks. They now have one more day left in the Sprint so they ask the Product Owner for more work.

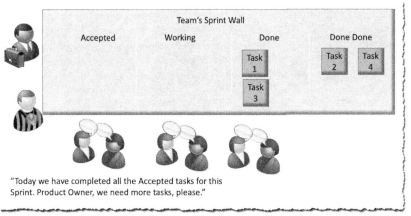

Figure 25 Team Asking The Product Owner For More Work on Day 6.

Still Day Six:

The Product Owner is obviously happy at the news, so given the amount of time left in the Sprint, brings two small-ish Product Backlog Items from their Product Backlog for examination, negotiation and probable acceptance by the team into their Sprint Backlog.

You might be wondering whether the whole team should call another Sprint Planning session to deal with this? Of course, they could have done but as the jobs were small and there is only a day left in this Sprint, the team took a more pragmatic view. Besides, Scrum.org says that every Daily Scrum should incorporate some minor re-planning.

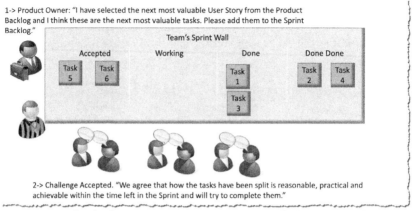

Figure 26 Daily Scrum Day 6 - Interaction And Negotiation Between The Product Owner And The Team.

Given the small size of the tasks, the team thinks they are both achievable within the time left in the Sprint, and accept them into the Sprint Backlog and will do their best to finish them.

Which is great news for the Product Owner. For tomorrow's **Sprint Review,** they will be able to tell the stakeholders that they have not only achieved all the planned tasks for the Sprint but have also done some bonus tasks, too.

3: The Sprint Review Meeting

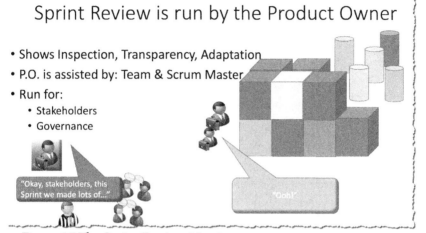

Figure 27 The Sprint Review Meeting

The Sprint Review is the progress demonstration meeting in Scrum. But it is also the governance meeting as well. The work that has been achieved during the Sprint is publicly demonstrated to the team and whoever the Product Owner wishes to invite.

The Sprint Review is run by the **Product Owner**, not the Scrum Master and not the team. Of course, they may help (and it makes for a _much_ better meeting if they do), but it is important to remember that it is run by the Product Owner.

The Sprint Review meeting is where the work that has been done during the Sprint is shown to the outside world, especially the stakeholders. This is the demonstration of what has been achieved, and what has not been achieved, during the latest Sprint.

From the governance perspective, the following happens. For example:

* * *

1. The Product Owner announces which **increments**[103] have been achieved (everything that has achieved "Done," or "Done, Done") from the list of items that were accepted into the Sprint backlog by the team for this Sprint.

2. The Team discusses what went well, what problems were encountered, and how they were solved.

3. Product Owner announces and discusses what is left on their Product Backlog.

4. Relevant stakeholders for this stage in the work will have been invited to attend by the Product Owner. Different stakeholders have different needs at different times. For example, if you are building a house then the people from the Planning Department won't be interested in coming to the same Sprint Review that the people from the Building Society will want to come to. It's simply sensible to invite the relevant people to the relevant Sprint Review.

If the Product Owner has confidence that there is value in carrying on, then there will be another Sprint. It is expensive to run a team, so a judgement should be made by the Product Owner that the projected work will deliver more value than it will cost. The Product Owner alone decides if there is enough value.

Notes For Scrumnasts:

(A Practical On The Sprint Review)

If you are an inexperienced Product Owner, you could do a lot worse than use the same format that most TV news programmes have used for decades. I find it lends your project a very professional air. I use it all the time, it is what I teach new teams to do.

---

[103] New for Scrum 2020, when a task has been completed (meets the definition of done, it becomes an *increment*.

* * *

It is:

As ever, the Scrum Master opens the video meeting application as an administrator five to ten minutes before the scheduled time. Then they admit the known participants one by one. Do not mass admit everyone, there are 'lurkers' who may wish to cause mischief and disruption.

Promptly, at the advertised start time, the Scrum Master formally opens the meeting as the chairperson. The Scrum Master then introduces the Product Owner to the meeting and hands over to them.

The Product Owner Follows This Structure:

1.   Tell them what you are going to tell them (the introduction - five to ten minutes maximum).
2.   Tell them (the details - thirty minutes maximum)
3.   Tell them what you told them (the summary - ten minutes maximum)

As in all meetings, shorter is *always* better. However, there is also a Scrum.org stipulated time limit of a maximum of:

1. One hour for a one-week Sprint.
2. Two hours for a two-week Sprint.
3. Up to four hours for a four-week Sprint.

Less is more. These timings are the maximum allowed. You can and should try and make them shorter if possible. Trust me, everyone will thank you if you do. You want to leave them wanting a little bit more, not a whole lot less.

If I have a team that are working in two-week Sprints, because we are using video I make sure there is a ten minute break just before the hour at the fifty-fifth minute. I also try and make the second session a maximum of forty minutes. It's like theatre and classical music: the second act is always shorter.

* * *

Generally, I don't recommend that you do four-week Sprints because of the heightened risk of the work veering off in the wrong direction during the Sprint making it hard to catch. I also think that a series of video sessions over a four hour period would be hell on earth.

Finally, again, it is really important for the good running of Scrum that the Sprint Review is run by the Product Owner. If you don't do this and someone else runs it, then it is uncanny just how quickly the project can get itself into a real mess within a short amount of time.

4: The Sprint Retrospective

Sprint Retrospective (the Debrief)

- Run by: Scrum Master/Fixer/Agile Coach
- Run for: Benefit of Team and Continuous Improvement
- Happens: At the End of the Sprint
- Benefits: Opens the Loop for improvement
- Artefact: The 'Thriving Index" ('Happiness Index')

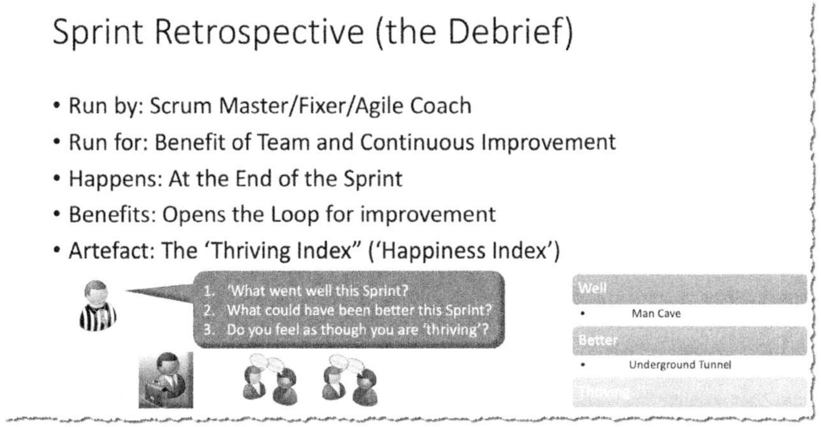

Figure 28 The Sprint Retrospective

The **Sprint Retrospective Event** is a type of debriefing session. The purpose of the debrief is to try to discover the team's emotional temperature, how they feel the project is going, could the ways of doing things be improved, and how involved and engaged they feel in the project.

If you are an old-school, 'Theory X[104]' manager, why would you care?

Teams are meant to be permanent, and if individual members of the team are approaching burn out, that is going to negatively affect productivity for the whole team. Having a team break up because of exhaustion means you may have to replace all or part of the team. That will wreck any production projections you will have made. It will also be ferociously expensive and the client will not be happy with that. You will want an early warning of that possibility.

Unhappy projects and unhappy teams are less likely to succeed. Long before they can put their feelings into words, a team's 'spidey-

---

[104] From "The Human Side Of Enterprise" by Douglas MacGregor. Theory X managers believe all workers are lazy and need to be shouted at.

sense' can give you an early warning of any upcoming problems. You need to know this in order to manage and support them better.

Now to be sure, there is normally always a point in any project where team morale dips. It normally comes mid-way to two-thirds of the way through the projected length of the project. Frequently, there comes a point when they come close to breaking, when the team realise that *they* are the only people who can bring the project to a satisfactory conclusion.

The team realise they have no option but to dig deep and overcome all the problems that seem to be in front of them. Morale will slowly rise as they begin to see a string of small triumphs as they complete work items.

People actually need stress in order to thrive. But they need the right *kind* of stress and the right *amount* of stress. All living organisms are designed to cope with stress, it's how we progress and grow. A fair amount of the right kind of stress can actually be exhilarating. The right kind of stress is where the reward is much bigger than the input ("that walk up to the top of the hill was really hard, but, wow, look at that view!"). But too much of the wrong kind of stress, where you get less back than you put in, is detrimental.

We need an early warning of anything like that. There is a tool that allows me to frequently take the temperature of the team and also the individuals within the team too. The tool I use is the "**Thriving Index**," which I will talk about below.

Knowledge workers have an inbuilt interest in working smarter. They know that if they can work smarter then they normally get paid better, for longer and get considered for more work. I like to take advantage of that fact when managing them.

Which scenario is more likely to produce better ideas on improving productivity? A team of five to eleven people caught up in doing the work coming up with solutions because they are coming up against problems in the course of their work, or me, working on my own, late at night, dreaming up potentially daft work 'improvements'? Personally, I'll take the many pairs of eyes looking for a set of solutions any day.

Why this is different to what you are doing in your company right now:

You know that ghastly annual staff survey that your Human Remains department make you endure once a year where everyone lies through their teeth because, even though H.R. swear blind it is anonymised, everyone knows it really, really isn't? And if you get too minty and honest in your responses then they are going to track you down and nail you, sucker? Well, the **Sprint Retrospective** is nothing like that.

The Sprint Retrospective is really is an honest, frank discussion between equals on how the team feel their work life is going. The big difference that gets their buy-in is that their views actually count for something because they can actually change how they work. That matters because it means that they have some control over their working lives, the best hours of their day.

By the way, you will all probably have to do quite a few Sprint Retrospectives before you really get true honesty from the team. After all, this is a basic issue of trust. They have all been working for a considerable amount of time in environments where frankness and honesty are often rewarded with a P45[105]. However, once they see real, positive changes happening to their ways of working, they will begin to open up.

Baby step improvements

Even if you and your team only increase your effectiveness by 1% every Sprint, at the end of 20 or 30 Sprints you will have made an *astonishing* gain in productivity.

* * *

---

[105] For non-UK readers, a P45 is your "Golden 'Off'" certificate from your employer.

I once doubled the amount of work that a team produced within 6 weeks. The secret? Paying very close attention to doing the Sprint Retrospective really well. That was the secret. Every suggestion that the team came up with was put to the vote, if it was in my power to grant it and the vote passed unanimously, we tried it for a Sprint. If it was successful during that Sprint, then we voted on it again on whether to make it permanent. Again, if it was passed unanimously then it became permanent.

Of course, behind that vote, in order to pass something unanimously meant that those who were keen on a proposal had to lobby other members of the team outside of the Sprint Retrospective by buying coffee in order to discuss the idea. This forged and strengthened the informal bonds between people in the team which in turn also helped team morale

After all, if military and civilian pilots, ships' captains, army officers, and people whose lives depend on doing things right can incorporate a debriefing into their core ways of working, who are we to argue with the principle?

The Sprint Retrospective Meeting

When:

The Sprint Retrospective is held after the Sprint Review and prior to the Sprint Planning meeting for the next Sprint. I always hold the Sprint Planning meeting for the next Sprint the next day, otherwise you have three very intense video meetings on one day. This is absolutely exhausting for everyone.

Purpose - To Support The Three Scrum Pillars Of Transparency, Inspection and Adaptation

To honestly and openly inspect how the sprint went with regards to people, their relationships, the processes, and the tools being used.

* * *

Identify and order the major items that went well, could have gone better, and to list any improvements that the team think would improve the ways of working.

Create a plan of action to implement any improvements that the team comes up for how a team does its work.

A good way of 'punctuating' the Sprint, to bring it to a close and ready to begin the new Sprint afresh.

How Long Is A Sprint Retrospective?

(as mandated by scrum.org)

Forty-five minutes maximum for a one-week Sprint.
Ninety minutes for a two-week Sprint.
Three hours for a four-week Sprint.

Notes For Scrumnasts

Video: It's a good idea that people join by video for this event. If any of the team dial in by telephone, then this will deaden the atmosphere.

Working online is obviously nowhere near as intimate or natural as being in the same space as the rest of the team. As the team leader, you need to be able to see and gauge the quality of the non-verbal communication going on within the team. Part of that is being able to all see those little visual tics, the rolling of the eyes, the doubtful, involuntary glances that happen as people respond to what is going on. All of these things are essential visual cues to what is happening beneath the surface of the team. I just tell my teams that I need to see all the non-verbal communication going on so that I can serve them better as a leader. Do not allow your people to call in by audio only.

* * *

Honest Reflection:

The real point of a debrief is to try to achieve continuous improvement. Continuous improvement is a very big deal in Japan where it is called "kaizen."

What you may not know is that in Japan, it is considered impossible to achieve any improvement without going through a period of reflection *first.* The word for reflection in Japanese is *"hansei."* In Japan, if your child 'only' got 96% in their mathematics test, then you would ask them to spend some time reflecting upon why they only got 96%, before they retook the test.

If we are to achieve continuous improvement in our teams, then I think it is vital that we do the same. That's why we need to do our best to try to and make honest reflection a key component of the retrospective.

This meeting is held at the level of the team as a whole, and not at an individual level. In order for the Sprint Retrospective to be successful, you *cannot* run it as a witch hunt. If that is what you intend to do then, frankly, you are better off not bothering doing a Sprint Retrospective at all.

What we want here is true progress for the team, so you need complete honesty within the team. If you want honesty, then you need to make sure that it does not turn into a hostile or point scoring environment. After all, we are Scrumnasts, not bureaucrats or technocrats. We have real work to do.

Below are the watch words which we use in my teams. I send these out to everyone before *every* **Retrospective** begins. I think they set the right tone for the meeting and I recommend them to you.

"Regardless of what we discover, we understand and truly believe that everyone did the best job that they could, given what they knew at the time, their skills and abilities and the situation at hand." - Taken from Norman Kerth's "Project Retrospectives" 2001.

This Is How I Run A Sprint Retrospective:

Having finished the Sprint Review, the team, the Scrum Master and the Product Owner take a one-hour work break and some refreshment, we then reconvene on Zoom. Try and encourage them to eat something in the break. It makes a big difference to how well the meeting will go.

Remember that all video communication is MUCH more exhausting than face to face so we do not want to make the Sprint Retrospective meeting too long. Again, the Sprint Review happens before this and can be very tiring, so it is good to have a break beforehand.

I tend to read out the Norman Kerth's quote above first of all. This sets a positive note and also some boundaries for the meeting. Then I thank the team for all their hard work over the previous Sprint and try and find praise for anyone who spoke during the Sprint Review. We are now ready to go into the three questions that have to be answered.

"What Went Well..."

I cover the "What went well" question first because I want them to start off with the positives. This seems to anchor a positive mood on the team, which will be important as we progress.

I ask the team to write in some suggestions on Zoom (and they can anonymously privately message me on Zoom if they prefer,) about what they felt went well during the last Sprint. They can write as many or few points as they like. I need to make some form of formal record of those. It is also a good idea to make a count of how many of these positive ideas came up.

Then I read each of them out back to the team and ask them to rank them in order of importance from their perspective. Again, I make some kind of record of that too. Having done that, we move on to

"What Could Have Gone Better?"

Again, this is from a team point of view so make sure that everyone knows that this is not a personal witch hunt the first few times you run it.

We are looking for things that affect the team productivity more than individuals. For example, it could be things like bureaucratic clumsiness, ordering system from a supplier not very good, lack of training, unexpected events, Zoom problems, team sickness. Again, get them to message you there on Zoom or Microsoft Teams and count them.

Again, I read them out back to them and ask them to rank them in order of importance from their perspective. Having done that, we move on to

"Which One Of Those Things Would Have Made The Biggest Difference In Making Your Work Easier?"

I cut and paste their suggestions into the Zoom chat board (or Microsoft Teams), and get them to vote on them. Once I get the top one, I feed the winner back to them and then ask if they have any idea how we could change our ways of working to make this better.

Notes For Scrumnasts

Are there more "What Went Well?" items than "What Could Have Gone Better?" items? If so, well done. This is a very rough and ready, but useful, straw poll for how the team is feeling. If there are more positives than negatives it normally means no-one is about to jump ship from the team. If there are more negatives than positives you may need to have a quiet word with one or two of the team who may have the jitters.

The Thriving Index

Although it is not a formal part of the Sprint Retrospective, for me, this is a crucial part of the ceremony because this is where I find out the team's temperature.

* * *

I have heard other Scrum Masters and Product Owners refer to this as the 'happiness index.' I don't. Let's be frank: we are talking about work here. You may believe that millennial bunkum about work having to be fun, but I don't. I really enjoy work, and I enjoy working with my teams but work is work. Sometimes it is fun, but there are times when it really, really isn't. This is why I am more interested in whether the team members are thriving rather than whether they are having fun.

Thriving is the state where you are receiving more than you are putting in. Your work may be challenging but it is giving you more back than you are putting in. You may be going through all sorts of challenges but overcoming them is making you a better and more skillful worker.

So, this is what I do: I ask people whether they felt that over the last Sprint:

1. **Did their skills grow?**

2. **Were they able to overcome challenges** and feel that somehow, they were better equipped for the future as the result of working in the Sprint?

Then I ask them to give me a number between 1 and 10 on how positive they feel about their work. It is very important that you get them to give you that number privately, because if it is done publicly, there is a tendency for the group to take the first number they see as their anchor, which will skew the results.

Once you have all the numbers, simply add them all up and divide by the number of people who voted. If the number is above 5 then I count that as a healthy team with a positive outlook. Every team is different, and your team might count 7 or 8 as an average. What you are looking for is a drop from the average figure, or huge oscillations going from Sprint to Sprint. Unlike the annual staff survey, if you do get a big drop then, because you are doing this every Sprint, you will be able to see this early and it will not be hard to do something about it.

5: Sharpening The Tools[106] (Optional - Not Core Scrum)

- Where Does The Idea Come From And Why Might You Need It?

When you are working with online teams the opportunity that everyone in the team used to have for sidling up to the client for that quick, necessary quiet word are very limited.

I thought that it was best to formalise a time in the day when the Product Owner was available for such chats and more. It also gives the Product Owner a time slot in their day when they are supposed to be working on their Product Backlog. Thirdly, online teams need a time boundary for their working day. We start our working day with the Daily Sprint, and that is great. What I needed was a boundary to signal the end of the working day as well. I call this time "Sharpening the Tools."

Sharpening the Tools[107] is not a new idea. I nicked it from my grandfather, who started it when he was overseeing the building of Cwmbran New Town in the 1950s. Obviously, if you are building a town from scratch, that is a huge amount of work and, of course, you always want to get the best quality of work out of your teams of house builders.

As you can imagine, the physical work that house builders do is very demanding. The quality of physical work done at the end of the day can never be as good as the physical work done at the beginning of the day. People make mistakes when they are tired, and such mistakes are costly. Often, some of the work had to be redone the next

---

[106] If you are going for a formal Scrum Master or Product Owner qualification then don't mention this. This is not part of formal Scrum.

[107] To be clear: this is not a formal component of Scrum so you don't have to do it. However, this IS a formal part of what we do at Scrumnastics.

day, which is counterproductive.

In my grandfather's mind, the last half-hour of work was a danger zone that could potentially undo a great deal of the good work done in the afternoon by the men. Instead, for the last half an hour at the end of a hard-working day, he got the men who worked in all the house building teams to mend and sharpen their tools ready for the next day. Sharp, clean tools are much more productive tools than blunt, dirty tools, and when the tradesmen started the next morning, just when they were at their most productive, their tools would also be at their best and razor sharp too.

He reckoned he gained an extra boost to the various teams' productivity that was worth far more than that half an hour's pay that he technically lost. It also cut down on the work that had to be redone.

Now if you are a "Theory X"-type manager[108], you are probably hopping up and down right now at what you see as the total iniquity of this. Time to buy a copy of MacGregor.

Scrumnastics: Sharpening the Tools.

Our Sharpening the Tools ceremony is a fifteen-to-twenty-minute meeting done at the end of every working day and is where we do our refinement of the items on the Product Backlog. The members of the ceremony are the team, the Scrum Master and the Product Owner. Sharpening the Tools only deals with items already on the Product Backlog.

Here are three benefits I have found to holding the Sharpening the Tools ceremony.

1. Reserves a dedicated time for looking at upcoming work.

* * *

---

[108] *Theory X and theory Y managers: See Douglas MacGregor's still brilliant "The Human Side of Enterprise," 1960. - Go and buy it, it will make you a much better manager

2. Promotes a 'helicopter view' perspective for the team. Sometimes in Scrum, team members can become a little blinkered and too laser-focussed on what is in front of them in the Sprint. We do want them to focus on what is in the Sprint but we do not want them to obsess about it - this really helps. If they are more aware of what else is coming up it may have a bearing on how they work on things in this Sprint.

3. Gives a formal end to the working day.

One of the best parts of having this ceremony is that it gives a dedicated time for the Product Owner to develop the Product Backlog, which they don't formally have otherwise.

The other good thing is that it gives the team a good long look at the work that is coming up for the next Sprint. Bringing the Product Owner's dreams into reality requires a lot of considered thought on the part of the Production Team. There is a big difference between 'what' they are required to make and 'how' they are going to make it. Ideas need to percolate in people's minds, often for a night or two before they can figure out just how they can turn a dream into reality.

This is also an opportunity for the Product Owner to clarify their ideas and so clear up assumptions before any real work is done.

THE WHEN - THE SPRINT

The Sprint

Figure 29 The Sprint

What A Sprint Is:

The Sprint is the time period in Scrum within which all work is done. Working in Sprints allows you to manage time, resources, quality and budget. It is the container inside which everything in Scrum happens.

The whole team should choose how long a Sprint can be, but once chosen it always remains the same. It can be seven days, fourteen days and anything up to a month long, but no longer.

* * *

A sprint echoes Walter Shewhart's and William Edwards Deming's "**Plan**, **Do**, **Check** (sometimes Study), **Act**," work cycle, which is used by most Japanese and world class manufacturing companies.

How Does It Echo Walter Shewhart's And William Edwards Deming's "Plan, Do, Check, Act"?

Each Sprint Must Have A:

1. Sprint Planning session. - {"Plan"}
2. A set of Daily Scrums where work progress is updated - {"Do"}
3. Sprint Review {"Check"}
4. Sprint Retrospective. {"Act"}

Every Sprint should be given a meaningful name of the intended work, not just numbered. (At some point your actions will be examined. It is a lot easier to remember and report what happened in "Sprint 10 - Coming Out of the Ground - Dig Foundation Trenches and Pour Foundations" than "Sprint 10," especially when you are on sprint 32).

This also ties in with the Scrum 2020 manual that says that every Sprint should be given a 'sprint goal' (that is, a purpose, or a 'reason why' the sprint is being done.). Teams deliver better quality work when they have a reason why and a purpose to do it. What you are also trying to do here is eliminate the tendency of many projects for doing useless, busy work. Useless, busy work is _really_ expensive.

"A Complete Slice Of The Pie"

Each Sprint should be focussed on delivering "one complete slice of the pie," (a useful thing that might even be a deliverable product). If you think about it, to deliver "one complete slice of the pie," would need a recipe, contain all the necessary ingredients and all the work processes involved in turning the raw ingredients into a pie. You need to apply a similar mindset to the sprint's endeavour.

Coming up with a "one complete slice of the pie" is something that needs some thought and planning by the whole team.

Why Bother To Do It? Two Main Reasons:

1.   What would happen if the project were cancelled after the next sprint? At least with the one slice of the pie idea, you would have something tangible to show to stakeholders, such as a complete door assembly for a house, with glass, locks, handles and paint all installed. If you tried to resurrect the project later, you could point to that completed door.

2.   To eliminate doing that peculiar brand of grandiose, but useless work that only gets done when a project starts to go badly wrong. If you ever hear of a project where it is reporting things like "ordered 250 doors," or "bought seven tons of flour," or "hired web developer," you can be sure that the project hasn't made any real progress or done any real work. Instead, someone made a bold gesture with your money.

A Project is a collection of Sprints.

The Sprint Goal: Naming Your Sprint

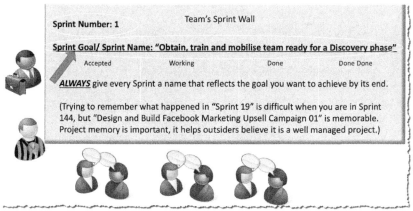

Figure 30 Naming Your Sprint - The Sprint Goal

This is one of those small, subtle, insignificant looking things that many Scrum teams put in the "that's really not important, let's ignore it and not bother," box. But not you, Scrumnast.

Like a lot of those small things in life, it turns out to have a much bigger benefit than you might imagine if you actually do it, and also a bigger negative effect if you don't.

Remember how I have been banging on and on about how the Product Owner (and any leader, for that matter), needs to come up with a 'reason why?' or purpose, for the product being built? Well, the reason you do it here is that it gives a mini 'reason why,' or purpose, but this is just for the Sprint.

If you bother to do it then when you look back, you not only know what each Sprint was meant to achieve but it will also add a sense of story, or narrative about the product being built - and people like that. It lends a certain confidence to the team and bathes you in a light of 'these people knew what they were doing,' and you should never underestimate the power of that. It is always good to have your reputation enhanced.

How To Go About It

By the end of the Sprint Planning session, the production team should have a good idea of what the Product Owner wants to achieve in the upcoming Sprint.

It is very good practice to bake this idea into the Sprint by putting that as the Sprint Goal as the name of the Sprint. This gives you an easy way to judge the success of the Sprint at the time of the Sprint Review. For example, your goal was to make and train a team, did you do achieve that?

As I have said above, naming Sprints is a good habit to get into, and one day you will be very glad you did, especially if you get into those difficult conversations that start, "what happened when, and where's all my money gone?"

What To Do In The First Sprint ("Sprint -1")

Whenever I have a new team, I start with a Sprint for training people in Scrum, mobilising them and forging them into a team. I give that as the Sprint Goal.

It answers the question "What did we do in Sprint -1?"
Answer: "We trained everyone, mobilised them and forged them into a team ready for a great second and subsequent Sprints."

Training may not be popular in business anymore, but Peter Drucker, the original business guru said, *"If you think training is expensive, try ignorance."*

Not yet convinced? How about the old business story of the HR director trying to get their training budget approved?

Finance Director: "What if we train them and they leave us?"

H.R. Director: "What if we don't train them and they stay?"

Training a team at the start ensures that everyone knows what they are doing rather than just pretending they know. Pretending leads to confusion within the team and confusion is never efficient.

A side effect is that it allows the Scrum Master to lay down the ground rules for good working behaviour that I expect from the team.

Also, although everyone swears blind on their CV that they know all the Agile ways of working inside out, actually, most people really don't. They say they know how to do Agile because it gets them jobs.

Of course, the bland phrase "knowing Agile" is a bit like liking ice-cream. I always want to ask, "That's great to know. Which flavour?" As we know, there are many flavours of Agile, and although many are similar, they are all very different.

Besides, we are talking about Scrum here, which is just one of the many Agile frameworks. they are all different to each other so the team may as well learn Scrum properly.

When I put a team together, I need to know that they know how to work in Scrum which means that they know who is responsible for what, how to behave, how to work, and where to go for help.

The Sprint As A Timeline

A lot of books on Scrum show the Sprint as a graphic with big circle with lots of little circles within it, rather like the picture on the next page.

It confused the hell out of me the first time I saw it, and also every person I know who has ever been on a Scrum course. The problem with drawing time as a circle is that most people think of time as being linear, not circular. After all, we talk of things like 'timelines.' So, just for a change, let's show it like this:

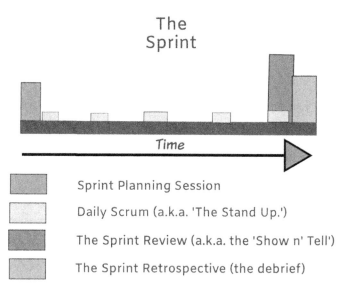

Figure 31 The Sprint As A Timeline

This diagram is meant to show you that a Sprint is a unit of time (that is what the arrow is there for), and that time goes in a straight line. The amount of time in a Sprint can be a week, a fortnight, three weeks or a month.

Inside a Sprint four different types of fairly short, but very specific meetings happen. I have shaded them in the picture. These meetings are known as 'events' in Scrum.

The first meeting is the **Sprint Planning** session for the Sprint, the five small boxes show when the **Daily Scrums** happen, the last but one box stands for the **Sprint Review** and the very end one stands for the **Sprint Retrospective,** because that is always the last event in a Sprint.

A Sprint is a fixed length work period. Sprints are always kept at the same fixed length for the duration of a project. The most common (by far) are one week and two week long Sprints. The ruling body of Scrum, scrum.org, stipulates that a Sprint is NEVER more than 30 days long.

Each Sprint is a little like a project in miniature. Within a Sprint you plan, you design, you work, you update, you deliver a small but complete "slice of the pie," and then you hold a debriefing session. You then repeat the process in the next Sprint.

The Sprint

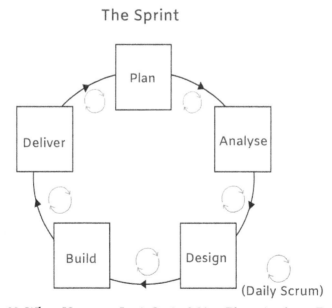

Figure 32 What Happens In A Sprint? You Plan, Analyse, Design, Build, Deliver.

So, a Sprint is an amalgam of work done in a period of time, and a set of specialised meetings. Each of these meetings has its own distinct purpose. If you don't do all the events, then you are not doing a Sprint and so you are not doing Scrum.

The Sprint always starts with the planning session ceremony. This planning session is never more than one hour long for a one-week Sprint, two hours long for a two-week Sprint and four hours long for a four-week Sprint. This is not a long time, so a good amount of time is spent in the Sprint on understanding and preparing upcoming items that are due to be worked on in the next Sprint. Please see the "5: (Optional) Sharpening the Tools," section for more details.

The Daily Scrum is held at the beginning of every working day. It is a short progress, and update reporting meeting. A minor amount of planning or adjustment might be done here too.

The Daily Scrum is a good way to start the day if you are working online. It is a free way to give a 'we are now at work' signal to everyone. Don't underestimate just how helpful this will be for some people in your team. If they are working remotely then they have lost all the traditional micro reinforcements that tell them they are at work. Doing this helps.

The Daily Scrum is <u>never more than 15 minutes long</u>. It is always best to hold it early in the working day so that everyone gets the message that the working day has begun. Always start it at the same time. A sure hallmark of a sloppy Scrum team lacking direction is a team which has Daily Scrums at randomly changing times.

All members of the team must attend and I ask that they are all connected to video and online at least five minutes before the formal start of the meeting so they can catch up with each other before we start work. Do not allow any persistent late turning up or not showing up at all. Attendance reinforces work and team discipline. Turning up on time, every time, is a mark of respect from one member of the team to all the others. Not turning up without a good excuse is a mark of disrespect to the team as a whole.

The quality of the work produced in a Sprint will always be higher if the Product Owner attends the Daily Scrums. Having the money person there always does. It also helps enormously with communication and co-ordination.

At the end of every Sprint, two more meetings are held. The first is the Sprint Review ceremony. The Sprint Review is where the Product Owner and the Team demonstrate what has been achieved during the Sprint to the stakeholders. This meeting is ALWAYS run by the Product Owner, and no-one else. Stakeholders may be present if the Product Owner has invited them. Stakeholders do not have speaking rights at this meeting unless the Product Owner grants them.

Wise Words for Scrumnasts:

The Sprint Review

I have seen a lot of projects where the Scrum Master ran the Sprint Review on their own, or worse, the team just demonstrated what it had done to itself with no Product Owner and no stakeholders. This is rarely successful and is bad practice.

It rarely works because part of the point of the Sprint Review is that it is not only a demonstration of the product, but it is also a governance meeting. This means that you need people with budgetary responsibility (such as the Product Owner,) to attend.

Other organisations may try to do this, but not you, Scrumnast, not you.

The Sprint Review ceremony is part demonstration, part governance, and also partly a risk management meeting. If the work achieved in the Sprint has been acceptable then the Product Owner will okay the spend to carry on into the next Sprint, if they decide that there is enough value in carrying on.

If there have been problems in the Sprint, these are able to be seen before too much time has elapsed and remedial measures can be put in place immediately in order to bring it back on track.

* * *

To err is human and, despite what sillier, more traditional project managers may tell you, every project will 'wobble 'a little from time to time. It is not the wobbling that is the issue, it is how soon you can steer everything back on course. In any project the tide will come in and the tide will go out. That's what we earn our money as management to do. We bring things back on track. The Sprint Review, when done properly, is a little technique that allows management an early touch on the steering wheel for any needed correction.

Short Sprints:

The shorter the Sprint the shorter the period that the project has to veer off course and so the more opportunities you have to mitigate risk. By having shorter Sprints, the smaller the potential value put at risk and the easier it is to bring the product back on course. This is why I prefer to run week-long Sprints rather than two week-long Sprints. If you find that the work follows a fortnightly rhythm, rather than a weekly rhythm, it is pretty easy to move from a week-long Sprint to a fortnight long Sprint. But doing it the other way round is a lot more difficult.

The Sprint Retrospective:

The very last meeting of the Sprint is called the Sprint Retrospective. This event is often more successful if it is run in a more informal way. The Retrospective is a debriefing meeting where the team honestly reflects on how the work in the Sprint went, what went well and if there were things that could be done better next time. In Japan, you cannot achieve improvement without first reflecting on what you have done.

I also add something called the "Thriving Index," which basically takes the team's temperature and asks them if they believe they have 'thrived,' during the last Sprint. There is more on this in the events section.

* * *

A Sprint Retrospective is a debriefing session, which includes honest reflection. It is not a witch hunt.

If you run them well, then doing retrospectives can give you astonishing levels of increased productivity over time. I have doubled productivity of a team inside six weeks mostly by using retrospectives well.

If you choose to run them as witch hunts, then your people will not co-operate in them, and it will be a complete waste of everyone's time.

Scrum focusses on producing work incrementally, Sprint by Sprint. Each Sprint normally builds on the work of the previous Sprints, with the aim of producing "One Complete Slice Of The Pie" as the Sprint Goal.

What does the strange phrase "One Complete Slice Of The Pie" actually mean? Let's think about what a slice of any pie contains. The ingredients have been mixed up, put into a tray and baked. A pie is a completed thing, not the bare ingredients. You are always aiming for a working completed thing.

It probably seems obvious and common sensical to you, to aim for some kind of working increment each and every time, so why even bother talking about it?

Unfortunately, the history of wider product development all over the world is littered with projects that go off track and when they do, oh, when they do, just watch out for the weird, extraordinary and vainglorious things that are occur.

Thirty-five doors ordered and delivered for your new house before it even has any walls? - That's a project in trouble.

New government QUANGO building a spiffy new website proclaiming how they will change the world before it has even one member of staff? That's a project in trouble.

You may say "Oh, those are ridiculous examples, they wouldn't happen in real life." Unfortunately, they do. More often than you'd think and both examples are both real examples I have seen other project managers try as tactics to give their projects a kick.

So, what's the real reason why we aim for one complete slice of the pie in each Sprint? Easy. It gives you better financial project management because you only plan, work on, order and pay for the things that you need when you need them. Also, if the Product Owner decides to finish work at the end of a particular Sprint and not carry on, they and the project, are left with completed work.

Working incrementally as you do in Scrum is very close to the Japanese management term "Kaizen[109]," which is often translated as "continuous improvement," or literally "Change, Good"

If Scrum is all about doing incremental work, what happens when doing increments is no longer appropriate?

What do you do when an overwhelming event appears from nowhere, like a Covid-19 lockdown? What is the point in trying to work incrementally when the old-world order may have changed forever? You need a different tool: the **Kaikaku Sprint**.

---

[109] In Japan, it is considered impossible to achieve continuous improvement without hansei, which stands for 'reflection.' You cannot have continuous improvement without reflection.

Sprints and The Toyota Production System

I am a fan of lots of different leadership and management frameworks, especially Scrum. However, the greatest of all of them is the Toyota Production System.

The Toyota Production System is all encompassing. It is breath taking in its depth, breadth and scale and nearly always has an answer to every question of management. But the thought of trying to implement it fully, from a standing start is overwhelming task. After all, it has taken Toyota more than seventy years and thousands of excellent managers to implement it at Toyota.

But, whenever I am at a loss on how to get round a problem that Scrum does not address, I always go searching through the Toyota website. I know the people at Toyota have probably already thought deeply about the problem before I have and have almost definitely come up with a solution.

Even better, Toyota are so rightly proud of their management system that they publish the system online, on their website. The answers are all there for us to read.

Here is an example where I used the Toyota Production System website to solve a problem. I think you may find it useful.

Problem: Scrum Is Fundamentally About Iteration And Continuous Improvement. Continuous Improvement (Through Iteration) Is Brilliant 99% Of The Time, But What Do You Do When A Covid-19, Or Similar Event Happens?

Trying to improve on the same thing simply won't work, because you can't carry on as you did before. So, what do you do?

Well, what I did was to go straight to the Toyota Production System on the Toyota website where I reread about their two different types of working period.

At Toyota, they have two kinds of working periods:

1. *Kaizen*, which is always combined with hansei[110], for continuous improvement (Kaizen is used 99% of the time).

2. *Kaikaku*, which is used for an emergency period (- literally "emergency change"). When there a need to make a rapid respond to changing external events, *that* is a Kaikaku period.

At Toyota, when they declare a Kaikaku period, the management immediately stop production and swarm all over the problem until it is resolved.

So we swarmed over the problem until we had a solution.

Never Assume, Always Test.

When the lockdown was announced, we _thought_ we were in a position where we could carry on working. But of course, there is a massive difference between *thinking* you can do something and _knowing_ you can do something. Testing that something works in real life is the only thing that matters - evidence beats eminence and/or faked expertise.

Before lockdown, we worked remotely all week. But the difference

---

[110] "Hansei," is a Japanese term for reflection. In Japanese culture, "hansei," goes hand in hand with kaizen. You cannot separate the two. If your child 'only' gets 95% in a maths test, a Japanese parent would ask them to do their hansei, so that they can reflect on where they went wrong and so improve for next time. You cannot have kaizen without hansei and I have improved our Sprint Retrospectives immensely by adding this idea. I think you should consider it, too.

this time was that, prior to lockdown, if we really needed to meet up then we could. During lockdown there is no possibility of that.

One of our teams is made up of very bright Scrum Masters. I wanted to take advantage of all their brains in order to focus on the problem. That is different to how Toyota would do it, but we don't have the numbers of managers that Toyota have.

What We Did When Lockdown Was Announced

I stopped the current Sprint[111] so that we could look at all the options to make sure that we could still work as teams.

It is one thing to rely on technology when it's important but not crucial. It's quite another to have to rely on technology when it becomes essential. All technology fails eventually. When it does it normally fails over in a nasty heap just when you need it most. That is, when you put it under more stress than before.

Our proposed solution was:

Once we had explored everyone's thoughts and ideas, we found one or two great workarounds, where needed.

I did a full **Sprint Retrospective** session (I talk about Sprint Retrospectives elsewhere) via Zoom so we could pause and reflect, we could debrief, and make sure that all the team were willing to carry one and support each other.

I proposed that all Scrum Masters be able adopt the role of **chairperson** for all of the events. This was formally adopted by the teams.

I also used Zoom to hold a **Thriving Index** poll to gauge the spirit of

---

[111] As Product Owner I have the right to stop a Sprint.

the team (again, I talk about this elsewhere).

That covered the human, or 'soft skills' side.

So that was when we began testing. And I mean everything. Twice. That was the hard skills and the technology side.

Luckily, we have a training and mobilisation procedure that we use for setting up new teams for clients called "**Sprint -1**." We just adapted it to use for the **Kaikaku** Sprint.

Once we knew we could go back to work and that everyone was as happy as they could be, I formally closed the kaikaku sprint and we went back to working inside of normal (kaizen type) sprints.

THE WHAT - THE ARTEFACTS

The Three Artefacts[112] in Scrum

An artefact is Scrum's word for the work that is done by the complete Scrum team, meaning the Product Owner, the Scrum Master and the production or developer team.

There are two different types of work in Scrum.

There are the actual things you are making which is the real work of the team. But there is also the work that surround the core work such as reports on the progress of how the work is progressing, which you could call management work, (or 'meta-work,' - literally the work about the work).

In Scrum, there are three different artefacts. They are:

1. The **Product Backlog** - A list of the work required for the creation of the product or service to be delivered in the next and subsequent sprints. It is almost always in a 'not quite finished' state because changes are always expected to occur.

2. The **Sprint Backlog** - The list of items, and their work states, being worked on right now in this sprint.

3. The **Increment(s)** - Once a piece of work is finished to a previously agreed, required minimum acceptable standard[113] in a Sprint, it becomes an **increment.** The whole point of a Sprint is to create one or more increments. Everything else is secondary.

This agreement of 'done' is like a miniature work contract. It is agreed among the whole team (including the Product Owner) during the Sprint Planning Session event, which is the first event of a sprint.

A good definition of done stops the team from 'gilding the lily,' where a product gets more expense spent on it for little extra return on

---

[112] Or Artifacts, in American English.
[113] known as the 'definition of done'

the investment.

The **Product Backlog** is owned and maintained by the **Product Owner**.

The **Sprint Backlog** is owned and updated by the **team**.

The **Increment**(s) are produced by the **team**.

Scrum Teams And Their Backlogs: Showing Work Progress During The Sprint.

Progress Of The Work In Scrum Is Shown Through The Backlogs

This picture shows the Scrum team in the triangle, the Product Owner is responsible for creating and updating the Product Backlog and the team is responsible for updating the Sprint Backlog.

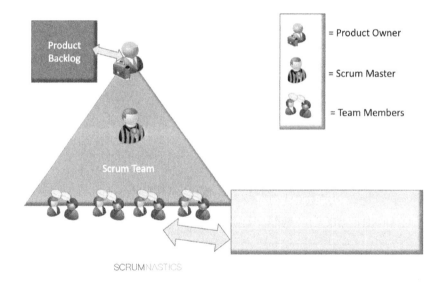

Figure 33 The Product Owner And The Developer Team And Their Backlogs

The whole Scrum team display their plans and progress via their respective walls (probably done online in a software package like Trello).

* * *

Work being done in this Sprint is shown on the Team's Sprint Backlog (the box at the bottom right of the picture). This is owned by the team.

Future work is shown on the Product Backlog (the square box to the upper left of the Product Owner) and is owned by the Product Owner.

Backlog? That Sounds Ominous...

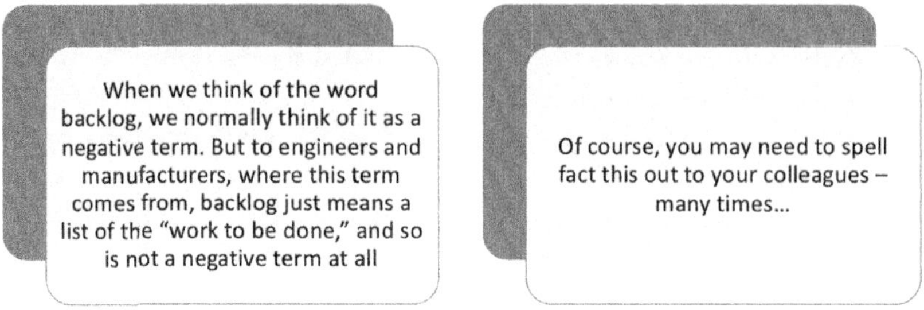

When we think of the word backlog, we normally think of it as a negative term. But to engineers and manufacturers, where this term comes from, backlog just means a list of the "work to be done," and so is not a negative term at all

Of course, you may need to spell fact this out to your colleagues – many times...

Figure 34 Solving The Problem With The Word 'Backlog' In Your Organisation

Let's face it, 'backlog' is an ominous sounding word, so let's be clear: in Scrum, the **Product Backlog** is a **visual plan**, and the **Sprint Backlog** is a **visual work status report** on current work.

Unlike traditional project management plans they are not spreadsheet horoscopes[114]. They are visual reports meant to be understood at a glance by everyone. They look great - it's just that they have terrible names.

In most work environments, the word backlog has a very negative connotation. It brings up visions of delays and impending failure before you have even started your working day.

However, the term backlog actually comes from a production engineering environment and here it just means stuff on the list yet to be done.

---

[114] What we called the subcontractors' astonishingly optimistic project plans when I was a programme manager.

Artefact 1: The Product Backlog

As we have said elsewhere, the Product Backlog is nothing more than a high-level visual plan of what is to go into the product.

Here's a dirty little secret: every client I have ever had, and everyone in senior management _hate_ the word backlog. The word has very negative associations with delays. Now successful people love to be associated with success, not failure. That's why we don't call it the Product Backlog in front of our (very successful) clients.

Instead, we call it the "**Visual Product Plan.**" Why do we call it that? Because if you say the word plan our clients nod and smile and give us money. If they hear you say the word backlog, they shake their heads, frown and show us the door.

Internally, amongst ourselves, because we are all Certified Scrum Masters and Certified Scrum Product Owners, we call it the backlog. What you call it is entirely your concern but I'm betting if you replace the word backlog with the word plan, you are going to have an easier time of it.

As you read this section. Try reading every sentence that has the word backlog in it twice, but the second time replace the word backlog with the word plan. Smoother, isn't it?

Scrum.org says you definitely need to do a Product Backlog but then it doesn't actually tell you how to do one. You are supposed to take the time to work out your own way of doing your very own, bespoke, Product Backlog.

In other words, one that is completely appropriate for _your_ business. But in my experience, very few people do because they just don't have time.

What tends to happen in real life is that the Product Backlog just gets ignored.

That's a pity. The Product Backlog is a great, simple planning tool that help you co-ordinate your work effort, drive out ambiguities and help everyone gain clarity. Clarity will make your project run better throughout its life. It will probably also help you deliver a better product at the end, too.

"The Product Owner bring the dreams, but the team brings the means.[115]*"*

Inexperienced (and sometimes bewildered) Product Owners sometimes leave their Product Backlog as the original list of crudely thought out, ill-defined features which they never bother to revisit again. That's such a real shame because it is only the process of grinding out the details and *refining* the backlog that brings clarity. This saves everyone money, time and anguish. It is very important that you make sure that the Product Owner understands that everyone needs to spend time wrestling with the items on the Product Backlog in order to make them understandable. Remember Konosuke Matsushita's maxim "out of the heads of management and into the heads of labour"? Well, this is where that happens.

One of the other benefits of a good Product Backlog is that it also stops managers wasting productive workers time by asking them to make yet another stupid spreadsheet report instead of being productive. The backlog is a visual plan, and if you do it properly, its flexibility can accommodate all sorts of levels of detail within the planning process.

So, this is the way I do a Product Backlog. There are many other ways but this works for us. It is what we teach our own teams to do. It is also what I teach when I am helping our clients set their own teams up. They seem to like it. They find it useful, and I hope you do too.

I use a lot of principles from **Kanban**[116] in it. Why Kanban?[117]

---

[115] This is a quote I use when training Product Owners.

[116] (Japanese for 'signal card')

[117] Kanban is a completely different management framework and nothing to do with Scrum. The Toyota Way, a much larger management framework, contains elements of both Scrum and Kanban.

Because, of all of the **Agile**, **Lean**, or other hundreds of self-managed team frameworks, Kanban has the strongest visuals in showing how work is progressing. Besides, Toyota originally developed Kanban and, frankly, if it is good enough for them, then it's good enough for us.

I deliberately tried to make it free, easy to build and work with. After all, you are busy enough.

Our problem:

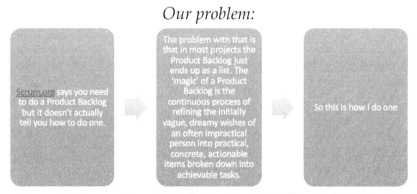

Figure 35 No-one Actually Tells You Precisely How To Do A Backlog On a Scrum Course.

Although the Product Backlog belongs to the Product Owner, it is only when the whole Team get involved in refining the Product Owner's (often woolly) ideas that they actually become achievable.

As we often like to say, *"**The Product Owner may bring the dreams, but it is the team that brings the means**."*

This high-level planning is one of the key parts of Scrum that if you get it right, *everything* you and your team does from then on becomes so much easier and smoother.

The good news for you is that while a lot of companies get this wrong, you will be doing this right. You know that feeling when you learn just one skill and you find you can apply it to many situations? This is one of those skills.

* * *

How We Make A Product Backlog

I'm going to use a piece of software called **Trello** to do this. It is not the most sophisticated piece of software but that can be a good thing because it will force us to refine our craft as Agile managers, rather than hide behind a software tool. It is free, pretty good, and that means you can try this for yourself without spending any money - but, of course, you can choose to use anything you like.

What We Are Going To Do:

We need *five* different areas on our working space to capture all the stages for the preparation of our work.

We need one area to capture all the initial ideas (no matter how crude, unrefined or batty they first seem) as a sort of master scratch pad.

We need a separate place to put the pick of the most promising of those ideas so that we can concentrate on them. We will put them in this second area so that we know they are ready for further consideration and development without being mixed up with everything else.

We will need another two areas to develop those ideas from 'dreams and wishes worth looking at' into a developed and refined state of being practical and achievable items. One of these areas will focus on looking at the idea from the perspective of the customer (or the person who will use it) and one will concentrate on items that are needed but maybe hard to see from a customer's perspective. Both of these places become the lists of items that are ready to be considered in the **Sprint Planning** event.

These areas on our workspace are:

Figure 36 The Scrumnastics Five Column Product Backlog

1. "First Thoughts:" -

This is the capture box, where we put everything to begin with. All the Good, all the Bad, and all the Ugly ideas.

2. "For Refinement:" -

The Product Owner and the team take the most promising and valuable items from the **First Thoughts** column and put them here. Then then develop and refine them further until they become both concrete and better understood by the whole team.

3. "Product Backlog Items:" -

An unfortunately ugly piece of Scrum jargon that means, "bite sized chunks of work of a size that can be completed inside a Sprint." This is where we can further refine our ideas. **Product Backlog Items** are meant to be 'vertical slices' of work, also known as a 'complete slice of the pie.' The item should produce a complete thing of value and not just an ingredient. So, a fitted front house door, complete with hinges, windows, and locks would be a slice of a pie. Ordering 25 doors, or 50 door hinges, would not[118].

4. "User Stories:" -

---

[118] Evidence of ordering vast lists of components rather than evidence of useful things actually being created can be a tell-tale sign of a project going horribly badly wrong - keep an eye out for this

Although User Stories are not technically anything to do with Scrum, they are one of the many things that can be 'plugged in' instead of the official "Product Backlog Items," (PBIs) and many Scrum teams prefer to use them instead.

Why Would I Want To Use User Stories Instead Of Product Backlog Items?

A User Story is a very high-level, simple, method of focusing on a particular consumer and what they want for your product. It tells how they would want to use a particular feature, and what *benefit* they get from using it.

It tells you who they are, what they want to do, and why they want to do it.

It is deliberately non-technical. A User Story focusses on the person and what they want to do, not the bundle of tasks that need to be completed in order for them to be able to do it.

Why is this important? If you ask any excellent salesperson, they will tell you that people don't buy how many features a thing has, they buy the benefit from buying.

A 'Product Backlog Item' is just that, an item, or a package of work from the Product Backlog. That could be any feature that the Product Owner wants to put in. However, a User Story is different. It is a written from the viewpoint of someone who is going to buy and consume something.

Unfortunately, there is often a chasm between what buyers are looking for and what producers want to put into a product. Producers want to fill their products with features, but buyers often don't want features, they just want the benefits of the features.

For example, someone buying an electric drill is probably not that bothered with all the super-duper *features* like a quick-release chuck, or the specific power, or super high speed number of revolutions. What they actually want from a drill is the *benefit* of a hole in the wall, how they get that hole is not that interesting to them.

Like a Product Backlog Item, a User Story should be of a size that can be completed within a Sprint. If it is too big for that, then it is called an epic. Epics should always be re-examined, refined and broken down further until they become an achievable size in a Sprint.

A User Story -

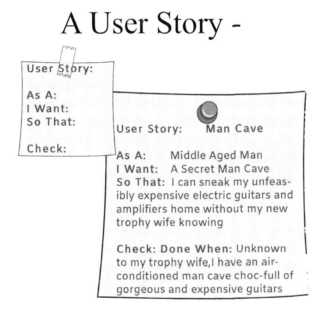

Figure 37 The User Story Card: "As A, I Want, So That..."

A User Story is made up of three parts, known as the "3 C's ," which are:

Card: It must be on a card (an electronic card is fine).
Conversation: It must only have enough information that the person accepting the work must talk with the person who wants it created to iron out the details. This is meant to minimise assumptions, all of which will prove very costly.

* * *

Check: This thing is 'done' (complete) when... The 'Definition of Done." The Product Owner writes down what the acceptance criteria are for the thing before work starts. In essence it is a miniature work contract. This stops any 'scope creep,' (or "Mauve-ing," as my good friend, Ben Memmott, calls it,) - where things do not ever get finished.

If the user in a user Story was a future owner of a dream house, one user story might be for a "**Man Cave**," which could look like:

<u>User Story</u> "Man Cave." (The title of the User Story)

<u>As A</u>: Future Owner of a Dream House

<u>I Want:</u> An underground, air conditioned, dry, 20 metre by 20 metre Man Cave with a separate, underground secret entrance, with its own electricity, water, air supply and powerful wi-fi

<u>So That:</u> I can sneak in my growing collection of unfeasibly expensive custom built acoustic and electric guitars and amplifiers (and any Harley-Davidsons I might be tempted to buy,) without my trophy wife seeing them so prolonging my marriage

<u>Done When</u>[119]: I can pick up my Harley-Davidson 883, my Honda VFR and my three PRS electric guitars from the shops where they are being held in storage for me and move them in without anyone seeing. (This is the 'check,' and is written on the back of the card. The check is the Product Owner's acceptance criteria for any piece of work and forms a mini contract of work).

A Test For Your User Stories: The "Invest[120]" Acronym:

A good user story should be able to pass each letter in the **I.N.V.E.S.T.** acronym:

---

[119] Done When: This is the Definition of Done. When this is achieved the item becomes an Increment"

[120] This came from Bill Wake, a general good guy, all the way back from 2003.

* * *

"**I**" for **Independent** - of any other User Stories you may have. It stands by itself

"**N**" for **Negotiable** - cannot be completed without a conversation or negotiation

"**V**" for **Valuable** (or vertical) - There must be money value in the work - no busy work allowed

"**E**" for **Estimable** - The knowledge workers can 'size' the job, even if only approximately

"**S**" for **Small** - Can be completed within one iteration - called a Sprint

"**T**" for **Testable** - Will It pass the 'Check' - the 'Done When' above

Notes for Scrumnasts

If you are going to use User Stories, they only really work on living things, so make sure they are focussed on real human beings or animals and never inanimate objects - don't try to force or mangle them to fit. If you do feel as though you need to mangle an item, then put it in the Product Backlog Item column instead.

I was once asked by a company how could they write a User Story for a computer server. I simply said, "Er, you can't." - That illustrates a common problem: sometimes we get so "down in the weeds," that we stop thinking and just try to 'shoehorn' the problem into something that doesn't fit. We consultants don't get many easy jobs, but that was one.

"Ready For Sprint"

The final column is called *"**Ready For Sprint:**"* To be in this column, items have been really worked on and are understood by the whole team. The item has passed the "Definition of Read[121]y" test, which means it has a "Definition of Done." It is now refined enough to be a

---

[121] This is the Product Backlog's equivalent of the 'Definition of Done' that appears in the Sprint Backlog. Once a Product Backlog Item, or a User Story has been refined enough to be acceptable for consideration, we put it into the "Ready For Sprint" column.

candidate for the Sprint Planning session in the next Sprint, but only if the Product Owner thinks it is of high enough value.

Items for this column can come from *either* the "**User Story**," or the "**Product Backlog Items**" column.

The Product Owner and the team are also agreed that the User Story or the Product Backlog Item are of a size that can be completed inside the time available in the Sprint.

If the team say it can't be completed, then it needs to be re-examined and broken down again. For example, the "Man Cave," example above is probably too large a job to be finished inside one Sprint. That makes "Man Cave" an **epic**. As we have said above, epics always need to be broken down more, sometimes a great deal more, so that they have a good chance of being done inside a Sprint. There is not much point in the Product Owner forcing the issue. If the team say the scale of the job can't be done, then the Product Owner has to accept that.

Now, of course, you can call these headings whatever you like, but I have tested these particular headings in many, many projects and they work for me and my teams and the projects that we have done.

I haven't insisted on any copyright on any of these, so feel free to use them.

But When Does This Pre-Planning Thing Happen?

There is no formal pre-planning or refinement event in Scrum, so just when is this pre-planning work between the Product Owner and the team to be done, exactly?

It is *supposed* to be done informally during the present Sprint in time for the next Sprint. But the problem with that is that the team are always focussed on, and busy with, what they are doing in this Sprint. That makes it hard to find time right *now* for something that might happen in the future.

* * *

This is a real problem: I see a lot of projects that go awry because too little (or no) refinement has been done. Why? Because a lot of ideas need to be wrestled with before they become achievable.

If you don't give enough time for the team to understand what is in the head of the Product Owner, then you have to rely too heavily on getting everything right in the Sprint Planning session. In my experience, this is rarely successful.

What tends to happen is that when the Sprint Planning session comes around, everything becomes rather rushed and heated. Inevitably, costly assumptions are made. Working when based on assumption is not the way you want to work. Those assumptions are often wrong and really costly, especially when the work has to be undone and then re-done again.

An Extra Event When Working Online - "Sharpening the Tools"

As you know, since 2016, we have all worked remotely and online 100% of the time. We found that to accommodate that properly, in addition to the standard Scrum events, we needed an event that did two things:

1.   A dedicated time in the day when the team and the Product Owner could refine the Product Backlog so that they could refine what was coming up for the next Sprints.

2. A way of formally closing down the working day.

Why Did We Need It?

I saw some in the team began to work later and later into the evening. Now, there will be some reading this who are thinking, "brilliant!" and take advantage of it. However, long term I find it just fosters resentment, 'busy work,' a lack of fresh, creative thinking and, in the end, individuals burning out.

People burning out in a team is ferociously _expensive_, not just in money, but also in lost time and poor morale which affect the whole team for a very long time. That's why I don't want my people working late into the night. I need their very best creative ideas for our clients every day, and so I want them bright and fresh the next day, every day. Besides, I know that my people will be subconsciously mulling over work at night anyway, so I am not losing out.

To be clear, they know that if I receive any kind of '11pm texts' (which are the norm in other consultancies), I will be _very_ unhappy with them. I do not want any virtue signalling from members of the team.

So, for the last 15-20 minutes of every working day, the team, the Product Owner and myself as Agile Coach/Scrum Master come together on a video call and we examine how the Product Backlog is coming along and we refine the ideas it contains and slowly move them along to a state where they are ready to be considered for the next **Sprint Planning** event.

When the **Sharpening the Tools** event finishes, it marks the end of the working day.

For more on this please see the section in the book marked as, "5: Optional: **Sharpening The Tools**."

Practical Demo: Making A Product Backlog (Plan) in Trello

Let's see what a Product Backlog could look like if, say, you used a piece of free(-ish)[122] software called **Trello** to build it.

You can use Trello to make a Product Backlog and a Sprint Backlog. I recommend that the Product Backlog and the Sprint Backlog are given different background colours to make it clear which one people are looking at.

The basic idea is that we need a process where we can turn the sometimes all-too-vague ideas of the Product Owner into something tangible and achievable by the practically minded "do-ers," of the team. This is why we have four 'buckets' for the team to work and develop.

Instead of using just one "To-Do" list in one column, which is very common, each of the buckets represents that some refinement of thinking on the item has happened for it to get in there. This thinking becomes more and more refined as you move from left to right.

From left to right these buckets are: "**First Thoughts**," "**For Refinement**," "**User Stories**," and "**Ready For Next Sprint**." (I have left out "**Product Backlog Items**" because it made the screenshots too complicated to show on the page).

* * *

---

[122] Like with all cloud-based software, there is a free plain vanilla version and, if you pay money, you get more features. Everything we do here is in the free version, so you can try this out for yourself.
I have no financial connection with Trello - I don't recommend any particular project management software.

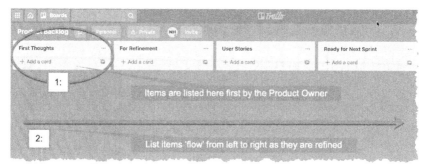

Figure 38 The Scrumnastics Product Backlog In Trello With "First Thoughts"

The first bucket on the top left is called "**First Thoughts**," where the Product Owner can put all of their initial ideas. Think of it as a kind of scratch pad. It is an informal bucket for the Product Owner to list all the things that they want for the product to have. Once the Product Owner has captured their ideas here, their next job is to prioritise the most important and valuable ideas by dragging and dropping them to the top of the list.

Imagine that our Product Owner is someone who wants to build a dream house with all the wonderful things that might go with that. Our team is a set of house builders. The Product Owner's first stab at a list might look something like this.

First Thoughts Bucket:

Figure 39 The First Thoughts Bucket

The second thing that has to happen is that the Product Owner now reorders the list so that the most valuable items are at the top and the less valuable are at the bottom. The Product Owner is probably the only person in the team who has the best idea of the market value of the items, so they are the person who needs to do this.

The Product Owner's "First Thoughts," reorganised in order of value, top to bottom.

Figure 40 First Thoughts Items Ranked By Value

The next bucket along is called "**For Refinement**." This will contain the most valuable things according to the Product Owner. These **MUST**[123] have been dragged and dropped from the "**First Thoughts**" bucket. (It is best to drag and drop the individual items over from the "First Thoughts," bucket rather than adding them a second time. This is partly because it is very easy to get duplication, and partly because we want to capture a sense of flow in the ideas).

* * *

---

[123] It is _crucial_ to the process that everything starts from the left and moves to the right once it has been considered. When I see items spontaneously appear in different places it is because it is a project that has lost direction. But not for you, Scrumnast.

For Refinement

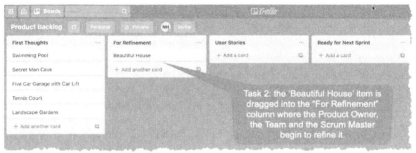

Figure 41 The "For Refinement" Column/Bucket

The "**For Refinement**" bucket is the point that the team get involved in clarifying, ironing out wrinkles, and generally firming up the content of the Product Owner's imagination into a set of more concrete and achievable solutions.

The Scrum Master often has to point out to the Product Owner that everything may seem easy when looked at from their high-level perspective, but this often masks hidden complexity. Most things appear easy at a high level, the hard bits are always in the details. The difficulties and potentially expensive components are often only uncovered when you drill down into the details in order to actually produce something in real life.

When dealing with a production team, *nothing* is more wasteful and expensive than having ambiguous definitions. If something *can* be misunderstood by someone in the team, it probably *will* be misunderstood by them. We don't want that. We want to eliminate and wipe away any assumptions before practical work starts. Drilling into the details, prodding and poking the ideas over time in order to gain clarity is how certainty takes shape.

Time spent on this may seem wasteful but spending time here gaining clarity is a *lot* cheaper than delivering a poorly understood product. Another benefit is that sometimes a Product Owner won't realise how impractical a particular idea is until they have to explain it to someone who has the skills to build it. Product Owners tend to be people of vision while production teams are made up of practically minded knowledge workers who know they only get paid when they deliver reality. That knowledge sharpens the mind.

Obviously, there is always a bit of a gap between these two perspectives. Sometimes this can be a chasm. This is partly what we are trying to unearth here.

For example, what does the phrase "Beautiful House" actually mean? What does it conjure up in everyone's minds? It could mean almost anything. Is it a twenty-five-bedroom mansion? Is it a straw-bale walled eco-house with a living roof on a ten-acre smallholding? Or a steel and glass, open plan 'statement' embedded in a cliff overlooking the sea? It could be any of these or anything else. We need to get into the details to define and clarify. This definition is the job of the Product Owner, not the team.

Drilling Down Into The Details.

In badly defined projects, teams are sometimes presented with a demand to go off and make a product with not much more than the vaguest of definitions. When they do actually produce it, the management then throw a hissy fit because that wasn't what they had in mind.

This will not do for Scrumnasts. The production team are knowledge workers and telepathy really is not in their job description. We need to remember Konosuke Matsushita's wise words, "Out of the heads of management and into the heads of labour." This is why defining the specifications of the product is the job of the Product Owner, and getting to those definitions of the specifications from the Product Owner is the job of the team.

We may not need to get down into nuts-and-bolts territory at this stage, but we do need enough definition from the Product Owner that a team can make a good attempt to talk sensibly about it.

I find that you really need some dedicated time every day for the team to speak with the Product Owner to get an idea of what the

Product Owner has in their mind for an item in the "For Refinement" bucket.

That is why we use the "**Sharpening the Tools**," ceremony at the end of every working day.

Often the Product Owner might say one thing one day, be challenged by the team and, when they have reflected and let the idea percolate in their mind overnight, they often change their mind the next or get a better idea. Sometimes.

But getting dreams and visions tied down into reality needs time for reflection to let the ideas percolate.

What To Do With The "Beautiful House" Item?

It is fairly common that when you initially capture it, an idea starts off as small, and then grows and grows and grows. Accommodating this can be a nightmare in a lot of so called 'Agile' project management software. However, Trello is really kind in dealing with things like this. Let's pretend we have captured one item called "Beautiful House."

It's unlikely that the team of builders can build a whole house in one Sprint. This is really an epic. As we know, User Stories (the building blocks of the product), are meant to be achievable in one Sprint, so we can't really call this a User Story yet.

What we can do instead is to call "Beautiful House" an "Epic." Epics are very big user stories that have to be broken down into Sprint sized pieces.

In Trello, we could make individual cards for each of the steps that go into making "Beautiful House," or, we could keep the card for beautiful house and open it up by double clicking on it to add something Trello calls a checklist. This is what we will do here, because it just keeps things tidier.

* * *

The "Beautiful House" card can be opened up by double clicking on it. When you do click on it, your screen will look something like below.

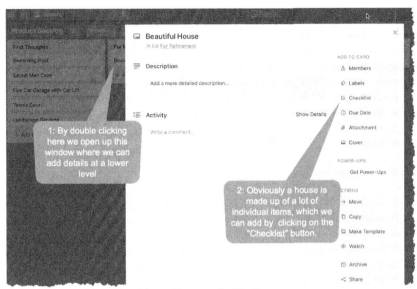

Figure 42 The "Checklist" Feature In Trello

As luck would have it, we have this **Checklist** item which allows us to add as many items as we like to our card.

Click on the **Checklist** button and your screen will look like it does below:

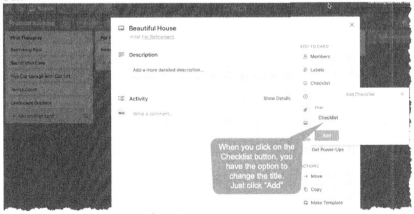

Figure 43 Filling In A Checklist

* * *

Just add your own title and when you are happy either press the
Return (Enter) key or click on the green **Add** button.

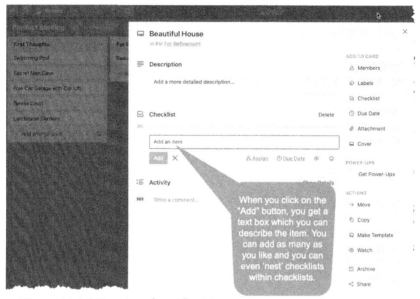

Figure 44 Adding Another Checklist

And you can add as many as you like…

* * *

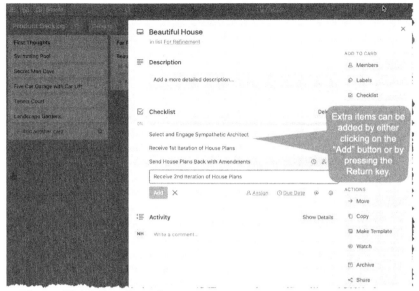

Figure 45 Adding Extra Items

One of the many clever things about Checklists in Trello is that you can rearrange them if you get them out of order at any time, by dragging and dropping them.

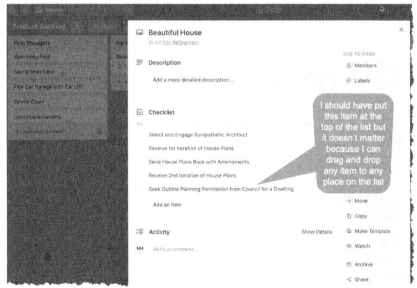

Figure 46 You can re-order and re-rank at any time

So, by dragging and dropping the item to the top of the list the Beautiful House Epic card now looks like this:

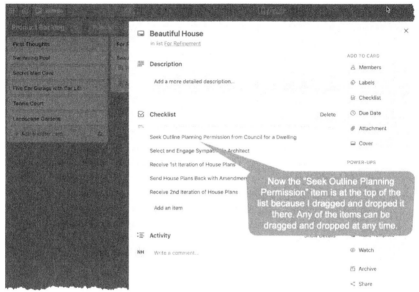

Figure 47 Re-ordering A Checklist Item

Notice that on the left of the various Checklist titles, there is a tickbox that can be checked to show that an action has been completed.

So Why Is The Flexibility Of These Checklists And Cards So Important?

Planning is an elastic business.

* * *

What starts out as one, simple little concept can quickly multiply and become a whole raft of product needs once you start to really grind out and refining the idea. This means you need really flexible and 'kind' software. Here's our problem: most planning software isn't very flexible or kind.

The fact that Trello has these lower level checklists means that we can capture items at lower levels, and if once you start to really examine an item you realise it really needs to be its own User Story or Product Backlog Item, you can promote it to become it's own Trello card by clicking on the "Make Card" button.

Multiple Boards and Portfolio Planning:

Portfolio planning is just planning for the very highest level. In traditional project management, the top level you can operate at is the **portfolio** level. The next level down is the **programme** level and below that comes the **project** level. This raises questions about how much and to what level you should actually plan and, once you have, how should you coordinate the different plans for the levels?

Luckily, Trello allows you to have multiple boards, and each one can communicate with other boards. In fact, you can pass cards between them.

We will see this in the next demo called "Practical Demo: Making A Sprint Backlog In Trello." In it I will use another Trello Board to make a Sprint Backlog. Here's the important thing to remember: we can take a card from our Product Backlog and export it to our Sprint Backlog.

And if we can export a card from one board to another board, we can export a card from any board to any other board, whether we call it a **Product Backlog,** a **Sprint Backlog,** or a very high level **Portfolio Board** to a lower level **Product Backlog** board.

Finally, Trello keeps a record of when a card is moved from one board to another board complete with who moved it and a time and date stamp. For me, that really beats the 'good old days' when we used sticky notes on a white board.

Yes, But I <u>Hate</u> Trello...

Of course, you don't need to use Trello. I am just using Trello for demonstration purposes. You could use any one of the other Agile project management software tools. (There are lots to choose from).

But please bear in mind that very few computer programmers actually have an Agile mindset. In fact, most have a rather bureaucratic mindset and what they write and deliver often reflects this. This can certainly be true when it comes to Agile project management software.

Product Backlog (Product Plan) Refinement - Don't Neglect It!

Obviously, there were lots of steps and a great deal of work involved in the refinement process. Were they all done solely by the Product Owner?

That's a lot of pressure on someone who may not be technical at all which is why they were done by the whole team, which included the Product Owner.

The items were refined iteratively, probably over quite a period of time and it was largely done through the "Sharpening the Tools" ceremony.

It illustrates our saying, *"the Product Owner brings the dreams while the team bring the means"*

Of course, it's not just me that says this. I really took this idea from working at Panasonic. You will remember what they had written in the foyer of their offices:

*For **the essence of management is getting ideas out of the heads of the bosses and into the heads of labour.** We are beyond your mindset. Business, we know, is now so complex and difficult, the survival of firms so hazardous in an environment increasingly unpredictable, competitive and fraught with danger, that their continued existence depends on the day-to-day mobilisation of every ounce of intelligence."*

Konosuke Matsushita – Founder Panasonic

Product Backlog Refinement:

Words To The Wise Scrumnast:

* * *

(I know I have said this before, but this really needs to be grasped).

Knowledge workers (the team) are paid to employ their skills and *not* their imaginations. They are largely practical people who do practical things. That is the same whether they are carpenters, computer programmers, mechanics, electricians or even musicians. They are technicians.

Therefore, you really need to work hard to make sure that what you, as the Product Owner, have in your head becomes a set of clear, concrete requests that are as unambiguous as possible. Why? It will save you time and money.

This is where the Panasonic quote about getting ideas from, "out of the heads of the bosses, and into the heads of labour" happens.

Ambiguity costs **_big_** money and I don't want that to happen to you. If a wrong assumption *can* be made, then it almost certainly *will* be made. In any kind of transformation or project, assumption is the mother of most disasters.

You also need to be careful to use their language, not yours. Cringe worthy, empty headed managerialist phrases like "ideation," do not impress a bunch of hairy blokes who can transform a few bits of 2 by 4 wooden planking into your dream cabin in the woods during the merry month of May depending on your choice of words.

Knowledge workers do big deeds. Being able to do big deeds leave them unimpressed by big words. In order to get the very best from them you need them to respect you - which is hard if they think you're a plank. Speak plainly, but respectfully to them: it is a key to effective leadership.

Over time, the very top items on the Product Backlog will become continuously refined and reworked by the team so they become clearer and more well defined.

Some of the items at the bottom of the Product Backlog list may bring so little value that they will hardly be worked on at all. This is not a waste of time; this is an effect of true prioritisation. It means that they are listed, but you haven't spent any time on them. Sometimes, when working with some stakeholders, it is politic to list items of little value just to show that you have evaluated them - even if you don't actually do anything with them.

The most valuable items will be refined and refined and refined. When that happens, they will either become "Product Backlog Items" or even "User Stories.[124]" which means that they are ready to be worked on.

---

[124] We will cover this in the "Artefacts" section.

Artefact 2: The Sprint Backlog (Sprint Plan and Work Status Report) In Trello

The Sprint Backlog[125]

Figure 48 The Sprint Backlog: Accepted, Working, Done, and Done Done Status

The Sprint Backlog is the 'information radiator[126],' of what is happening in the Sprint right now. In other words, it is the plan for the Sprint that also shows the current work status of the job(s) that are scheduled to be done in this Sprint.

Again, Scrum doesn't actually tell you how to actually do a Sprint Backlog, so this is the way *we* do it. If you can work out a better way then please use it, but this will do just fine while you are at the beginning.

The Sprint Backlog has four columns to reflect the state of the work

---

[125] Although you can't see it here, it is coloured in blue, to distinguish it from the Product Backlog. This makes sure everyone can tell at a glance that it is a different backlog to the Product Backlog

[126] This is a phrase they actually use on Scrum courses.

in this Sprint, as it was reported by the end of the last Daily Scrum.

The columns we use are: "**Accepted**," "**Working**," "**Done**," and "**Done, Done**."

Accepted is for items that have been accepted into the Sprint and are going to be worked on but haven't been touched yet.

Working is for items that are currently being worked on by one or more members of the team.

Done is for items that have been completed.

Done, Done is for items that have been completed but needed some kind of third party certification or perhaps a quality assurance check before they can be considered finished. For example, you may have a qualified electrician install the electrics in a new house, but they would have to be certified as safe before they can be used.

Making A Sprint Backlog (Plan, Work Progress And Status Report) In Trello

Figure 49 The Sprint Backlog - At The Beginning Of A Sprint

THE SPRINT BACKLOG IS THE STATUS BOARD OF THE WORK BEING DONE IN THE CURRENT SPRINT.

AGAIN, SCRUM SAYS YOU SHOULD DO A SPRINT BACKLOG BUT DOES NOT TELL YOU HOW TO DO ONE

ALL ITEMS THAT GO INTO THE SPRINT BACKLOG MUST COME FROM THE PRODUCT BACKLOG BY WAY OF THE SPRINT PLANNING SESSION

Figure 50 The Sprint Backlog - The Basic Rules

The **Sprint Backlog** is the team's visual, at-a-glance, latest current status report of this Sprint's work tickets.

Remember: the Team *can only pick their work from this list, and nowhere else*.

If you stick to this rule, then everyone knows that the Team and the Product Owner will have gone through a proper process of planning and negotiation in the Sprint Planning session for what work should be done and how it should be done.

In other words, some kind of thought, investigation, and 'sizing up' the jobs will have already been done. Please do not underestimate the value of this. Sizing up is a time-honoured exercise in risk mitigation.

* * *

The Team will do their best to complete the items within this Sprint. If they don't complete all the items, they can be re-planned for the next sprint.

One of the benefits of the Sprint Backlog is that it is so visual, and easy to understand. Anyone, even those uninvolved, should be able to understand at a glance the current state of play. The Team, the Product Owner, the Scrum Master, any Stakeholders and other teams too, can immediately see where work is up to.

Again, just like the Product Backlog, all the items start off in the leftmost column. If they are accepted by the Team in the Sprint Planning session, then they move to the "**Accepted**" column. They move rightwards through the columns as they are worked on and they progress through the "**Working**" column, and when completed they get moved to the "**Done**" column. There is also a separate "**Done, Done**" column for those things that need outside approval.

Let's pretend we are part of a project to build a "Beautiful Dream House." The future owners are in the early stages of the build, so it's just the happy couple that make up the team at the moment. They have bought the land, but they don't have planning permission for a house yet. And they haven't chosen a team of builders or an architect either.

Let's kick off with starting some initial tasks. This is **Sprint Number One** which we will call "**Mobilisation**." In this two-week long Sprint, they would like to achieve the following:

1. Send off an application to the planning department.

2. Engage a great firm of architects.

3. Get some preliminary, rough sketches from the architects to see if they are on the same wavelength.

4. Even if they are on the same wavelength, then the couple might want to make a few changes once they have seen the drawings

* * *

How Would We Record That?

Well, in the Sprint Planning Session, they would have looked at all the items on the separate Product Backlog to see what they could do right now. They know the work is fairly simple at the moment, and it is only the couple doing it, so there isn't much to argue about yet. They can simply drag the item across into the "Accepted" column, so it looks like this:

Figure 51 Into Status "**Accepted**"

And they can also drag the other items that we think we can achieve in this fortnight long Sprint as well, so the Sprint Backlog looks like this:

Figure 52 Adding Items To The "**Accepted**" Status

It is pretty simple to get an architect, and they could also make a planning application so let's put those in the "Working" column to show that they are doing something with them.

Figure 53 "**Working**" Status

After ten days of searching for an architect and interviewing quite a few, they have chosen a firm of architects that they both like. They have sent them a rough set of plans to look at, so we can all check that everyone is clear on the upcoming commission.

They are looking at them to check them over, so they move that item to the "**Working**" column. The outline planning application has taken a bit longer than we anticipated, but they now have that in too. That means that these two tasks can move to the "**Done**" column.

Figure 54 "**Done**" Status

By the next day we have looked at the initial house plans and seen a few small errors that need amending. We have highlighted them and sent them back to the architects. The council have also come back to us about the planning application and told us that it will need some time for consideration. We have done as much as we can on that item for now and it is out of our hands, so we are awaiting a "**Done, Done**" response.

Figure 55 "**Done, Done**" Status

It may not be a very complicated Sprint Backlog, but it will do for now in order to get us into the habit of working out a Sprint Backlog using Trello.

* * *

Sprint Backlog Procedure Crib Sheet:

When Are The Work Tickets On The Sprint Backlog Board Moved?

The items are moved during the early morning Daily Scrum[127] event. *Make sure the person in the team who has done the work is the person who moves the items.*

It may sound like an insignificant and infantile thing to focus on, but this small exercise of 'giving credit where credit is due' will make a big difference to the quality of the work and how fast it will progress.

Being online, we use the Daily Scrum event as a video meeting to start our working day. The whole team will join on Zoom, or Teams, and they will also all have the Trello application open so that they can see work tickets move.

Where do the team get the work items from?

For items to get accepted onto the Sprint Backlog, they must have come from the Product Backlog *and nowhere else*. You can tell a disorganised or chaotic project because new work items appear as if from thin air. We don't want that, we want order.

After all, the Product Backlog is where the often imprecise, vague dreams of the Product Owner are refined, processed and transformed by the team into bite-sized chunks of achievable, worthwhile valuable work items ready to be worked on and created during the Sprint by practical, productive people.

---

[127] Remember, 15 minutes *maximum*.

How do they get accepted into the Sprint? The Sprint Planning Ceremony.

The Sprint Planning ceremony is exactly what it says, a planning session for the Sprint. Prioritised items from the Product Backlog are brought to the team for consideration for the Sprint. The Product Owner is responsible for bringing the prioritised items (prioritised by both importance and by value) to the session.

The work items are sized by the team by how large a job they think it will be. Numbers used are 0, 1, 2, 3, 5, 8, 13, 21, 34, 55, and 100. (don't try and use man days as an estimating tool. Human beings are unfortunately useless at estimating how long a job will take. Just ask anyone who has ever engaged a builder to do any work.)

There must be some negotiation between the team and the Product Owner on how many things can be done in the upcoming Sprint. There is always a creative tension between the Product Owner and the team doing the work. Product Owners normally want everything done by tomorrow and teams want to push back. Most Teams want to deliver an achievable amount of work so the Product Owner must trust the team to be truthful and accurate in estimating the amount of work they can really achieve.

The Product Owner does not have the power to force the team to take on more work than they can handle. The Scrum Master must push back against the Product Owner and defend the team's view if they do this.

Please don't neglect this

Wise Words for Scrumnasts:

A sure sign of a badly run or chaotic project is that items magically appear from nowhere onto the Sprint Backlog, without undergoing any planning, sizing or refinement process. *Your project will suffer if you let this happen.*

* * *

Weak Scrum Masters often allow this when they don't have the necessary heft to stand up against their panicking middle-managers. This may be uncomfortable to you to deal with, but this behaviour is not acceptable. In this case, your responsibilities and accountabilities are to the good running of your project and to your team, not to the Product Owner.

THE WHY - ETHICS

The Working Culture And The Five Scrum Ethics

"All anyone asks for is a chance to work with pride." - William Edwards Deming.

The Five Scrum Ethics are:

1. Focus

Meaning that team members concentrate on completing one task at a time and will continue to work on it until it is either finished or as complete as it can be for the time being. Multi-tasking[128] is frowned upon (because everything, all human beings, and even computers, are terrible at it).

2. Openness

The team are open to inspection at all times through the Scrum events, and we are transparent about our problems, knowledge and our progress at every stage.

3. Courage

It takes courage to own up to mistakes. It takes courage to give bad news early. It takes moral courage for a set of team members to refine, challenge and iron out a Product Owner's often imprecise, vague, dreamy, wish-list and transform it into an agreed set of achievable, concrete tasks that can actually be delivered.

---

[128] Multi-tasking: doing multiple jobs simultaneously - All of them badly.

* * *

4. Commitment

I don't just mean commitment to the work. That is a given. Great teams don't happen by chance. It takes time, commitment, and a certain amount of 'rubbing the corners off' from everyone within the team to create, develop and maintain a high performing Scrum team. Great Scrum Masters value the commitment that the members of the team have towards each other.

5. Respect

Everyone in the team is treated with respect. Mistakes will be made because:

1. To err is human

2. Unforeseen events will occur, and circumstances will change.

Nevertheless, we believe that those in the Scrum team work to the best of their abilities with the knowledge that they had at the time.

But why stop there when we have already explored David Sirota's research on what employees actually want?

At Scrumnastics, (Though Not A Part Of Core Scrum,) We Have Also Added David Sirota's Recommendations To Our Scrum Ethics. These Are:

Equity:

People wish to be treated fairly when at work. Equity means getting the right recognition and reward for their efforts, both from their managers and from their colleagues in the team. It also means that there are no favourites.

Achievement:

We all need purpose in our lives, and the largest component of the waking day is spent working. Why wouldn't your team want to get their purpose with a sense of achievement and pride from their work and a small measure of control over what they are doing?

Camaraderie:

Money is important, but people don't just come to work for the money. They also come to work for the company and to be social. This has been especially important during the lockdowns. Human beings are social animals who thrive when well socialised and do not do well when isolated. And we have all been isolated. Fostering a sense of _belonging_ in the team has been crucial to the wellbeing of all of us.

There is nothing more despised than the false and affected manager who thinks they should be in charge of fun. Let your team talk to one another independently without you being there. I encourage my team to video call each other during the day, and they often have a "Zoom Coffee,[129]" in addition to attending **Scrum Events**. To reinforce this, we call all the Events the '**Minimum Viable Contact[130]**.'

You do not need to be their best friend, but you certainly do not need to be an oaf, either. The British were once famous for what would now be called '**Minimum Viable Politeness[131]**,' or basic manners. In other words, small talk. It turns out that those stiff, stilted, formal conversations about family, the weather and what have you, are actually really valuable. I use them in the five minutes before any of the video events.

---

[129] I owe this idea to Sarah Lambert, who works at the European Commission. She told me in summer 2020 that she and her colleagues just spontaneously started doing it and they found it incredibly useful.

[130] Yes, I know that it is easy to get carried away with the "Minimum Viable …," idea, but I think this one serves a useful purpose.

[131] Okay, I know I am pushing my luck here…

The Working Culture

This can feel a bit 'touchy-feely,' especially to British people, and may seem to be something that you would rather avoid. Please don't - there's gold to be had here if you do it right. It may make you feel uncomfortable, but this is the facet of Scrum that actually offers the greatest potential rewards for productivity.

This can either be the easiest or the very hardest of the five faces to get right. How successful you are with this really depends on two things:

1. The Work Culture Of Your Organisation.

2. What Type Of Leader And Manager Are You? A Theory X, or a Theory Y?

1. The Work Culture Of Your Organisation

If you have an open and supportive work culture, then this will be an easy job and you will wonder why I am making a big issue of it. But if you have a toxic work culture then this will be very, very long hard slog.

Of course, you *can* establish a great work culture in a Scrum team within a wider toxic culture, and sometimes, that's the real job you will have been brought in to achieve, but it is hard to maintain, and you and your team will always have to be vigilant about the danger of becoming infected by colleagues outside of the team.

The establishment of a working culture in Scrum is the responsibility of the Scrum Master. However, maintaining that culture is the responsibility of the whole team. In a toxic work culture, it is definitely not for the faint hearted. Establishing and maintaining a healthy working culture requires courage and commitment on everyone's part in order to challenge bad behaviour when you see it.

Sometimes the hardest part is getting the senior management in the organisation to admit that how people are being treated in the workplace is not healthy.

Of course, most modern work environments are very healthy and not at all like this, so if you are thinking "what on earth is he on about?" All I can say is, "lucky you!"

2. What Type Of Leader And Manager Are You? A Theory X, or a Theory Y?

What type of leader or manager are you? It is a serious question, because depending on what personality type you are, this is going to affect how easy you are going to find implementing this.

Are you a 'Theory X,' (you think your people need constant chasing because they are lazy and work shy), or a 'Theory Y'? (where people want to actualise themselves and come to work for more than just money)

This question goes all the way back to the ideas raised by Douglas MacGregor's classic management theory book "The Human Side Of Enterprise," first published in 1960.

The "Three Pillars of Empiricism:" Transparency, Inspection, and Adaptation

Transparency

This has two sides to it, the internal and the external.

Internal (within the team)

1. Everyone in the team needs to know their responsibilities and

accountabilities. The Product owner manages the product, the team do the work and the Scrum Master leads the team and is responsible for the good order of Scrum.

2. Everyone in the team need to know and understand the Artefacts. These are the:

   i.   Product Backlog,
   ii. The Sprint Backlog
   iii. What defines an **Increment** (i.e. what is the **definition of done** for the item).

3. Everyone in the team needs to know what the ultimate goal for the Product is, and what the goal for this particular Sprint is.

4. Everyone in the team must attend all the Events. These must be established and conducted in an open and honest atmosphere. This is especially true for the Daily Scrum, because that is where any problems will surface *first*.

External (The Stakeholders And Budget Governance)

The Sprint Review event is where the latest work on the product from the latest Sprint is demonstrated to all the interested external parties, such as stakeholders. The Sprint Review is also a governance meeting where the running of the project and the product is made transparent.

Although it takes a lot of courage to do, experience tells us that it is *always* better to deliver any bad news early. If you deliver bad news early, you may be able to do something about it. If you let an issue grow and fester until the money has all gone, it will be too late to do anything. Although people do not like an "Oh, dear," moment, they always prefer it to an "Oh God," month.

Inspection

There are inspection tools in Scrum.

* * *

The **Product Backlog** is an at-a-glance visual plan.

The **Sprint Backlog** is an at-a-glance visual update and progress report that gives the latest news on the product.

The **Daily Scrum** event is where the team (including the Product owner) inspect progress every day and any issues that can not be solved by the team are given to the Scrum Master to solve.

The **Sprint Review** event is where the latest work can be inspected and interrogated, and is run by the Product Owner. It is held at the end of every Sprint and is where all the latest work is shown.

The **Sprint Retrospective** is where the team have a debrief for the Sprint and inspect how the work went amongst themselves. Although often neglected, this event offers the most powerful set of tools for improvement and increased productivity.

Adaptation:

The world turns and everything changes. That is just how the world is. That pristine specification for the mahogany centre piece that sets up the visual theme for the whole trophy house? It will change. That British Racing Green paint scheme your client specified for their 'restomod' E-type Jaguar? They will prefer red tomorrow.

In the world of traditional project management, that isn't how things work, which is why so many projects deliver products that don't work. Traditionally run projects fail to deliver what people want *today*, because they are so focussed on what they wanted yesterday.

In Scrum we realise that things will change, so we might as well welcome it. We welcome changes to:

1. **Our ways of working together**. Government announces another lockdown? No worries, we have a section in this book on that. We also have an event that happens in every Sprint. It is called the **Sprint**

Retrospective, in which we reflect on our ways of working as a team, and we see if we can improve upon them. Every Sprint. In Japanese, they call this _**hansei**_. For the Japanese there can be no 'continuous improvement,' or _**kaizen**_, without a period of _**hansei**_.

2. **The demands for what our product should do**. It is a fact: People want more every day. Has your competitor just brought out a new product that does everything your forthcoming product does? Then you had better make yours better, cheaper, faster, safer, greener, cleaner and better designed, or you won't compete and then you will be out of business. When is the product you are working on judged by what is happening externally in the world? During _every_ Sprint Review.

You have to make sure the Product Owner is aware that the Sprint Review should always examine what is happening in the wider market.

That's the real secret of the beauty of making a **Minimum Viable Product**, otherwise known as the **MVP.**

What is an MVP? Let's pretend we are setting up as an ice cream maker. Before we get into all the wonderful, exotic flavours, what we need to prove is that we can make a great tasting, good looking, plain vanilla ice-cream. We don't worry about raspberry sauce, the 99 flake, or any of the other stuff.

Your Sprint Review reveals that your competition suddenly makes an even better plain vanilla? That's okay because you know how to make a great ice cream. Looks like its time to make a strawberry one. Adapt.

Although there's not really space to go into it here, we specialise in working in the fascinating area called "Blue Ocean" strategies, as developed by W. Chan Kim and Renee Mauborgne. This is where you aim to make your products feed in the blue oceans, where there is lots of food, rather than compete in the yucky red seas, where the feeding frenzies happen.

Scrumnastics: Join Us?

If you would like to see more videos on leadership, why not join the Scrumnastics mailing list? I post videos regularly on Youtube, FaceBook and the Locals platform.

Who knows what social platforms we will all be using next year? But if you join the mailing list you can be sure I will email you the latest links to the latest videos on the latest platforms.

You can sign up to the Scrumnastics mailing list at scrumnastics.co.uk (no, we don't sell your email, and every email has an unsubscribe option).

Have a real business that you are serious about growing?

Scrumnastics Elite: Open to directors and senior managers with real businesses. Maximum 6 members per club.

COURSE THREE: "SCRUMNASTICS ++" - LOTS OF TEAMS LOTS OF PHASES

Scrumnastics ++

Well Done! Here's To Your Success!

Congratulations! Welcome to Course Three.

You now know how to *lead **and** manage* a small team.

You now know what the 35% of leaders and managers who actually *can* and *do* make a difference know. The rest is simply practice.

By the way, leading and managing a small team is actually *harder* than leading and managing a large team. There are lots of bad managers who can't lead small teams, but nearly all managers who can lead a small team can go on to successfully lead larger numbers of people. The secret is in creating more than one team.

Onwards And Upwards...

Of the many clients I have had, five clients, three of which were business owners, told me that their only ambition was to lead and manage their one team well. All five got back in contact within a year to ask me to help them lead and manage multiple teams either because:

1. Business demand had grown so much

2. They were now seen as the up-and-coming management talent in the company.

So, if you are thinking, "all I will ever want to do is run one team," or "my business will only be the one team," that is _exactly_ what these people thought too. Look what happened to them.

Nevertheless, if you are going to lead and manage large teams, we need a few more tips and techniques, but all of them build on what you already know. We are just going to extend what we already know in Scrum and Scrumnastics.

* * *

We are going to extend them across time and extend the number of teams we are going to lead and manage. In management jargon, this is called **_scaling_** growth.

The best bit is that having done all the groundwork in the other courses, I think you are going to find this pretty straightforward.

Let's crack on.

Scaling

... is management jargon for making a team bigger.

Why make a team bigger? Probably because you need more skills and greater capability than you have at the moment. Ten or eleven people can obviously do more than three, but there will be compromises on speed of delivery and the team will be harder to manage, harder to co-ordinate and harder to administer.

If you are working online, then it becomes even more difficult to lead, manage and co-ordinate ten or eleven people, especially in the Events.

Scrum.org Say, "Two Teams Of Five And Six Beats One Team Of Eleven"

Scrum used to say that the maximum size for a team was eleven, including the Product Owner and the Scrum Master. Since the 2020 update, they now recommend that if you do need that many people, you should use two, up-to-six-person teams instead. They also say that the two teams need the same **Product Owner**, **Product Backlog** and **Product Goal**.

That takes care of a project where the two teams are working on the same project, but what about where you have multiple teams working on different projects? We will talk about that here in **Scrumnastics ++**.

At The Other End Of The Scale - What Is The Minimum Size Of A Scrum Team?

You don't really need to use Scrum if there are only two of you. The communication and co-ordination difficulties between two people are minor in comparison to larger teams. I am not trying to belittle the potential for problems between two people (which can still be big,) but trying to implement Scrum for a duo is probably overkill.

The Three Person Scrum Team: The Easiest way to start with Agile

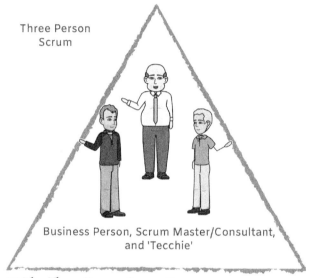

Figure 56 The Three Person Scrum Team

This is how I started out working with Scrum, all the way back in 1995 with Panasonic. I used this format really successfully for years when I was a data architect. I think it's the smallest, feasible way to start with Scrum.

To do this, as ever, you need a team that has a mixture of skills. You need:

1. Someone who has some business focus

2. Someone with the particular technical expertise you are after

3. A third person who has knowledge of Scrum.

* * *

Because there is so little management overhead in a three-person team, the Scrum Master can normally also do another job as well.

The pace of a three-person Scrum is *rapid*. We frequently use them to do short, pilot projects called 'Discoveries,' for marketing and I.T. Clients. You can achieve an astonishing amount of work in a short space of time with a three-person Scrum.

In fact, if you want or need to try out Scrum before committing to it, the cheapest, virtually risk-free way is to do a quick three to four sprints[132], three-person Scrum. Pick a pressing need like "Will anybody actually buy this new thing?" and get a **Discovery** project together so you can see for yourselves.

We will talk more about **Discovery** projects later on in this section.

---

[132] I recommend you make the Sprints just a week long. I bet you will be *amazed* at the pace of work.

Using the GDS Phases of Sprints To Minimise Risk and Grow Your project

A Scrum Team growing as it moves through GDS phases

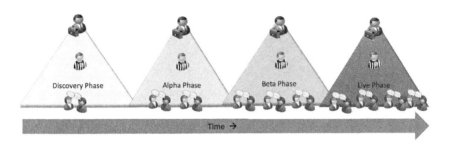

Figure 57 Moving Through The GDS Phases. - Notice How the Team Grows From Left To Right

The **Government Digital Services (GDS)** phases are not specifically Agile or Scrum. A lot of Agile and Scrum purists will be upset by me even mentioning them here. The purists will tell you that Scrum is about improving and evolving a product or service incrementally. This is all very fine until you come up against a real client who wants to know that you can manage their money properly.

If Scrum has a weakness, I think it is that Sprints can sometimes become a little frenetic and frantic in their pursuit of constantly iterating the work. Scrum 2020 has attempted to mitigate this by insisting that each Sprint having its own Sprint Goal. I think this is a great addition and it really helps.

However, your client budget holders will need convincing you know how to run a project before they part with real money. They tend to like having confidence that you know how to manage their money and just telling them that every Sprint has a Sprint Goal so that's alright then, tends to make their eyes glaze over.

* * *

The **GDS** phases are a set of pretty good project control structures that you can use to mitigate risk. They are especially helpful when you are starting out when you and your team have your training wheels on. By the way, we still use them in every project we do because our clients like them and it gives them confidence in us.

Let me say again, there is nothing in Scrum or Agile that says you ought to proceed in this way. But if you want to avoid pure terror in your first few projects, the following set of stages are recommended by the U.K. government's Government Digital Services (GDS) board and are helpful when you are starting out.

Please note: All government digital services are mandated to use these and the U.K. Government have abandoned PRINCE2[133] for digital projects.

Notice that every phase always has a **Product Owner** and a **Scrum Master**. Hopefully, it will have the same **Product Owner** as the project progresses. After all, the Product Owner is meant to stay with the product even once it is live. The numbers in the production team get larger as you add capabilities to the team.

You can string a number of Sprints together into a daisy chain to make up the following phases.

The GDS Project Phases

Government Digital Service (GDS) splits a project into five stages that map onto a project life cycle. The five phases are **Discovery, Alpha, Beta, Live**, and **Retirement**.

* * *

---

[133] PRINCE2, or **PR**ojects _**I**n_ a **C**ontrolled **E**nvironment version 2 is a project management methodology written by the UK government for UK government run projects. It has been exported to over 130 countries and has been a triumph as a project management methodology.

1 Discovery Phase: - 3 - 4 person Scrum Team - running for 2 - 3 Sprints

Answers the questions

1. "Does anybody actually want this enough to pay money for it?"
2. "Is there really a need/desire for what you are doing?"

-The Discovery Phase allows you to 'fail fast[134]' if an idea turns out to be a white elephant or a 'vanity project' that has no actual support in the marketplace. We are trying to avoid 'sunk cost,' where you spend so much money on a failing project that those involved just can't stop because their careers are on the line.

These kind of projects are often promoted by those managers in the organisation who might be pretty useless, but still have the power to sack you. You might see failing fast as wasteful but, it is a lot less wasteful than spending three years making a white elephant.

If the answer is "yes, there really is a demand," then you move onto doing an **Alpha** phase. If it is "no there isn't," then you stop. Or you modify the project. You can count it as a success that you have saved yourself the expense of building a vanity project or a white elephant.

This is what is known as "failing early." In the real world, you can do all the planning you want, but you will not know if there is a real demand for a product until you have tested whether real people will actually pay for it. If they won't, it is far cheaper and better to quit while you are ahead and return the finite resources you could have burned up creating something that no-one wants or needs.

In government, the main effort of this phase is focused on user research. However, I don't have much faith in polls or user research, because people fib. We would rather rely on getting some input from salespeople or service engineers (both of whom will have a better nose for what their clients actually want, than most user researchers).

---

[134] i.e. stop wasting time and money on pipe dream projects. You try it and if it succeeds you carry on. If it doesn't you move onto something else which might work.

* * *

Main feature of the team: should have Salespeople/Customer Feedback/User researcher.

2 Alpha Phase: - 4 - 6 person Scrum Team - running for 3 - 6 Sprints

Answers the question:

"Do we have the ability to easily make it, or do it ourselves without bringing the company/organisation to its knees?"

It should also answer the sub questions of:

A: Do we have the capability to make it ourselves or not?

B: If not, who/what do we need to get/partner with in order to get that capability?

C: If we do have the ability, how quickly can we make a rough prototype, show it to potential users and get their feedback?

Again, this phase attempts to guard against ruinously expensive 'sunk cost' projects, which goes, "You know, I'm sure we're nearly there now. It would be a shame to lose all this work so why don't we just spend another £xxxx million just to get it over the line?"

This is another risk mitigation phase. We now know there is a demand, but can we build it? For example, we may have proof that there is a huge market for a smart phone that sells for 20% of the price of other smart phones on the market, but can we build it without risking the whole company?

Main **Increment**: Two sides to team:
1. People who can actually make a rough demo/prototype
2. People with the ability to ask the market whether they like the demo/prototype.

* * *

3 Beta Phase: - 7 - 11 person Scrum Team - running for 8 - 15 Sprints

Answers the questions:

1. "But will they buy _our_ thing?"

2. "Can you build the smallest acceptable (plain vanilla) set of features into a product and see if it sells?"

You now think you have the capability and capacity to build this (perhaps with a partner or a consultancy). Now prove it. Build a real working prototype as a Minimum Viable Product (or 'M.V.P.') - (8 - 15 Sprints).

Main Increment: A working prototype to Minimum Viable Product standard (which can be very 'rough and ready').

A Minimum Viable Product (MVP) has no gimmicks, bells or whistles. It is the bare bones product. If you were making ice cream then the MVP would be a plain vanilla ice-cream. That is, no flake, no raspberry sauce, no nuts and no other flavours.

You need to know how much you can build this plain vanilla product for, so that you know whether you can make it for a profit or not. After you have achieved that, you can add the extras to earn extra money.

We are testing that we can make a product for a certain amount of money and that we could sell that product for a larger amount of money. Car manufacturers often use this technique and build show cars to show the public at motor shows in order to gauge response. Although they are rarely fully working cars, they are more than happy to take a deposit from the customer. Probable Team size? 8 - 11

4 Live Phase: As many as you need for the production facility - runs for life of product

* * *

Where we are: We have proved that there is a need, and we think we can do it, and we know what it looks like because we have a prototype that people like.

Product Launch/Go Live/Get the Client to take possession.

You know that there is a demand, you know that you have the ability to build it, you know how much it will cost to build, whether you can make a profit on it and you have real feedback from real people who have seen the real thing and want it enough to give you real money (Porsche was able to do this with the prototype Porsche Boxster,). Okay, now you can go and build the real thing.

There is a world of difference between making a prototype and getting ready for making the real thing on a production line. If you have a factory, this means passing the work from the team that does development and onto the people in manufacturing who do the work of making things. If you are doing craft work, or complex work, this will probably mean that you will need multiple specialist teams that will all need coordinating. How do you do that in Scrum? We use **Scrumnastics ++**, but you could use **Scrum Nexus®** or **Scrum At Scale®**.

You then constantly refine and improve the product from feedback from users and add the features that they ask for. The product is never static. New benefits and features are added as time goes on.

5 Retirement Phase:

This is where you manage the phasing out of the product in a well-managed and well controlled manner, rather than let it collapse in a heap.

All products have a life cycle, and there comes a time when adding more and more new features actually subtracts from the original, clean design.

* * *

Perhaps your competition has moved the whole industry on, or perhaps consumers are starting to get bored with the look of your product and it is time for a newer, cleaner, better, faster, cheaper-to-produce product to take over. There is a nagging suspicion that the product or service is not as slick or as elegant as it was when it was first released.

The product or service is now brim full of features, but some have been obviously bolted on as time has gone on as afterthoughts.

Nevertheless, there will still be life (and sales) in the existing product. There will be some consumers who still love the existing product, may hate the new one and so will want to buy the old version of the product while they still can. You want the changeover from one to the other to be elegant so that you, and they, still feel they are getting value.

This is where we gracefully withdraw the item from the market (hopefully to be replaced with another product that is better, faster, cheaper).

Again, car manufacturers, especially Ford, are brilliant at this and their product retirement strategies are well worth studying. Instead of letting the existing model production fall over in a heap, car makers make 'run-out' models. These have all the optional bells and whistles, that originally cost a fortune, are added to tempt those buyers who would rather have the tried and tested than pay good money to simply be a guinea-pig for the new product.

It is well worth studying how they bring out special editions towards the end of life of existing car models. Those which are loaded to the top with leather doodads and electronic widgets to bedazzle the public but basically, they are there to flog off old stock.

Scrumnastics ++ - Co-ordinating Multiple Scrum Teams

We know that Scrum Teams can stand alone and can manage themselves. That is one of their strengths. However, what do you need to do when you have multiple Scrum Teams that are doing different things, such as what you have to do a programme or portfolio level? How do you 'scale' them up so that they co-ordinate properly?

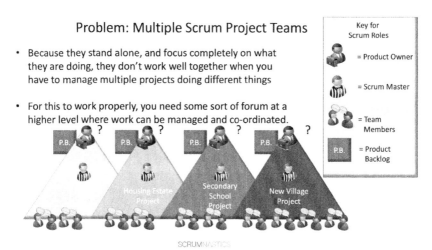

Figure 58 How Do You Co-ordinate Multiple Scrum Project Teams?

So, how do you co-ordinate them?

Well, as we have already seen, the 2020 Scrum guide officially says that you can split work into two separate teams, but you must keep the same Product Owner and the same Product Goal.

This can work really well for two six person teams and it gives us a good start, but what do you do when you inherit and have to turn around a project with 60 or more staff[135]? That obviously won't work.

You could turn to and use the official "**Scrum At Scale**," or "**Nexus**," frameworks, which are the official scrum.org and ScrumAlliance frameworks for scaling up to many teams and I think you should definitely explore them to see if they appeal. You could also explore the "Scale Agile Framework," (SAFe) which does wonderful things with blocks of work called trains.

Or, you could do as some of my clients have done and rely on the intrinsic strength of the triangle-type team structure in Scrum with its Accountabilities (roles), the Events, and the Sprint.

This is what I did when I was asked in 2016 by a government department to come up with a new "way of working" (a way of getting things done) because their own official, bureaucratic structures didn't work anymore[136]. .

They already knew Scrum and it had worked for them so they liked it. I had done a project with them the year before which had been a great success. I suggested they try the official Nexus or Scrum At Scale frameworks but when I showed the two frameworks to them they just shuddered and said, "We already know how to do complicated, we need simple."

How did we do it? Basically, I just stuck another triangle on the top.

* * *

---

[135] My record was inheriting 84 staff on a project. What did I do? I split them into small teams.

[136] The bureaucracy was so bureaucratic that even the bureaucrats couldn't make it work anymore. Just take a moment and let that thought sink in... Does it hurt your head as much as it hurts mine?...

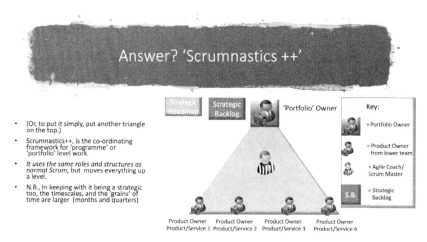

Figure 59 That Infernal Triangle - Again.

Remember in the Scrumnastics course where I said that the basic unit of a Scrum team was a triangle and that the Scrum team structure is 'fractal?' Fractal means the same structures appear at both a large or smaller scale

Well, that is what allows you to stick another triangle on the top.

The difference is, all the people who are developers/team members/production team in this top triangle ARE THE PEOPLE WHO ARE PRODUCT OWNERS IN THE LOWER INDIVIDUAL TEAMS.

Simple, right?

Well, it is a *bit* more complex than just sticking another triangle on top because you have to think about the difference in rhythm between high-level management and low-level management, but I'll talk about that below.

And, of course, you have to pay attention to the status needs of the senior management, so you have to give it a posh name like "**Portfolio Management**," or "**Scrumnastics ++**," or, even better, "**Portfolio**

Scrumnastics ++[137]."

I hope this picture of "Portfolio Scrumnastics ++," makes it clearer:

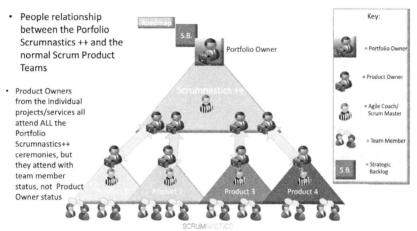

- People relationship between the Porfolio Scrumnastics ++ and the normal Scrum Product Teams

- Product Owners from the individual projects/services all attend ALL the Portfolio Scrumnastics++ ceremonies, but they attend with team member status, not Product Owner status

Figure 60 "Scrumnastics ++" The Product Owners Of The Various Teams Appear As Developers When They Are In The Scrumnastics ++ Triangle.

The 'Rhythm' Of A Portfolio Level Scrum Team

Portfolio really just means strategic. But being strategic, you really need to pay attention that the rhythm of tactical level (projects) and strategy (portfolio) should not be the same for the vast majority of the time. Tactics should never drive strategy.

Apart from emergencies and crises, this strategic level shouldn't use the same length of sprint as the lower levels. It should be longer, in order to foster a longer cadence and a calmer perspective.

Typically, if the sprints are a week or a fortnight long at the project level, we say that the sprint for the portfolio level should be a month.

* * *

---

[137] They are all exactly the same thing. Why not? They all work.

The events should also be on a monthly rhythm so you get:

1. Portfolio sprint planning event
2. Portfolio sprint review event
3. Portfolio Retrospective event

We treat the Portfolio Scrum sessions slightly differently to the other events, because a Scrum is an update and progress meeting. That means that it needs to be more frequent than the other events.

In normal times, you should aim to hold the **Portfolio Scrum** sessions _weekly._

However, in times of a project crisis, Portfolio Scrum sessions can temporarily move to happening daily, just like the Daily Scrums for the normal project level.

When Portfolio Scrums are being held on a daily basis, they should occur immediately after the project Daily Scrums so that the latest information can get passed upwards immediately.

However, once a crisis has passed, and things are beginning to calm again, the Portfolio Scrums should go back to occurring weekly again as soon as possible.

When they go back to weekly, it is normal practice to hold them immediately _before_ the project level Daily Scrums so that strategic information can be passed down to the Scrum teams.

It is important that the Portfolio scrum does go back to the normal rhythm as soon as possible. After all, if your strategic level is playing to the same drum beat as the tactical (lower level,) then it is easy to lose that '40,000 foot perspective' that strategic oversight is meant to give.

What are the different tools available?

The Tools:

The Portfolio Owner's Tools:

The Portfolio (Strategic) Goal/Roadmap: Gives a sense of long term vision to the projects and ties all work to the goals

The Strategic Backlog: Gives strategic level order. Refinement is achieved through tinkering

Portfolio Sprint Planning Meeting : Where the possible meets the achievable

Portfolio Sprint Review meeting (A Show n' Tell)

The Team Member Tools:

The Chasm of Negotiation: delivering the art of the possible means accepting only the achievable

Just as in KanBan, there is NO MULTI-TASKING. Each task is done until no further work can be done

The Sprint Wall: What the team have:

• Accepted
• Working On
• Done

The Scrum Master's Tools:

Portfolio Scrum (Stand Up): Where progress is proved, colleagues are updated and blockers are highlighted to the Scrum Master

Portfolio Retrospective: The core improvement framework

• What we did well in this Sprint
• What we could have done better in this Sprint
• Going forward, what would we improve to make our work easier or better?
• Are we thriving? (The 'Thriving Index.' Are we in 'Eustress,' or in 'Distress' as a team?)

Figure 61 The Tools At The Portfolio Level.

As you can see, everything just about identical apart from putting the words "Portfolio" or "Strategic" in front. But that is its strength.

The only things that are different are:

1. The rhythm of the events.

2. The Portfolio level team members are Product Owners from the Scrum teams.

Anyway, the slide below is the one I showed the client and that's the system they used.

* * *

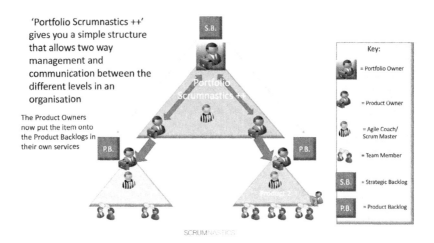

Figure 62 "Portfolio Scrumnastics ++"

To be clear, they were already enthusiastic about the speed and power of Scrum projects, so the idea of being able to re-use Scrum for senior management really went down well.

There was also a side benefit: once the project teams knew that the senior management had bought in to Scrum, the following pleasant surprises happened in the department.

1. Confidence in Scrum as a system of management shot up in the normal Scrum teams.

2. Overnight, I went from being reluctantly tolerated to everyone's best friend and being invited to every single event.

3. Productivity shot up because they knew the boss was using the same system that they were.

4. Suddenly everyone wanted to become a Certified Scrum Master or a Certified Scrum Product Owner

I didn't realise that there would be such a virtuous circle. The change in atmosphere in the department was amazing once they knew that the bosses were using exactly the same system.

* * *

Everyone relaxed into using Scrum.

What, then, are the similarities and differences?

Scrumnastics and Scrumnastics ++

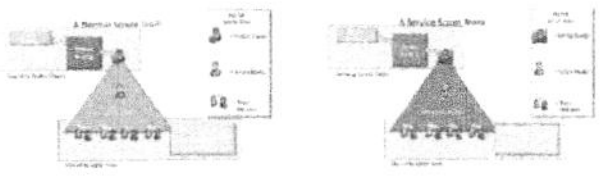

- They both have identical walls and team structures
- However:

Differences	
Scrumnastics	**Scrumnastics++**
Inward facing (project only)	Cross facing (across projects)
Short Sprints (weekly or fortnightly)	Long Sprints (monthly or quarterly)
Short Timescales: (Deliver Discovery, Deliver Alpha, Deliver Beta, Deliver Live.)	Long timescales: Responsible for Total length of service (Discovery, Alpha, Beta, Live, Retirement)
Deliver Product	Deliver Service

SCRUMNASTICS

Figure 63   Differences Between Scrum (Scrumnastics) and "Scrumnastics ++"

Practical Stuff: D. I. Y. Scrumnastics And Triangles

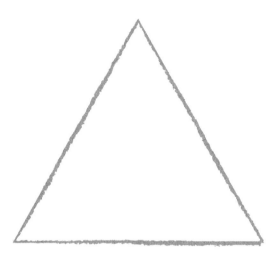

Figure 64 The Portfolio And Programme Manager's Friend: The Triangle.

Clients have often asked me to design their Scrum teams for them. I used to find it really hard until I came up with this method of using a simple, triangle. Now, whenever I am asked by a client to design a team, this triangle helps, and it saves me hours. Now you can do the same.

I Use The Triangle As A Shorthand Symbol For A Scrum Team.

I know that in any Scrum team, I will always need a Product Owner and a Scrum Master. Those roles are a given and putting names to those roles is a good start.

After that, I can pay attention to the particular skills I will need for the members of the team. Once I know the team member skills needed,

I can start to put names against the skills.

What kind of project will it be? Will it be something like:

A quick deep dive "**Discovery**" project to see if there really is a potential demand for a new product and rule out a potential 'white elephant,' or expensive vanity project?

A feasibility "**Alpha**" project to see how and whether a product could, or should, be built internally or externally with a partner? If with a partner, which partner?

Will it be a short "**Beta**" project to produce a working, life sized prototype?

Will it manage the "**Live**" manufacture and release of the working version of the product?

Is it to "**Retire**" an existing product and synchronise that retirement to give the new replacement the very best chance of success?

You know that each of them will require a different kind of team with different skills.

You already know that if you use **Scrum**, you are going to have a **Product Owner** and a **Scrum Master.** All you need to do now is identify the skills of the team that you need.

Are you going to do a **Discovery** phase? Then you need a small team that includes some people with kind of customer facing experience and skill. The point of a Discovery is to find out whether or not real people will pay real money for the Product Owner's dream. A small team can give you that answer rapidly.

Beware Of Putting Faith In User Researchers:

H.M. Government places great faith in using User Researchers in Discovery projects. - I don't, for the simple reason that people asked like to please the people asking the questions so you can get very inaccurate results.

I think it is safer to have some people who, as part of their job, talk with real customers. The right salespeople can be the best, but customer service people or field service engineers will do just fine too. Asking one of them a question and seeing them fall on the floor laughing as they clutch their sides is probably the cheapest way to find out whether a potential product should be built or not.

The Scrumnastics Multiple Teams Mapper Crib Sheet

I use this diagram on the next page to sketch out the teams that I will need.

Feel free to do the same.

Remember, every team _must_ have a Product Owner and a Scrum Master.

* * *

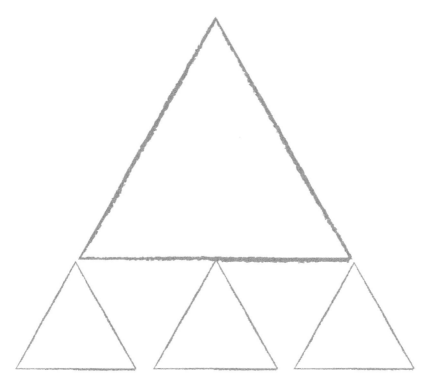

Figure 65 The Multiple Teams Mapper

The Multiple Teams Mapper:

Each Triangle is a Scrum Team. I have only drawn three triangles here but, I have used this structure to accommodate up to eleven individual teams, with eleven in each team. And, *yes*, it was extremely hard work, but it was a lot less hard work and a great deal more productive than trying to manage one team with 121 people in it.

If you need to, you could also scale the number of teams up again by adding a third layer above this one. I have actually done three levels, but that was due to the organisation having three levels of management in it, which they wanted me to map onto so they could try it out. It worked well for the time they used it, but they reorganised their company into a flatter structure after about six months, so that was the end of that.

* * *

The ability to co-ordinate the teams comes from each of the lower level Product Owners also being members of the master team triangle above. Remember: in this master team that lies above their own team they are only team members.

Wise Words For Scrumnasts

Have you ever wondered if there's a really good, practical reason why most team sports have eleven or less players? - I think it's because more than that it all becomes completely chaotic.

Scrumnastics++: - Join Us?

If you would like to see more videos on Scrum, Scrumnastics and extending Scrumnastics, why not join the Scrumnastics mailing list? I post videos regularly on Youtube, FaceBook and the Locals platform.

Who knows what platforms we will all be using next year? But if you joing the mailing list you can be sure I will email you the latest links to the latest videos with on the latest platforms.

You can sign up to the Scrumnastics mailing list at scrumnastics.co.uk

Have a real business that you are serious about growing?

Scrumnastics++ Elite: Open to experienced Directors, Senior Managers, Senior Scrum Masters and Senior Product Owners. Maximum 6 members per club.

COURSE FOUR: "LIGHTS! CAMERAS! ACTION! DOING REMOTE AND ONLINE MEETINGS BETTER"

Going Online The Easy and Effective Way

First, let's make an obvious point: working remotely/online/ virtually is harder and not as effective as working together in a near perfect office environment like the ones you see in the adverts. You know the kind of thing, easy to come to work, lots of space, great acoustics, great lighting, electronic white boards and breakout areas, all quiet and clean.

Obvious question: honestly, how close is your office space to that? I have worked in a lot of client offices and most of them have been truly *awful*.

They are often noisy, grubby, cramped, with lots of interruptions and actually very unproductive places to work. So although working from home in a remote team is not as good as the gold standard office like you might see on television, it can be a lot better than two hour commute on a soggy, cold Wednesday in February to a cramped, dingy, clammy, grubby, badly lit, noisy, typical British office.

Leading And Managing Remote, In-Office & Hybrid Teams

1. **In Office** - Many (but not most,) leader/managers can lead and manage a team that works entirely in an office without having to use some kind of managment framework. In my opinion they will do a **_much_** better job if they do use something such as Scrum, but many can do it. It is fairly easy for a good to great manager.

2. **Fully Remote** - As soon as you have to manage a completely remote team, I believe it is incredibly hard to successfully lead and manage a team without using a recognised management framework. The amount of management work and pressure on the business owner/leader/manager is astonishing in this environment. If you are not careful, your people will soon begin to see the inevitable holes in your leadership and management approach. When you use Scrum you

are using a framework that has been refined by millions of people around the world and for over twenty-five years. It just works. In comparison, a home grown system cooked up on a PowerPoint template by Ferrero and Rocher, your company's H.R. Business Partners,' just will not stack up against it.

3. **Hybrid** - *The most difficult environment to manage a team in is the hybrid* model. The hybrid model is where some of your team are in the office and some are working remotely. The key problem here is that some will be communicating with each other in person, and some will be communicating via video. Those communicating remotely via video are at a *distinct and complete* disadvantage to those communicating in person, *even if you are using something like Scrum.* Human beings have been doing face-to-face communication since our species has been on earth and we are *really* good at it. We have been trying to do video-to-video communication for about thirty years, it has only been of an acceptable quality since the past five years and we are just about getting to grips with it.

3a. If this is your team's situation then this, as the result of months and months of trial and error, is what we recommend: *disperse all your face to face workers to different parts of the building for all of the Scrum events.* Make sure that they cannot see or hear each other other than via video. The effect of this will be that everyone is at the same disadvantage as the remote workers and it forces everyone (including the in office workers,) to use the video to the best of their abilities. This will be unpopular but you need to impress on the in office workers that the team as a whole needs to work at the pace and limitations of the whole team. It is the same idea as a fleet of ships only being able to go as fast as the slowest ship. The limiting factor, or the denominator here is that you have remote workers who should not be disadvantaged..

Why We Work Remotely. - Our Ten Reasons Why.

At Scrumnastics, we have been working online and remotely since 2016 because our clients just preferred it. Amongst a raft of reasons our clients wanted us work remotely were and are:

* * *

1. They rarely had any free space to accommodate us anyway.

2. Many of our clients had already been working from home for at least one day a week for years on a fairly regular basis. It was becoming more and more acceptable for them.

3. We embraced the technique of video-only meetings very early. We made a rule in 2016 that all meeting attendees had to use video and could not attend by phone. This really improved online communication because everyone could be seen, the often ignored but all too important non-verbal communication could be experienced, and no-one had the ability to 'zone out' of any part of the meeting that did not affect them (as phone attendees tend to do).

4. We used the Scrum events, and demonstrating them gave our clients confidence in our organisational and managerial strengths. For example, we always start our day with an online 'Daily Scrum,' which everyone attends using video and I recommend you do the same. Once they could see we were well organised in our working practices, they became very relaxed about us not working on site.

If you don't know them, Scrum's 'Events' (single purpose meetings) follow Walter Shewhart's and William Edwards Deming's[138] classic "Plan, Do, Study, Act"cycle:

> **Plan**: - Sprint Planning meeting
> **Do**:   - Daily Scrum
> **Study**: - Sprint Review
> **Act:**   - Sprint Retrospective

5. We always make sure that our clients know we have a true working culture. They know we are committed to working within Scrum's three pillars of **Transparency**, **Inspection** and **Adaptability**.

---

[138] Walter Shewhart and William Edwards Deming were the two original managment gurus of the mid twentieth century. Shewhart came up with the Plan, Do, Check, Act cycle but in the 1950's, Deming took it to Japan where many Japanese companies adopted it. Having a hard time competing against Toyota? Blame William Edwards Deming.

They also know that we follow the Scrum ethics of **Focus, Courage, Openness, Commitment** and **Respect**. To the cynical, that may sound like a load of hokum, but it does a great deal to promote the idea that we can successfully work off site for our clients. Finally, we also believe in the Sirota inspired values (that are detailed elsewhere in the book) of **Equity**, **Achievement**, and **Camaraderie** for our teams and our clients.

6.   The reliability and speed and quality of video software went from "not very good at all" to "pretty good most days" during 2016. We also learned that things went even better if you passed a lot of the hard work of sound and video capture to dedicated sound and video devices, rather than let your computer do the hard work.

7.   The speed and reliability of the internet network dramatically increased during 2016.

8.   In the wider environment, lots of global companies had been moving their salespeople to working from home offices and closing their offices since the 1990s. I was project manager for a Europe, Middle East and Africa (EMEA) part of a global rollout for Dow Chemical in 1995-1996 which did just that for all the cities from Dublin to Moscow and from Stockholm to Cairo.

9.   Not having to maintain office space cuts our costs *enormously* in comparison to our competition..

10. And let us never forget: Commuting in Britain is *appalling*.

So What Do *You* Do First?

When the first lockdown began in March 2020, there was an online panic buying spree for video cameras. You could not buy an external video camera for love nor money for more than 6 months.

There's just one major problem with that approach: if you want to have great video meetings, a great video camera is actually one of the very last things you should buy.

* * *

I know that sounds counter-intuitive, but it isn't. There are two side to doing this right: the skill, or craft side, and the technical side. On the skill side, you are better off learning a few, inexpensive tips and tricks to improve your knowledge before you go to all the bother of researching and buying any new video equipment.

In order of importance, and bang for your buck, the order of steps I recommend you do this are:

1: You Need A Chairperson To Run The Events (Meetings) Now.

The biggest threat to a team with going online well is that everything descends into chaos because everyone talks at once. You need someone in charge to chair the meetings to bring a sense of order.

If you don't have a chairperson then you will end up with bedlam. If you are using Scrum, the person most likely to be the best candidate for this is the Scrum Master. They already have a leadership and expertise role anyway, so it should not be too much of a stretch.

2: Make Sure everyone's Cameras Are At Eye Level - Buy A Stand, A Cheap Tripod, Or Get A Box (An Old Shoe Box Will Do)

- It is such a simple thing, and almost no-one pays attention to this, but it is important. If you make sure your computer's camera is at eye-level, then you get two benefits:

1.   Your face will be not be elongated or distorted by your computer's camera lens, (and nearly all computer/tablet/smartphone camera do that).

2. Your colleagues won't have to look up your nostrils when you are on camera and you won't have to look up theirs - which is even better.

* * *

3: Don't Overwhelm Your Wi-fi - Or Your People

That probably sounds obvious, if so, my apologies. But remember, domestic Wi-Fi is a LOT slower and a lot less robust than the commercial Wi-Fi in the office and is easily overloaded.

You are getting alot less than you think. The speed your internet provider promised you is a bit of a fib - it is always slower. Also, data transmission is measured in bits per second not bytes per second, whereas almost everything to do with computers is measured in bytes, because it is the familiar word. Most internet sales people do not seem know the difference between a bit and a byte and will nearly always refer to bytes when they mean bits. A byte is eight bits. That probably means that the number you think you have bought is actually eight times smaller than the number you are used to dealing with when it comes to computer things.

Domestic Wi-Fi is optimised for downloading, not uploading. When you are video conferencing, you are doing a lot of uploading so you are probably perilously close to the limits, anyway.

If you share your Wi-Fi, try and make sure no-one else in your house is making heavy use of it while you are having important work conversations. That means no NetFlix, no Amazon Prime features or gaming consoles please.

It also means turning off all social media on your computer. _Every_ social media app you have open checks in with its home servers every three seconds or so, even when you are on video. That can make a big difference at times, especially if you have four or five apps open at the same time.

As an aside, we have a rule in both of my teams that we do not allow social media during work hours - (and it was the teams who made this decision, not me). Because my teams work remotely, we all pay special attention to anything that might affect our mental health, especially during the lockdowns. Frankly, they feel that all social media apps should carry a mental health warning. Finally, social media works by distracting your attention and, as we are at work being paid by a client, we owe them a duty of care to focus on their work and not to become distracted.

4: Fix The Sound

This gives you the best bang for your buck when you are going online. There is a separate section below on this.

5: Now Fix The Lighting

You can make a terrible camera take great quality video by doing nothing more than adding some good, cheap, diffused light. There is a separate section below on this.

6: Okay, _Now_ Buy A Video Camera

Don't bother with buying an expensive 4k or 8k resolution camera. Buy an old-school high-definition (or 'HD') camcorder and a good HDMI box instead. There is a separate section below on how best to do this.

Keep Your Events (Meetings) As Short As You Can.

Ever wondered why using video to be communicating and managing your team is so much more tiring than being in the same room as them?

Well, apart from everybody having the stress of trying to get video conferencing software to work the same way, every day, a great deal of our brain power is actually used up in observing each other and what we are doing. After all, we are very social beings.

Our brains actually like to keep score of where everyone is in the pecking order in our various tribes, and whether anything has changed from yesterday, how everyone is today, and idly wondering where will everyone be tomorrow?

With home working we have taken people out of their rich, social, stimulating, three-dimensional world and we have replaced it with a small, crowded, dowdy, two-dimensional flat screen substitute.

Which means you spend energy in stressful ways you haven't before such as:

Brain energy: You have to spend a great deal of your precious intellectual bandwidth just concentrating on making out which person just said what and on which part of the very small screen.

Viewing: Most people are not participating in your video conference by using 60+ inch TVs with expensive studio lighting. Instead, they are using small screened smart phones, tablets or laptops which have, (mostly) appalling screen resolutions. Use them for too long and you will get eyestrain, 'nerd-neck,' bad posture problems and chronically low energy because of the oxygen debt that chronically poor posture will give you.

Listening: The actual sound quality of the human voice which is transmitted through digital devices is of a very low resolution. Your brain automatically 'upgrades' this quality to make sense of it and actually fills in a lot of the gaps, but, again, it is wearing because your brain has to work harder than when you are in the same room. In comparison to normal, face-to-face contact, it is very wearing, especially over an extended period of time.

Although using all sorts of technical devices can help, all you are really doing when you are using these things is mitigating the problems.

By far the biggest thing you can do to help yourself and everyone else is limit the amount of time you are online. That's the big thing.

Scrum's time limits were especially helpful when it came to the 'Events' (the special purpose meetings). They really came in handy when we started working online.

Try And Make Your Online Teams Smaller

Larger teams require more co-ordination, organisation, and managing. They need a lot more communication to work than smaller teams, even when working face-to-face.

There's probably a really good reason why football teams, American football teams, cricket teams and all sorts of sports teams have eleven players a side and no more.

If you've ever been to church, you will know that fellowship groups are nearly all ten, or fewer people. Why? Because if you go any larger, the quiet people don't speak, _and you need the quiet people to speak,_ because they often speak a lot of sense. If the quiet people don't speak then you don't get their input. That can spell disaster.

Also, don't forget that when you are using Zoom or Teams, or any other video platform, it is very hard to keep your focussed attention on more than six faces for any length of time. Eight is so much harder to do by comparison and a two hour long eleven-person team on a video call can be shattering for everyone.

So, are there any management 'rules-of-thumb' we can follow to give us some good practices on team numbers? As a matter of fact there are. I find military management is very useful when you need metrics for situations where you really need to make sure things are going to work.

Sir Ian Hamilton, when studying the British Army all the way back in 1922, came up with a term he called the *"Span of Control.,"* which we looked at in the Leadernomics section.

He thought the maximum number of people a manager could control was _six_ when managing low down on the hierarchy (meaning the Sergeants and Corporals managing the 'other ranks') and _three_ as you reach the top of the hierarchy (meaning commissioned ranks commanding other commissioned ranks).

Of course, we are not getting shot at, so why use the army as an example? Because military management structures have to be robust all the time and really need to work when the bullets are flying. I know we are not in the army, but it gives us a first, good rule-of-thumb for team size - which is between three and six for a team.

Secondly, although Scrum officially says that the maximum effective size of a Scrum team is eleven, Scrum@Scale (Jeff Sutherland's method of expanding Scrum) actually advocates running multiple smaller teams of about six as he says that they are so much more efficient.

Jeff Sutherland and Ken Schwaber probably see more Scrum teams than anyone else on the planet, so I think we should probably listen to them.

In Scrum's latest update, Scrum 2020, Jeff Sutherland and Ken Schwaber now say that although you _can_ manage a team of eleven, the *optimum* size for a team is really about six. They also recommend that if you need a bigger team than that, then you should consider splitting the team into two - but make sure you keep the same Product Owner for both and also make sure that the Product Goal is the same too. We have talked about Product Goals[139] elsewhere).

And, of course, we know that the "Three-person-Scrum" team is incredibly rapid precisely because it is so small. The Three Person Scrum is how I started out working for Panasonic in 1995. It is still the

---

[139] The Product Goal is the vision statement for the product, sometimes known as the 'strong reason why' you are making it

'go-to' format that we use when we do a Discovery[140] phase for a client.

As trained Scrumnasts, I think we should definitely be able to cope with eight in a team, but any larger and we should be looking to split the team into two teams.

What To Do If You Inherit A Project With Lots Of People.

I once inherited a project with sixty-four people in it. By the time I got it, the project hadn't delivered anything of value, was badly over budget, and was very, very late.

How did I bring it back on track? I split them up from one massive team into nine, separate areas of work which had nine separate teams to do the work.

Simple, eh? But suddenly, everyone had the 'space' to open up and do the job of work that they wanted to do and the lazier found they had no place to hide any more (- okay, there was a bit more to it than that, but that was the most important part).

As you probably know, up to 70% of human communication is non-verbal. It comes out in the facial tics, the eloquent snorts, the shaking of the head and all the other ways that people communicate without words. As someone who leads teams, I need to be aware of these tics, etc, to get any early warning signs of any problems that might be coming up in the near future with members of the team.

That means that I need to see people's faces and to be able to concentrate on their faces so that I can study them in real time. If I miss out on that, then I am missing out on **vital** information that could jeopardise a project later on. Concentrating on eight faces appearing on a fifteen-inch computer screen is about my limit. Six is a lot more

---

[140] A 'Discovery' is a short mini project where we find out whether people will actually pay real money for someone's brilliant idea. If they will then the client should crack on, if they won't then we recommend stopping and try something else.

comfortable to deal with.

Try And Use Scrum's Time Boxes

Even if you are not going to use Scrum when you are working online, it is well worth using their specialist meetings, which they call 'Events.'

As well as each different meeting having one and only purpose, the meetings are limited in the amount of time they are allowed to take.

Before the Scrum 2020 update, Scrum was happy to recommend that all the different types of meeting in Scrum had time limits, which it officially called 'time boxes.'

The last Scrum update relaxed the amount of emphasis given to these time limits, but my teams still like to use them because they find them helpful and a good rule of thumb.

Why do they like them? Well, the people in my teams are knowledge workers. Unlike managers, knowledge workers get paid for what they do rather than talking about what they are doing or planning to do. The less time they spend talking, the more time they can spend doing, so you can imagine my teams are really keen to limit the amount of time they spend in meetings.

We're all mature adults, so you will make your own minds up.

The Scrum Time Boxes (pre-2020):

Sprint Planning Event
>   2-hours maximum for a one-week Sprint
>   4-hours maximum for a two-week Sprint.
>   8-hours maximum for a month-long Sprint

* * *

Daily Scrum Event

15 minutes maximum (10-12 minutes is a good rule of thumb)

Sprint Review Event

1-hour for a one-week Sprint
2-hours for a two-week Sprint
Up to 4 hours for a four-week Sprint.

Sprint Retrospective Event

45 minutes maximum for a one-week Sprint
90 minutes for a two-week Sprint
3-hours for a four-week Sprint

"**Sharpening The Tools**" (not an official Scrum Event, but we use it) 10 - 15 minutes at the end of each working day with the Product Owner to examine, clarify and refine upcoming items on the Product Backlog that are going to go into future Sprints.

Cue Cards

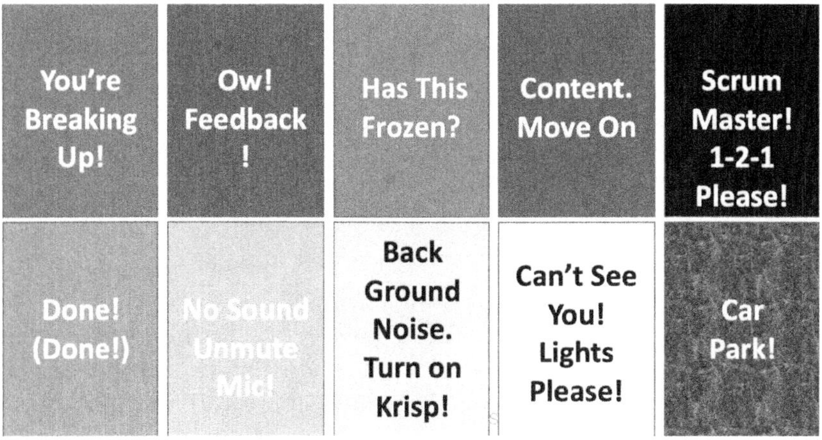

You're Breaking Up!	Ow! Feedback !	Has This Frozen?	Content. Move On	Scrum Master! 1-2-1 Please!
Done! (Done!)	No Sound Unmute Mic!	Back Ground Noise. Turn on Krisp!	Can't See You! Lights Please!	Car Park!

Figure 66 Scrumnastics Idiot/Cue Cards

We find these are really helpful when you are in a video meeting. They help to bring order in a potentially chaotic situation: when things have gone wrong with the technology.

These are cut-out-and-keep picture cards that can be used by the participants and held up in the middle of a video meeting if there are any problems.

Each member of the team carries them with them. We print them out on a colour printer and then encapsulate them in plastic at the printers to make them last longer.

Using Cue cards (or idiot cards, as they are known in radio and TV production) is the quickest, most effective way to point out any problems in the video meeting.

For example, if seven out of eight people hold up a card that says, "**No Sound – Unmute Your Mic!**" you instantly know that the person not holding up their cue card is the person who has the problem. You, as the chair of the meeting, can then sort this out.

* * *

The alternative is to waste minutes on trying to find out who has the problem, fixing it and then a few minutes more while you re-establish the working mood.

Note: I have found that you need to run at least two practice/ training sessions with your team to show them how to use them and get them used to using them without being self-conscious. Three sessions will make an even bigger difference in how comfortable they feel.

We have another card which just says, "I Want To Speak." We found that it is really helpful with maintaining good order of the meetings because it stops people talking over each other on the video call and the meeting descending into bedlam. Other people just raise their hand but that can also descend into bedlam. It's entirely up to you.

It will take some time for your team to get used to using the card but it really does help meeting discipline enormously.

There is also a website called www.collaborationsuperpowers.com who will be delighted to sell you some very professional looking cue cards for about $20 per person.

If you're a cheapskate like me, you can photocopy the ones that we made above, or make your own and get them printed.

"What Do You Mean, "Half of Video is Sound?"

It sounds daft, doesn't it? Oddly, most old-school TV and video producers really will tell you that "half of video is sound."

The idea is that people in meetings will put up with terrible video quality, but bad sound is such an instant turn off, that it ruins their concentration makes them lose interest. As a result, they stop listening to what is going on.

I know a terribly clever evolutionary psychiatrist who told me that the sounds of alarming noises have a higher danger priority than sight because things that want to eat you often come up from behind you where you can't see them. I have no idea if this is true or not, but I feel it might be.

You know those wonderful inbuilt microphones and inbuilt sound systems you get on most computers that mean you don't have to buy a separate microphone? They are terrible. The only thing they are good at is picking up every single sound apart from your voice. They pick up dogs barking, cars revving, jet engines screaming. They are really not up to the job of making your meeting sound professional.

Not only that, but the resolution of the sound they pick up is reduced by the computer as it changes it from analogue to digital signal before it is passed over to your particular video platform. At the other end the signal is changed from digital to analogue and then reproduced. This is a lot of work for a computer, especially when your computer is doing that while it is also trying to do everything else. When it goes wrong you get that unearthly 'Zoom' sound of digital distortion.

Even when it all works properly, when it receives the sound, the computer has to upgrade the sound, but it will not be what sound nerds like me call 'high fidelity.' Your brain has to work really very hard to raise what your ears hear to a point where it can decipher it properly. As I said before, this is very wearing on your brain, which means it is very tiring, especially for long meetings.

Here's the point: When the computer has to do a great many things at the same time it becomes overloaded. When it becomes overloaded you start to hear that unmistakeable, horrible, inhuman sound of digital distortion which is so very unpleasant and spoils everyone's concentration for minutes at a time.

While we are on the subject of awful sound: those brand name ear buds are definitely not high-fidelity and also become unpleasantly heavy if you wear them for extended periods of time. Try headphones, they may look ridiculous, but are more comfortable for extended wear. Part of what we are trying to achieve is you and your team getting to the end of the day without being shattered.

How To Achieve Better Sound Quality

As you may have guessed, I don't use the inbuilt microphone on my laptop, I use a dedicated sound recorder instead - Okay, I am a bit of a sound geek - I used to be a radio producer and a rock musician. But it is really worth me using it because I never have bad sound quality in my meetings. Once I plug it into my computer I can forget all about it.

The big brand names of the people who make these things are Tascam and Zoom, but Amazon has the Chinese knock offs from about £20. I have no idea if they are any good or not.

The really good thing about using dedicated sound recorders is that they do the job of processing the sound signals instead of your computer. The benefits of that are:

1. Your computer does not have to process the sound as well as doing everything else - so it reduces the risk of getting that nasty

digital distortion sound.

2. The signal that the sound device passes over to your computer is of a much higher quality than you would otherwise get, so your listeners ears and brains don't have to work so hard in meetings, which actually does a lot to help their understanding, especially towards the end of the day.

3. These devices have excellent, 'uni-directional[141]' (pick up sound from one direction) microphones which not only pick up your voice better, but they largely ignore background sounds, like dogs barking and aeroplanes flying overhead. If you prefer, you can also plug in a **'lavalier'** microphone (one of those 'tie-pin' microphones, like they use on TV stations).

4. They also allow you to wear real headphones, which produce much higher quality sound across the whole spectrum than the tinny sound you get from ear buds. Headphones are also more comfortable to wear than ear buds for extended periods. (Yes, I know they look a little silly but you can always pretend you are channelling your inner radio DJ.)

Seriously though, I have a client who is the Chief Executive of a company that has hundreds of different sites. During the lockdowns, he had been doing video calls for up to seven hours a day trying to keep in touch with all the managers.

When he was using ear buds, rubbish microphones and the sound that was like an old-style AM radio, he was so drained at the end of the working day that he was barely able to hold a conversation with his family after work. These tips helped. They didn't cure the problem - because the only cure would be to stop doing so many video meetings - but they helped.

* * *

---

[141] They only pick up sound from the direction they are pointing, unlike the 'omni-directional' type of microphones on your computers which pick up sound from all around your computer.

A Quarter Of Video Is Light?

Lights: Put Two In Front Of You And One Behind - (And Buy Some White Paper Chinese Ball-Type Lampshades)

Amateur photographers spend **fortunes** on their cameras. They always have to have the latest, greatest gear. But professional photographers and videographers do not buy the latest equipment. They often use cameras and video cameras which are relatively modest. But professionals often spend *really big money* on the lighting. *Why?*

One, simple reason. Great lighting can make a very modest camera take astounding pictures. But in poor light, even a fantastically expensive camera will always take awful pictures. When it comes to the quality of the image, it's all about the amount of light.

All cameras and video cameras are terrible in poor light in comparison to what the human eye can do. It is easy to think that what you are seeing with your eyes is what your camera is seeing. But it isn't.

Unfortunately, what you perceive as good light and what a camera thinks is good light are very different things. Your eyes may be telling you that you have lots of light and that everything looks great, but your camera will still take poor pictures.

Cameras really don't deal well with shadows, and in a home office ther will be *lots* of shadows. Worse, what the camera thinks is a shadow may be what you consider to be moderately well lit. There is a very good reason why professional videographers constantly walk around with a light meter in their hands when they are shooting.

So, if we want to look good, we need to supply lots of light. It also needs to be diffused[142] light, otherwise it can make everything look

---

[142] softened by passing through a screen or a lampshade

too harsh, and there needs to be more of it than you might think.

Actually, the cheapest way to add great light is to use two simple table lamps with white light bulbs and cover them with Chinese paper lanterns. Place the lights in front of you, out of sight of your camera, both diagonally at 45 degrees either side of your face and about a metre away from you. The difference in quality of your video image will be amazing even if you are using the inbuilt video camera. There you go: film star light for about £25.

"Yes, but I am not on TV and I don't what to be a TV personality, so why do I need to pretend like I am some kind of awful, reality TV wannabe?"

It's a good question: and the answer is that in a fair world, your dazzling, deep, incredibly intelligent and perceptive points really, really should stand alone, on their own two feet and transcend your appearance.

Unfortunately, they just *won't*. It *is* unjust, it is unfair, but it just is.

But the upshot is that you don't have to look like a film star, you just have to stop looking like you live your life as an homage to "The Godfather.[143]" The great thing is, you can do just that by avoiding the ghastly mistakes that others are making.

So, turn the lights on.

Lighting For Video: A Crib Sheet

* * *

---

[143] A brand new way of processing film was developed in order to get that honey-coloured, grainy, sepia tone that was used throughout "The Godfather," trilogy.

"Two In Front. One Behind."

Use <u>white</u> lights. Camera shops call these 'full-spectrum' light bulbs, in other words, white lightbulbs. White lightbulbs are about £20 cheaper to buy than full-spectrum lightbulbs. You do the maths. I did. I bought white bulbs.

Use a plain, white, or light-coloured background or a plain, dark coloured background behind you. White is really good. Personally, I use white.

You will probably need to soften the lights you have. One of the cheapest ways to do this is to use two white paper Chinese lanterns. They do a great job of diffusing harsh light from bulbs.

It's Not Actually Mandatory That You Must Have A Bookcase Behind You.

Yes, I know that it has become a convention to have a bookcase behind us on Zoom calls to show how well-read we are but that gives us problems:

1. Books are distracting. We want our audience to concentrate and focus solely on our face. Why? Because up to 70% of all human communication is non-verbal. The more they concentrate on your face, the greater chance they have of picking up that non-verbal communication and understand you better.

2. Book spines are dark, so leech out lots of the light that you have just spent money on adding.

3. Having lots of images behind us means that our video cameras have to work harder than if they have a plain background. This can result in that jittery and pixelated video that you often see.

4. Books are distracting - instead of listening to you they will be looking past you and over your shoulders trying to read your book

titles - and trust me, they are judging you while they do. You do not want your audience's attention to be distracted by your literary tastes (or lack of). If you have left that dog-eared copy of "Ninja Vixens" on your shelves, you will deserve what you get.

Don't Get Bookcase Envy - Plain Walls Are Fine

It is okay to use a plain, boring wall behind you instead.

Plain walls are fine, and actually more effective. Lined or striped wallpaper can also make your camera do weird things to your image so you might want to put an old, white or light sheet behind you if you have stripy wallpaper.

Similarly, don't wear a striped or spotty, or paisley pattern shirt or blouse. (They really send digital cameras absolutely bonkers).

One Behind You:

Put a white light to shine on your background behind you to add a '3-D depth of field.' On video, your people are looking at you through a two-dimensional screen where everything appears flatter than it is in reality. This is visually odd and again, makes your audiences' brains work harder than they need on non-essential things. This cuts their attention span.

Film and TV producers have been using this shallow depth of field technique since around 1910. None of us alive today have ever not seen this. In fact, we are so used to it we don't even notice it but we do notice it's absence. If you put a light behind your head, you will be taking advantage of over 100 years of visual language and culture - and that will make you look good.

Two In Front:

Put twice as much light in front of you (at about 45 degrees to right and left) as there is behind you. Cameras love light, although you may think that you are putting in too much light, it is highly unlikely.

If you really feel the need to buy proper camera-ready lights, Amazon sells lights and light boxes from companies like Neewer from about £25. These come with all the stands, the bulbs, the reflective light boxes and the diffusing gauzes, too. Although they are not as fashionable as Light Emitting Diode (LED) lights, the fluorescent light kits (again, complete with all the stands and gauzes) are much, much cheaper than LED lights. They also produce a much softer light (if you're over 40 this is a kindness for your viewers and a really good thing) and there is hardly any difference between the two types in power consumption or heat generation.

Trying To Compete With Sunlight - You Can't.

As long as you are a lighting professional, have lots of reflectors and really, really, really know how to use it, overhead sunlight, or sunlight from behind the camera is the very best light there is. Film companies love it and it is one of the reasons the film industry moved to Hollywood.

Artificial light can never compete with sunlight. Real sunlight will always overwhelm artificial lights.

Unfortunately, most cameras hate *direct* sunlight looking directly into the camera lens. Direct sunlight also really mucks about with the contrast of the picture and can make you look *really* washed out. You are probably better off controlling your lighting environment by keeping out of direct sunlight and using your white lights instead.

And The Very Last Thing You Ever Need To Buy…

(And a tripod…)

* * *

Tripods - A Video Nerds Best Friend.

Video pictures where the camera is moving around a great deal can actually make your viewers feel travel sick. The steadier the camera - the steadier the picture - the steadier your viewer's attention.

A cheap tripod will hold your camera steady. Using tripods is one of the cheapest ways of raising the 'production values' of your video conferences. Again, Amazon is your friend here, but eBay can be good too. - Specialist camera shops charge eye-watering amounts of money, for features you probably won't use.

And if you want to make your own video productions...

Eventually, you may well want to get into making things such as training videos for your team or your clients, or even advertisements for your social media presence. Ten years ago, this sort of capability would have cost hundreds of thousands of pounds. Now you can build yourself a complete film production solution for a few hundreds of pounds.

If you are planning to go down this route things start to get a bit more expensive (and a lot more complicated) but, on the plus side, the results really can be as good as a real TV station. There are three parts to this. You will need:

1. **Video camera(s)**: Okay, once you get into this territory, these actually need to be good (which means pricey).

2. **Digital Video Capture Box**: you must use one of these in order to get the signal from the video camera and into your computer (you can't just plug a video camera straight into a computer and get great results). These are about £60 - £300.

3. **Video Production 'Switcher' Software:** - such as **Ecamm** (Mac) or **OBS** (Mac or PC, and open source, so free,) or "**Mmhhmm**[144]."

---

[144] This really is the name of the software - brilliant, isn't it?

Switcher software gives you all the capabilities of a professional TV studio, including multiple cameras and backdrops. Of the three, **Ecamm** and **Mmhhmm** are definitely the easier to use. I use **OBS**, but I have been using this sort of software for years and I like doing video.

1.   Video Cameras:

The quality of a camera lens is really important. External video cameras, like the ones you plug directly into your computer, have buckets of clever electronics but sadly, most have quite average lenses. Camcorders, on the other hand, normally have brilliant lenses and they are also able to record sound brilliantly too. That means you can plug a good lavalier microphone straight into them so you don't have to worry about a buying a separate sound recorder. Personally, I would always choose to use a great camcorder over a dedicated computer video camera.

Although 4k (and even 6k) is all the rage as I write, all a 4k video will do is pick up *all* the imperfections in your surroundings and they will show EVERY imperfection and wrinkle on your face. If your team are under 21 then this will not be a problem, but if the team are more 'mature,' like me, then it can seem to your millennial audiene that they are watching a Freddy Kruger horror movie.

4k cameras can also generate a *huge* video signal which can quickly overwhelm your internet connection unless it is brilliantly quick. Although the picture may seem fine to you, the digital distortion that your colleagues get to see on their screens can make your picture appear pixelated, can produce buffering, or even freeze entirely.

Which is why I use the older technology 'HD' (1080p) cameras which will give you a much softer look and feel to your video images and the signal they produce will be a lot smaller than the 4k camera, so it is unlikely to overburden the video platform or your internet bandwidth.

Also, because no-one wants the 'old' HD format, even high branded (like Panasonic and Sony) cameras are really cheap.

* * *

But before you invest any money in this, remember that you will get a much bigger return on any investment by upgrading your sound and improving your light *first*.

2.   *Digital Video Capture Boxes:*

The size of the video electronic signal coming out of the back of a video camera is HUGE. Before it gets to your computer, it needs to be controlled by passing it through a digital capture box and then passed onto the computer. I use a BlackMagic Design Ultra Studio digital box, but then, I am a geek.

There are lots of other manufacturers, and prices start at about £60 for a single camera input. Boxes that can capture and switch between multiple cameras go upwards of a few hundred pounds. It may sound pricey, but if you buy one of these, then you have become your own television production company.

3.   *Video Production 'Switcher' Software:*

Want to handle multiple video cameras, have your logo appear on screen, show slideshows as well as they do on the TV and output your content out live to YouTube, FaceBook, Rumble or next week's latest social media thing?

Well, you will need some 'switcher' software, which is a television production studio that you run from your computer. If your ambition is to create video adverts or YouTube content then this is for you.

I use OBS, which is open source, free and brilliant but is probably not for beginners. I have also used Ecamm, which is excellent and also easy to use. As I write this it is $20 a month. I also love the brilliantly name "mmhhmm," which is around $10 a month.

As ever, there are a million YouTube tutorials on how to use all three.

* * *

Making An Online Digital Office To Become A Digital Nomad - A Crib Sheet

(Because this is a crib sheet, some information will be repeated from elsewhere in the book)

Sound (And Video):

Strangely, and maddeningly, as I have said time and again, half of the perceived quality of any video communication is actually due to the quality of the sound. That probably makes no sense, nevertheless, it is true.

People will put up with appallingly bad video quality as long as the sound is acceptable but they will rapidly get distracted or even stop listening completely if the picture is brilliant, but the sound quality is bad.

When we are working online that presents us with a problem: the sound systems on computers are mostly awful. Worse, most microphones on computers really aren't actually very good at all.

Most inbuilt onboard microphones only pick up a small portion of the richness of the human voice. Secondly, these microphones are designed to be 'omni-directional,' which means they pick up sounds from 360 degrees around the computer rather than from the one direction where your voice is. This means that the sound of your voice can easily become polluted with the sounds of noisy neighbours, dogs, aeroplanes or what have you.

Worse, the integrated circuits inside your computer, that convert your voice into digital signals, are also abysmal. They also put quite a strain on our computer while they are working.

So What Can We Do?

* * *

Well, the first thing we can do is use external microphones that plug into our computer. This will give much better results than just using the onboard microphone, so that is a plus. These can be bought from around £15. Personally, for microphones, I use Rode equipment. Rode is an Australian company, they make brilliant gear and no, I am not getting paid to say so.

Although using a microphone is a great first step, unfortunately, we will still be sending the sound to your computer to process. Now your computer is already working very hard if you are doing a Zoom or a Teams call. The strain on your computer's resources may make it cut out your voice or give us digital distortion, which sounds horrible and harms peoples' concentration.

To cure that we can add a dedicated sound recorder (like the picture below). Although the branded devices from people like Zoom and Tascam are pretty expensive, the unbranded ones start from about £20.

The Bronze Level: Just Additional Sound.

This is my basic sound recording kit. I am not recommending that you buy it, but it is what I actually use. Everything fits into that little bag on the right and it means that as long as I have my MacBook with me, as long as I use the onboard camera, I can work from anywhere.

* * *

Figure 67   A Zoom H4 Sound Recorder, A USB Cable, A Carrying Case And Two 'Dead Cat,' Wind Noise Protectors. The Steel Rules Are 25 cm Long To Give You A Sense Of Size.

What Are The Benefits?

1. Sound quality - you and your team will have better sound quality than using the inbuilt onboard systems on your computers.

2. Light and Portable- it all fits into a 20 cm by 10 cm bag

3. Ease - everything just plugs right in and you are ready.

4. Recording - You can keep a separate recording of all the sound recordings you make.

5. No feedback noise: the 'uni-directional' (which means it picks sound from just one direction) microphone just picks up your voice and, because it is pointed away from the speaker, will not induce that horrible feedback loop that plagues so many video calls.

Sound Recorders process the sound itself and then pass over the processed digital signal to your computer. This takes a lot of strain off your computer and stops it from having to do that job at the same time that it is doing everything else. This really relieves the strain on your computer. This gives two benefits.

1. Firstly, the sound quality will be immensely better, so your online communications will be superior to those who will not be doing this.

2. You will be safeguarding your meetings from the distraction and interruptions of digital sound distortion. People will put up with video freezing but bad sound really has a negative impact on any meeting.

Try and use headphones rather than earbuds for your online meetings. Earbuds are convenient but they are definitely *not* high-fidelity sound quality. They produce very little in the middle and bass frequencies, and your brain finds this very stressful. Ear buds are also a lot more uncomfortable than headphones when worn for any length of time (try wearing them for an hour and then taking them off - the relief is amazing) - and this also puts negative stress your body.

Of course, headphones themselves are also an artificial environment, so they should not be worn all day. My limit has always been about two hours, even when I was wearing them every day when presenting radio programmes.

If your people live in a noisy environment, then there is a brilliant app called "**Krisp**" which can reside on your computer.

Krisp cuts out background noises from neighbours and noisy dogs. I had someone who worked for me who lived in an apartment in a block of flats in Barcelona. Knowing that the neighbour's noisy children and barking dogs could no longer be heard in her meetings *transformed* her online confidence. This application is about £5 a month per user. It is a bargain for those that need it.

However, the very *best* thing to do is to always pass your sound through a sound recorder before it gets to your computer. Sound recorders do the sound processing rather than your computer/tablet. Sound recorders also have uni-directional microphones rather than omnidirectional microphones such as iPads and laptops have. Zoom and Tascam are the names that I know amongst the brands.

The "Silver" Standard:

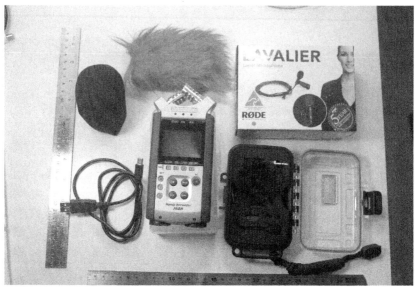

Figure 68 Zoom H4 Sound Recorder, A Rode Lavalier Microphone, The Carrying Case, A USB Cable To Connect To The Computer, and Two 'Dead Cat,' Wind Noise Protectors.

To be clear, you don't *really* need to add a lavalier microphone. If you have a sound recorder you already have superior sound equipment to 99% of all online users. However, a lavalier microphone really can make a big difference to the sound quality, and really do take it to the next level. By the way, the lavalier microphone plugs into the sound recorder, not into your computer.

Just as the sound recorder has a set of 'dead cat' covers (the fluffy things in the picture above), the lavalier microphone will have a miniature dead cat, too. For sound recorders, you don't really need them unless you are outside. However, for lavaier microphones, you really should use them all the time because they can pick up the rustling sounds from your clothing.

When you put one on, just make sure that you attach it firmly to your shirt and don't let your jumper or any jewellery rub against them, because they will pick that sound up and make it sound like you are in a force nine gale.

The "Gold" Standard

Figure 69 Sony HD Camcorder, Zoom H4 Sound Recorder, A Rode Lavalier Microphone, A Carrying Case, A USB Cable To Connect To Your Computer, And Two 'Dead Cat,' Wind Noise Protectors.

Video Cameras:

As you can see, I use a high-definition Sony that is simply _years_ old. It is still brilliant: it is simple to use, just works and produces great video. Even better, it captures sound as well and I can plug a lavalier microphone directly into it.

You want to use video over just using audio because you want your audience to pick up as much non-verbal communication as they possibly can. Remember, 60% of human communication is non-verbal. Picking up on the non-verbal cues makes for a richer environment when communicating online.

* * *

People really do get a lot of emotional cues and clues from the raised eyebrows, the eloquent sniffs, and the pursed lips that happen automatically when people are communicatiing face to face. You want to supply as much of that as you can when they are in an online environment.

Keeping attention on your face is very important for the following reasons:

Although we are often not conscious of it, when we step into the worlds of television, video and cinema, we step into a world that has a rich visual language that we may not be conscious of, but we are all familiar with.

We want to take advantage of that visual language and cultural heritage that has been built up. Cinematographers spend eye watering amounts of money in getting what they call a "**shallow depth of field.**" This is where only the subject's face is in focus and everything in the background is subtly out of focus.

If, for example, you have a load of books behind you then you are going against that whole tradition. Your people won't be able to help themselves but try to read the titles behind you to try and guess what kind of person you truly are. You want to avoid that. After all, we are at work: we wish our colleagues to concentrate on working rather than trying to discover whether that book behind your ear is "The Gulag Archipelago," or "Fifty Shades of Grey."

I know that under lockdown Zoom has developed a visual vocabulary such as having bookshelves behind you but actually it's nonsense. Be different, use a plain wall.

Finally, something that you may not have considered. That video-screen that people are watching you on, is flat and two-dimensional. Of course, we obviously live in a three-dimensional world. If we can do something our side of the camera to emphasise a 3D effect, we create a sense of depth in our video and that will make everything look a lot more natural.

* * *

We can do this by putting a light behind us in order to light the background up. Point it away from you towards your background or backdrop. The lighter the background you use, the better the sense of depth you will get.

Look, you don't *really* need all of this stuff to begin with. Even the cheapest camcorders will cost hundreds of pounds for each for the team and frankly, you are better off buying some cheap lights, some white paper Chinese lanterns and getting them to use their computer's inbuilt video cameras. Even buying dedicated video lights will only cost you around £30-£40 per person in your team.

Camcorders and the other gear you need to make them work definitely come under the nice to have category rather than the need to have category. Remember that you will also need to buy a digital recorder box and choose and learn some switcher software, but when you have them you will definitely be in the big league.

How can I justify it? Well, I use them in order to do my training videos and also to talk with existing and prospective clients. Prospective clients are always impressed that when they talk with us we look and sound like we are in a TV studio. That is pretty special in any industry but is unique in ours.

If you do spend the money, you will soon find it makes a *real* difference to your online events.

————

Scrumnastics - Join Us

If you would like to see more handy videos, why not join the Scrumnastics mailing list? I post videos regularly on Youtube, FaceBook and the Locals platform.

Who knows what platforms we will all be using next year? If you join the mailing list you can be sure I will email you the latest links to the latest videos with on the latest platforms.

You can sign up to the Scrumnastics mailing list at scrumnastics.co.uk

COURSE FIVE: BONUS MINI COURSE: KANBAN AND KANBAN...

Introduction To Kanban and kanban

This is meant as a short-ish bonus course within the book, meant to give you a 'taster' for another popular management framework. Why? Because knowing another system will make you a more skilled and so a better manager.

I will also give you some links and recommendations to encourage you to find out more if you wish to . We are going to have a look at a management framework called Kanban ("Kanban Methods,") and also how it differs from traditional kanban ("kanban systems").

Most Of This Book Has Been About Scrum. So Why Would You Want To Know About *Another* Management Framework?

For the professional manager, there are lots of different environments and situations in your organisation that you may need to manage. Different situations require different management tools. Sometimes you may be cautiously pushing forward into new and strange territory, so you need a system where you can pay close attention to how things are going. As we know, Scrum is really good at helping you with that.

But at other times you may be managing a mature product or service which has already found its market and is selling well. In this happy situation you may be constrained by how much of the demand you can supply. Although you _can_ use a framework like Scrum for this you are probably better off using something else.

* * *

Just as a handyman uses different tools if they are doing woodwork or plumbing, professional managers need different tools for different management environments.

Broadly, we can split our management needs up into two different types of management tools: *Push* **Systems** and *Pull* **Systems**.

1.   **Push Systems**. This is the situation where you are cautiously 'pushing' towards an as yet uncertain future by exploring and finding a way forward. Scrum does this well.

Whether you are developing of a completely new product, or doing a business transformation or project, Scrum will suit you fine.

Whenever you start out and you are doing something where you:

1. Cannot be certain whether you can successfully create the thing.
2. Once you *have* created it you have no idea whether there will be a demand for the thing.

In these situations you need a good way of managing time, risk, teams and money to maximise their effects and make sure nothing is wasted.

Frameworks such as **Scrum** fit this situation very well. Because they employ the age-old "**Plan, Do, Check, Act,**" cycle they help you mitigate all your risks.

2.   **Pull Systems**. Pull systems are more appropriate when are in a more mature environment where (say,) you already have a product or service that you can offer. You already know there is a demand for the product or service and you are in a steady state of producing and supplying it.

However, your ability to produce and supply more of it is constrained by the resources you have. You need to make the very best use of those resources so that you can maximise them. Think of a factory with a production line, or a product support department. The different situation requires a different kind of management framework.

* * *

I know we haven't distinguished the differences between them yet, but Kanban and kanban are _both_ pull management frameworks.

Unfortunately, We Have Kanban *And* kanban. However, The Common Theme That Connects Them Is 'Flow.'

What Is The Difference Between kanban and Kanban?

1. **kanban**. (spelled with a lower case "k") Is the original one. It is often referred to as *kanban system*. It forms a core part of Toyota's Just-in-Time production system, which is itself part of the wider **Toyota Production System**. This whole system was mainly developed by one of their chief engineers, Taiichi Ohno in the 1950s and the 1960s. To try and help distinguish it, this original method is often called the "<u>kanban system</u>."

Incidentally, a kanban is a Japanese word meaning an indicator, or some kind of signal. The presence of this signal means that something should *now* happen, or something *has* happened.

Some books say that a kanban is a card but that's not *quite* right. A kanban can be a card, a light, or anything that can give a signal. We are actually so used to them in our everyday lives that we are unawhere of them.

If you look at the back cover of this book you will see it has a computerised bar code, called an International Standard Book Number (ISBN) which can be used to provide all sorts of signals. It can signal to the printer that it is the correct book to print, to the shipper to make sure they pick and transport the right book and the picker to make sure they send the book to you.

A similar bar code is printed onto the packaging of just about everything you buy at the shops, especially at the supermarket. That barcode (or kanban), is the reason you can serve yourself at those grim terminals. But when you scan that code, it not only adds the price to your bill but also tells the stock taking system that it has one less of those, how long it has been on the shelves and a host of other things. In other words, a kanban can provide all sorts of signals.

At Toyota, kanbans are one of many management tools they have developed over many decades that all combine to allow them to do '*Just in Time*' manufacturing. They have been so successful within Toyota that virtually every other manufacturer has adopted them and kanbans are now used throughout the world of production engineering.

Now we know a little about the older of the two systems, we can learn more about the newer one. However, before we do I have to tell you that this is the one I prefer. Why? Because it has excellent tools to help you drive out waste in your working procedures. These are called "**Muda**," "**Mura**," and "**Muri**," and we will meet them shortly.

2.   **Kanban**. This comes from David J. Anderson's 2007 book, "**Kanban**." This   Kanban (with a capital "K"), springs from the software industry. Software management consultants now refer to this one as the "**Kanban methods** ."

Kanban Methods: David J. Anderson

David J. Anderson successfully managed teams using Agile software development projects at Sprint, Motorola, Microsoft, and Corbis.

David Anderson is obviously a really talented and successful manager, and I believe his book is excellent. He is obviously very talented and is a really big deal in the software world. His book has spawned a whole sub-industry of software project management.

If you are working in software development then this is a book for your management library, but be careful when you talk about to the wider audience of managers from other industries, especially production engineers.

So, What Is This Kanban With A Capital 'K,' Then?

Kanban stands for Kanban Methods, it formally arrived in 2007, unlike kanban systems, which was developed over decades beginning in the 1950s in Japan. Kanban (with a capital 'K') is used widely in the software industry, rather than production. Ther is quite a lot of evidence to say that, just like Scrum, it is also emerging into the wider world.

The 'Principles And Practices'

Kanban Methods has principles and practices. There are two broad different principles (which break down into sub-principles) and six different practices. Let's have a look at them.

The two principles divide work into:

1. **Change Management Principles**

2. **Service Delivery Principles**

1. The Change Management Principles

These are how you change and improve your ways of working. There are three sub-principles within this group. They are:

Principle 1: **"Start With What You Do Now."**

You don't have to 'clear the decks' of any existing workflows or management systems you have in place in order to start with Kanban Methods. You just add it in on top of what you already have. I think this is probably the biggest reason why it is so appealing.

Principle 2: **"Agree To Pursue Incremental, Evolutionary Change."**

There are no 'big bang' initiatives in Kanban Methods. It is evolutionary not revolutionary. You proceed by taking baby steps and see whether they work.

Principle 3: **"Encourage Acts Of Leadership At All Levels."**

The assumption is that everyone has the potential to be a leader. Therefore leadership should be encouraged, even in the lowliest members of the team.

2. The Service Delivery Principles

There are also three sub-principles for Service Delivery.

Principle 1: **"Focus On Customer's Needs And Expectations."**

You deliver value by concentrating on what the customer values. If the customer values what you have produced it is likely they will buy it. Easy enough, but of course, this also means *not* doing things that the customer does *not* value and so reduce your costs by not doing them. As we will see for companies like Toyota, this is the key pathway to making or managing a successful product or service.

Principle 2: **"Manage The Work."**

You encourage your people's abilities to self organise how they do their work. In doing so you diminish the amount of (often irrelevant or wasteful) 'busy work' that comes when they are being micro-managed.

Principle 3: **"Regularly Review The Network Of Services."**

Just because you have built a way of managing things, doesn't mean it is over. Building a successful culture of service delivery requires a lot of adjustment over time so be prepared for putting in review procedures in order to continually improve.

The Kanban Practices

1. "Visualise The Workflow."

The easiest way to do this is to use a Kanban board. What is a Kanban board? Remember the Product Backlog and the Sprint Backlog that we did in the Scrumnastics course earlier on? Those are really Kanban boards. You have already seen them.

The traditional names of the workflow states in Kanban are "Requested," "In-Progress," and "Done," which are not so very different to what we used in the Sprint Backlog, are they?

There is a separate section on Kanban boards later on.

2. "Limit Work In Progress."

What is a Work in Progress limit? It is the number of items that you can produce when working at full capacity in that team or department or work station. If it takes a person a whole day to produce a thing and you have five people working there then your Work in Progress limit is five. If you want to produce more then you either have to get more people to do it or you have to re-evaluate how you are producing the thing. If your demand is for five things a day then that is fine. If, however, your demand suddenly rises to ten then the only realistic way to quickly meet that demand is to get more people.

Work in Progress limits are core to Kanban and if you don't put Work in Progress limits you really aren't doing Kanban - you are pretending.

3. "Manage Flow."

Flow is how the work moves through your various procedures from raw material or request to finished product or service.

* * *

Don't concentrate on the managing the people. Instead, concentrate on visualising how the work moves. Once you get practiced at this, it is uncanny how wasteful some of your procedures will appear. This is a great antidote to "but we've always done it like this."

4. "Make Process Policies Explicit."

Your people work with and within your work processes every day. But if your people can't understand your processes, how can they hope to improve them? It is a LOT cheaper to get your own people to improve your processes as you go along than it is to get a consultant in, but they need to be able to understand them, That's your job. So no 'management speak,' just plain old English will do just fine.

This is a great antidote to old-style "mushroom management[145]."

5. "Feedback Loops."

Those who work in potentially life-threatening situations all seem to have one thing in common: when the task is finished they have to do a debriefing session to say what went well, what could have gone better and what went wrong and why. A debriefing session is an example of a feedback loop.

If you want to progress, feedback loops are the most effective way there is to do that.

Kanban method's word for a feedback loop is a 'cadence.'They exist at various levels: such as team level, and service delivery level.

The team level cadence is where members of the team meet up in front of the Kanban board and tell each other what they were working on yesterday, and what they will be working on today. Remember the Daily Scrum in the Scrumnastics section? It is similar to that.

The second level of feedback loop, or cadence, is at the Service

---

[145] Keep your people in the dark and bury them up to their necks in manure…

Delivery level. You can have them for risk, actual service delivery and operations or whatever you need in your environment.

6. **"Improve Collaboratively (Using Models & The Scientific Method)."**

This is a complicated way of saying that the basis for progress is through trial and error and that real life evidence beats the eminence of experts.

While it is true that it is the only realistic way of proceeding, don't underestimate just how difficult this can be to implement, especially if you have a lot of high-status experts in your organisation.

Kanban Boards

John Anderson's colleague, David Davis, was the first person to come up with the idea that your workflow should be placed on some kind of white board. As well as flow, Kanban boards are one of the stand out features of the framework. Kanban boards are made up of cards, columns, work in progress limits, and swimlanes.

Kanban Cards

Just like in a Sprint Backlog, jobs appear as cards. Each card contains information about the task and its status, such as a description, when it has to be done by, who has been assigned the job, etc.

Kanban Columns

The Kanban board is split up into the columns of the workflow. Unlike Scrum, where the column headings say things like "**Accepted**," "**Working**," "**Done**," and "**Done Done**," in Kanban the columns headings say "**Requested**", "**In Progress**" and "**Done.**" Just like a

Sprint Backlog, the cards go from left to right until they are completed.

Work In Progress Limits

This is one of the two **big** differences between a Sprint Backlog and a Kanban board. These are the *maximum* capacities that you can cope with. If the your capacity limit says three widgets then you can only accept three widgets, and not five. Your capacity is your work. Work In Progress (WIP) limits can be quite sophisticated in that they can be different numbers for different stages of work. Of course, to get this to work properly you *must* be in a situation to know what these physical limits actually are.

Kanban Swimlanes

This is the other big difference between a Sprint Backlog and a Kanban board. It may be that you are managing a range of different activities, or teams or services. How do you accomodate these potentially very different things and still keep them on the one board? You use swimlanes. Swimlanes are horizontal lanes that you place on the board to split out the various themes that you are managing so that each theme lies underneath the one above. Why do you do it? So that each of the swimlanes can be measured as they pass through the "**Requested**," **In Progress**," and "**Done**" stages of workflow.

Although a simple Kanban board may look similar to a Sprint Backlog, by the time you get to adding in swimlanes they get a lot more complex than a Sprint Backlog, and you will need to use dedicated Kanban board software.

When Should You Consider Kanban Style Management?

As we know, the difference between Scrum and Kanban is that

Scrum uses a Sprint and Kanban uses the limits on **Work-in-Progress** in order to measure progress.

When the situation is right, I will use both management frameworks but when I do, I *ALWAYS* start off with **Scrum** and then move to **Kanban**. Why?

1. Scrum Is More 'Rigid,' And When Appropriate, That Is A Good Thing

When I am setting up a new team, (especially a team that will be working remotely,) I find that the team has so much to learn and pick up that members appreciate working within the simple but strong rules of Scrum to begin with, especially if the team members begin as strangers. Once the team has gone through quite a few Sprints together, they will establish their own team spirit and will have established trust between themselves. This often becomes self-perpetuating, so the initial need for all that rigidity goes away.

2. The Conundrum Of The 'Work-in-Progress' Limits

Question: When you are starting out with a new team, how do you know what the work capacity of your team will be? **Answer**: *You don't*. You will be estimating, in other words, guessing. The whole basis for choosing any numbers will probably be based on the old "If it takes a man two hours to dig a hole, how many…" saw. Your numbers will be optimistic or pessimistic, but they will almost certainly be wrong. Both of these eventualities are very demotivating and they will make you look like a foolish manager in the eyes of your team.

When you use Scrum, the **Sprint**, the refining of the **Product Backlog**, the **Sprint Backlog** and the 'Deming cycle' **Scrum Events** that allow a team to "Plan, Do, Check, Act," will let the **natural velocity of the work in progress** emerge over a number of Sprints. Once you know that natural velocity, you know the Work-in-Progress Limits and you can procede to a Kanban method.

* * *

On A General Note, You Could Also Use The Following To Decide

1. You are looking at 'pull work.' Pull work is work that is led by existing demand, rather than 'push work,' where you are driving into the future without an exact blueprint of where you will end up.

2. There is a finite, fixed capacity and you need to eliminate the bottlenecks in production in order to attempt to gain greater capacity.

3. You have a mature work environment where there are defined controls and processes that staff must follow in order to produce the work.

4. You are doing regulated work - where you are working in some type of Government based - or one step removed, pseudo-Government based (such as a QUANGO[146]) environment (like Law, Accountancy or Finance)

5. You need to work more efficiently and eliminate waste. This becomes more important as your delivery matures over time. What does a factory do over time? It shaves costs. What does a service based company do to remain competitive? It shaves costs. See the "**Flow And The Three Wastes**" section that follows.

Kanban and Scrum: The

---

[146] A QUANGO is an American political term and stands for "**Qua**si-**N**on-**G**overnmental **O**rganisation." This is where a third party stands in to do government work. In Britain it is probably more accurate to call them "QUAGO"s, as most are definitely closer to government. Think Social Work England, which runs and maintains the register of social workers in England.

Differences

Kanban	Scrum
No prescribed roles as such	Pre-defined roles of Scrum Master, Product Owner and developer (team member)
Continuous Delivery	Time boxed (regular length) sprints
Work is pulled through the system (single piece flow)	Work is pulled through the system in batches (the sprint backlog)
Changes can be made at any time	No changes allowed mid-sprint (unless all work in the Sprint backlog has been completed)
Cycle time (Kanban word for work rate)	Velocity (Scrum word for work rate)
More appropriate in operational environments with a high degree of variability in priority	More appropriate in situations where work can be prioritized in batches that can be left alone

Table 2 Differences Between Scrum And Kanban

You will probably notice from the table above that one of the characteristics of Kanban is 'single piece flow,' rather than batch work. This core concept of producing one thing at a time (or 'flow,') rather than in batches is very important in Kanban and is used as a key tool to eliminate wasteful work. In true kanban (Toyota), batch work is seen as extremely wasteful, even in white collar environments, such as finance, accountancy and law.

Although we don't have room for this here, there are some brilliant management books on Lean Thinking and the Toyota Way that I recommend in the "**Best Books On Management**" section which is at the end of this book. These books really do this justice.

When To Use Scrum, When To Use Kanban?

As I said above, I use Scrum to create, build and implement _new_ initiatives, especially with new teams, but when the processes have been developed and are robust and mature, I move to kanban.

Why?

Once the working procedures and processes are in place, it is unlikely you will need the Scrum structures. These manage time, budget, work and the future. However, your newly worked out processes are meant to do just that. To keep both the Scrum _AND_ the new processes is just duplication and wasteful.

Kanban is great when the processes _are_ implemented and demand is fluid. We can now concentrate on making those processes more efficient and eliminate waste in the system. In fact, there is a whole sub-industry of management consultancy focussed on how to reduce waste in white-collar working environments.

There will always be room for both approaches. Even in the software industry in these days of '**Dev Ops**,' many software companies still make a distinction between '**Dev**' (Development) and '**Ops**' (Operations). Similarly, many companies make the distinction between **projects** (change) and **operations**.

Toyota's kanban

As we know, Kanban is Japanese for some kind of signal that shows a change in status of a thing. Many are simply cards that represent 'something' should, or is ready to, happen.

Taiichi Ohno, Toyota's most famous and renowned engineer, developed the kanban system at Toyota (the Japanese car manufacturer). They came up with the idea from studying how supermarkets kept their shelves stocked in the 1950s and 1960s. Toyota wanted to apply the idea to efficiently hold parts for their car manufacturing in their factories.

The idea of a kanban is a core part of the Toyota Production System, which is what Toyota themselves hold to be the one thing that allowed them to become the largest car manufacturer in the world. For Toyota, it is not the cars that matter, it is the _way_ you build the cars that matters.

Actually, although the kanban system was developed in studying supermarkets, there were other influences such as by the Japanese admiration for the way that Spitfires were manufactured in the United Kingdom during the Second World War. (A system known as the 'two bin system,' more below).

Not All kanbans (small 'k') Are Japanese, Or That New.

During World War 2, the British designed and manufactured a brilliant fighter plane called the Spitfire, which helped them survive the Battle of Britain. The Spitfire had amazing performance but it was a nightmare to manufacture.

Britain obviously needed to make them as quickly as possible, so it introduced a system into factories called the "**two-bin**" system. Instead of components being put into one box, the two bin system is where every component was split into two boxes, or bins.

* * *

When the first one became empty, the workers started taking the parts they needed from the second bin and could carry on. The empty bin was a signal for someone whose job it was to replace the empty bin with a full one. This was as much a kanban as anything the Japanese devised.

Back To kanban

In kanban, everything is boiled down to various 'job cards,' which are used to record the various stages that the real job goes through as it is worked on onto completion. Even small components like nuts and bolts can have their own kanban cards. As the product moves through various stages, the changes are recorded on the various kanbans. There is little or no software used in kanban. The kanban system is a very tactile and kinetic system where cards are moved physically and become a 'visual radiators' of progressing work.

There is a heavy emphasis on restricting "Work In Progress," which is the number of items that your team is working on right now. It highlights your team's capacity for work, making you concentrate on smoothing the production flow in order to eliminate bottlenecks and overflows.

There is **_NO multi-tasking_**[147] allowed in true kanban, because it has been shown to be wasteful (the 'Muda,' in Muda, and Muri). Unfortunately, computers, and human beings, cannot actually truly multi-task (they just think that they can)

---

[147] Multi-tasking is where you attempt to do many tasks at once - all badly.

Flow And The Three Wastes: Muda, Mura, And Muri – Why We Should Care About Waste (Even When We Work In An Office)

Whether you are using kanban with a small 'k,' or Kanban with a large 'K,' the core idea you have to keep in mind is *flow*.

Good flow is the sum total of all those things that add *value* to a product or service **that the customer is willing to pay for**. Welding up a bunch of aluminium panels to make the body of a car? That's flow. Why? Because a customer needs to be carried around in their car's attractive, strong, safe body. Painting the car that electric blue colour the customer has specified and has *paid extra* for? Again, that's flow.

How about moving a stack of car doors from one part of a warehouse to another? While it may be essential from the warehouse manager's point of view, it is not a cost that the customer would be willing to pay for because they see no benefit from it. That means it is not flow: it is waste, which is bad flow. **Anything** that you do where there is a cost attached to it but the customer sees little or no benefit from it is a waste.

Anything that comes in the way of flow of the product or service being made is something to be eliminated.

Eliminate more waste from your production while your competitors don't bother and you will become more competitive than them.

Toyota's Production System concentrates really heavily on the constant search for the elimination of waste. Toyota are probably the most admired managers throughout the world so I think we should pay attention to them.

* * *

The wastes Toyota define are:

Muda: the waste of doing futile work.

Mura: the waste from the uneven nature of work (slack on a Monday, busy on a Wednesday, rammed on a Thursday).

Muri: means overburden, **_whether of machines OR people_**. Muri is the reason that I pay so much attention to the Thriving Index in the Sprint Retrospective in Scrum.

Muda (無駄)

Muda means wastefulness, uselessness and futility, which is contradicting addition of Value, the reason why anything is done in the Toyota system.

As we said above, value-added work is a process that adds value to the product or service **_that the customer is willing to pay for._**

If there is no value actually added in a work process, it is considered to be waste, so there is no reason to do it.

There Are Two Types Of Muda, Type 1 and Type 2.

Muda Type 1 includes non-value-added activities in the processes that are necessary for the end customer. For example, inspection and safety testing does not directly add value to the final product; however, they are necessary activities to ensure a safe product for customers. They should be kept but the processes should be made as efficient as possible.

Muda Type 2 includes non-value added activities in the processes, but these activities are unnecessary for the customer. As a result, Muda

Type 2 should be eliminated.

There are seven categories of waste under Muda Type 2 that follow the **_TIMWOOD_** acronym.

The seven wastes are:

Description	What they are:
(1) **T**ransport	excess movement of product
(2) **I**nventory	stocks of goods and raw materials
(3) **M**otion	excess movement of machine or people
(4) **W**aiting	there is little smooth flow between processes
(5) **O**verproduction	local over capacity - making items for stock
(6) **O**ver-processing	making over engineered items
(7) **D**efects	repairing faults in assembly

Mura (斑)

Mura means unevenness, non-uniformity, and irregularity.

Mura is the reason for the existence of any of the seven wastes.

In other words, Mura drives and leads to Muda.

For example, in a manufacturing line, products need to pass through several workstations during the assembly process.

When the capacity of one station is greater than the other stations, you will see an accumulation of waste in the form of overproduction, waiting, etc.

* * *

The goal of a **_Lean_** production system is to level out the workload so that there is no unevenness or waste accumulation.

Mura can be avoided through the 'Just-In-Time' kanban systems and other pull-based strategies that limits overproduction and excess inventory.

The key concept of a Just-In-Time system is delivering and producing the right part, the right amount of the part, and at the right time.

Muri (無理)

Muri means <u>overburden</u>, beyond one's power, excessiveness, impossible or unreasonableness.

Muri can result from Mura (unevenness) and in some cases be caused by excessive removal of Muda (wastefulness) from the process.

Muri also exists when machines or operators are utilized for more than 100% capability to complete a task or in an unsustainable way.

Muri over a period of time can result in employee absenteeism, illness, and breakdowns of machines. When it affects a team things become very expensive

Standardising work can help avoid Muri by designing the work processes to evenly distribute the workload and not overburden any particular employee or equipment.

Muri is the reason that I use the "Thriving Index," in the Sprint Retrospective.

You Mean That's All there Is To Know About Kanban And kanban?

Ummmm,… No, not really.

If I were to try to do complete justice to all things Kanban and kanban then this book would be the best part of a thousand pages long, and it is quite long enough already.

But I *can* give the highlights and point you and your research in the right direction. Even if you don't do any more research, just by reading this section you will know a great deal more thatn many consultants and many consultancies out there who really should know better than they do.

So, what to do? If you want to know more you could do a lot worse than buy **David J. Anderson's** book "**Kanban**." After all, he is the originator of Kanban as it exists within the software and the wider Information Technology environment. There is also a pretty cheap Kindle version of his book which I carry around on my phone so it is always with me.

There's also a great website from the people at "**Kanbanize**" (www.kanbanize.com). Just so you know, the Kanbanize website is a website that sells project management software specifically for the Kanban method. The site also has some excellent Kanban tutorials for you to try. I think Anderson's version of Kanban is great[148], but it is more focussed on the peculiar problems that are found in the software industry, which may not be the same as where you are working. For example, if you are working in a production and manufacturing environment then you may find it completely opposite to your experience of Kanban.

* * *

---

[148] But of course, I am a management geek and this is how I make my living.

But you also need to know more about traditional kanban, as used by people like Toyota, especially to highlight waste so that you can begin the elimination of Muda, Mura and Muri.

In the west, many thinkers split between pull and push systems of management and champion one or the other. But this is false. In Toyota, they use both pull and push at different times and in different situations because they know that they are simply different management tools for different jobs.

When you need a hammer, use a hammer. When you need a drill then use a drill. The clever bit is knowing not to use a drill as a hammer.

That probably sounds as though I am being glib, and I am not. I come across many situations where a team are convinced that they are in steady state production and so are of a mindset that they don't need some kind of Scrum like tool to get things done. However, when they re-examine the products and services being produced, there is often a huge amount of variability. Scrum is better for that kind of thing.

Similarly, there are many companies who are moving from some kind of craft based production (where the product can have a lot of variability) to offering fewer and fewer options so that the can control their production better. These are the people who need to begin to let go of Scrum-like frameworks and move more towards a Kanban like framework.

Scrumnastics - Join Us

If you would like to see more handy videos, why not join the Scrumnastics mailing list? I post videos regularly on Youtube, FaceBook and the Locals platform.

Who knows what platforms we will all be using next year? If you join the mailing list you can be sure I will email you the latest links to the latest videos with on the latest platforms.

You can sign up to the Scrumnastics mailing list at scrumnastics.co.uk

WHERE DO WE GO FROM HERE?

Where Do We Go From Here?

Now you know how to use Leadernomics, Scrum (Scrumnastics), and Kanban and kanban in order to set up, lead and manage one or more teams whether they are online or not.

Congratulations! Well done!

Like achieving any accomplishment in life, you' may be thinking, "but I don't know enough! I feel a fraud!" So just where DO you go from here?

Now what? Well, now we have the ability to lead, manage and deliver, we can grow your business. Here are just some ideas that we use with our clients

The Agile Contract[149]

What's the very first tool we reach for when trying to incentivise people?Money. Or rather, a bonus. This is a bonus scheme where we swap money for time.

The key is getting the client to agree to the payment of an early delivery bonus of 20% of whatever is left of the residual budget. This is crucial to the incentive for your people working. If they don't agree then they can't have the Agile contract.

The Agile contract gives the team a great incentive to work incredibly quickly and deliver great work. Whenever a client of mine has agreed to an Agile contract the work has ALWAYS been delivered early, including when we manage their people for them.

For example:

---

[149] I didn't come up with this, Jeff Sutherland, co-creator of Scrum did. However, it is such a good idea that we do use it as a core part of the Scrumnastics offer

* * *

Say we have a team that burns £15,000 per one week Sprint. The Product Owner has a total project budget £300,000 for the product. That gives us enough money for 20 Sprints to build something. If we need to go to 21 Sprints then we are in trouble.

In a traditional project management environment, the project managers on both sides of the table will have to have one of those difficult conversations. But both of them know that they have a 'sunk cost' of £300,000 and it is unlikely that the project will get thrown in the bin. The client will have to find more money.

Let's contrast that with the Agile contract where everyone in the team has half an eye on the bonus. It isn't hard to imagine that this will probably have an effect on team productivity. But it can also have an effect on the simpler solutions that the team will come up with. What if everyone got lucky and the team delivered a great product that the Product Owner loved but in only 12 Sprints instead of 20? That is a cost of £180,000 out of our budget of £300,000, leaving a £120,000 underspend. 20% of the underspend is £24,000, which is a worthwhile pot of money to be shared out equally among the team.

 Why would they work hard to do that? If they are consultants and contractors then that's commercial suicide, right? Well, not if you can get them more work it isn't.

I normally try and get the client to agree to put a bonus onto each of the project phases of Discovery, Alpha, Beta, and Live Production[150]. (Retirement phases tend to be treated separately). It may not seem like much but if you can deliver the results of a discovery early and get a bonus to the team early on in a project then that tends to add quite a bit of stamina to the team

As well as stating that we will work with our client with Transparency, Inspection and Adaptability (beat that, competition) we have an ace up our sleeve.

* * *

---

[150] The GDS phases, as detailed in the Scrumnastics ++ part of the book

Growing Your Business - And Your Capability

Once you and your team have got a bit of experience of using Scrumnastics under your belt, you need to start to think about growing your business by growing your teams. By far the most successful way to do this is to grow the team from the people you have.

The easiest way to do that is to think about succession planning. Succession planning is where you start to train your successors.

If you are working as a Scrum Master, keep a good eye out in your team for someone with the correct attitude and aptitudes to train up as a Scrum Master. Not everyone in your team will be interested in management, but it does no harm for everyone in the team to become a certified or a professional Scrum Master. To have members of the team knowing the reasons *why* a Scrum Master is doing a particular thing is always helpful.

I was once lucky enough to train an eight-person team who were eventually all able to become Scrum Masters. The spirit and support that they gave each other when they became Scrum Masters was amazing. As you can imagine, this is by far the easiest and cheapest way to create a management team but it doesn't happen very often.

If you can't find someone in the team itself, ask the people in your teams if they could recommend anyone they know that they would be prepared to work with permanently in a team.

You often get two benefits:

1. You get a name of someone who is a known quantity.

2. It often concentrates the minds of the waverers, and the reluctant leaders in the team and so they volunteer. A little bit of initial hesitancy can actually turn out to be a good thing, it often means they turn out to be first class leaders.

Offer a recruitment bonus. I do.

* * *

I know a lot of managers who love to use Employment and Contractor Agencies to get staff but I think the Agency model is actually completely broken. It's sad, but its time has passed. I recommend that you don't use Agencies for these reasons:

1. The quality of their people they supply can be really dire. Sadly, all of the people I have had to fire since 2013 have all come from Agencies.

2. The knowledge of most Agency 'account managers' is amateurish at best. If I want to use an Agency, I want them to save me time. I can't count the number of times I have asked for their top 3 C.V.s and received 12 inappropriate C.V.s from complete space cowboys instead. I can only believe the account managers were flogging used cars up until last week

3. You pay at least 20% of whatever you are paying in Agency fees. Worse, many Agencies cream money off the staff too to get double bubble. Yes, I know it is illegal to do so but many still do.

4. I would rather pay someone in a team 20% commission for the length of the contract. Knowing that the team member will be permanently working with their recommendation also tends to weed out the space cowboys.

Training And The Narrative

All projects are about change. Change takes people from 'here' to 'there' - that is, from a place we are not happy with, to a place that we hope will be better. That's the whole point of a project. But that is a risky business, so we had better prepare our people and our project as best as we can. What can we do?

The Project Narrative:

You will find your project will run a lot smoother if you capture and record all the reasons you have been asked to do the work, *__before you start__*.

Every successful project has a good narrative, and a narrative needs a beginning for it to work. It gives the project a memory, and that is important. If you don't capture how things were before you started, you may be amazed how quickly it will be forgotten. Let's face it, you and your team are there to make a bad situation better, otherwise you wouldn't be there. Although getting people to admit just how bad things were before you started, this is a process that definitely needs to be done. We call this process of capturing the origins, "reversing the hearse up to the front door."

Training:

"If you think that training's expensive – try ignorance." - Peter Drucker.

Your job will be much easier, and you will have greater success, if you train your team before you begin. There's lots of talk in Agile management circles about the need for Agile coaching and there's buckets of money being spent on that. But before you get to coaching you need to train your people *__first__*.

Bringing The Two Together: "Sprint -1: Mobilise the Team"

The two tasks for this Sprint are to:

1. Interview the CEO, or the project sponsor, and make a record of where they are and what the problems are.

2. This first Sprint only has to be one week long in total. In my experience, the actual training part will only take one or two days. It is probably a good idea to spend the rest of the week doing two miniature projects so that you can practice doing the events.

This Sprint is called "**Sprint -1: Mobilise the team.**" It doesn't take too long but you do need to do it.

Never Assume Agile Knowledge…

Don't assume that just because members of your team can talk a good story about having worked in Agile in previous roles, that they know how to *actually* work in Agile. As my grandfather used to say, "there's talking and there's doing." And now there are YouTube videos, too. Assume nothing and train them all. You will reap the rewards later.

When it comes to investing in some training, you may get resistance especially from your manager colleagues. It is very common for number-based managers to say something along the lines of "What if we pay for their training and then they leave?" My response has always been, "What if we don't train them and they stay?"

Sorry to bang on about this but it really is a lot easier to run a project if you train your people to know what is expected of them from the start. The biggest benefit of training early is that they won't need as much expensive coaching afterwards, because they won't have learned bad habits and they won't have to unlearn them. Unlearning is _hard_. It is really time consuming and really expensive.

Weirdly, this is actually how a lot of competition try to implement Agile. I know this because companies ask me to coach their dysfunctional teams. Of course, if they had been trained properly to begin with, they wouldn't have to call me to retrain and mend their teams. Trust me, this is expensive: management consultant expensive.

Wise Words For The Scrumnast:

But not you. You are going to train your team at the beginning. You don't actually need to send them on training courses, you can use what's in this book and train them yourself.

Before you start off, make sure to tell everyone that you are all going to be doing Scrum, and that it would be a really good idea to go and have a look on Scrum.org to see for themselves. This will show them their ways of working will be changing, and what their responsibilities will be.

People work so much better if they know where they stand because they don't fret with uncertainty. It is such an obvious thing but forgotten in many companies. Just train them.

Why? The simple reasons are:

1. It's MUCH cheaper to train your team at the beginning when they have no bad habits rather than further down the road and you have to get them to unlearn the bad habits.

2. They get up to speed quicker and become more productive more quickly.

3. They don't get into bad habits that slow the team down when they are doing real work and are very hard to iron out

4. Teams feel more valued and respected, both as individuals and as teams, if you give them some training and feeling valued and respected makes them work better and with more confidence.

Another Reason Why You Should Use Scrum:

You must know by now that I think Scrum is absolutely great. I have rescued a lot of projects by using it. It is robust, it stands firm, and I think it gives you the very best bang for your buck.

But there is another reason I think Scrum is great: Scrum is a brilliant stepping stone onto more sophisticated management frameworks. I have an ambition for you: I want you to use and understand Scrum and then be able to get to the stage where you can actually use the gold standard of all of the management frameworks, the Toyota Production System.

The Toyota Production System is *massive*. Anyone trying to implement it from a standing start would be daunted at the prospect. The Toyota Production System is simply too large and will take you far too long a time in order to get any return on your time invested.

Scrum Gives You A Path Forward

However, if you start off with a management framework such as Scrum, a great deal of what is in Scrum is already in the Toyota Production System. You could well be between one-third and half-way there.

As you can imagine, it's a great deal easier to build on top of a firm foundation than trying to start out with a clean sheet.

Now, the Toyota Production System is far too large for me to show you just how to implement it, but here is a very small example

From Scrum To Lean Management And Toyota

This is a graphic from Gary Convis, from Jeffrey L. Liker's book "The Toyota Way[151]." Now I am not expecting you to go into this right now, but look at that shape. Oh, look it has a triangle…

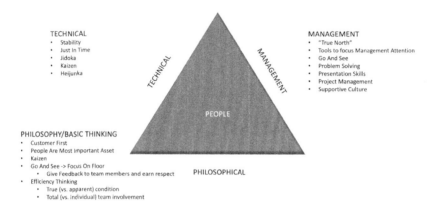

Toyota Production System Triangle (source Gary Convis, former President of TMMK)

TECHNICAL
- Stability
- Just In Time
- Jidoka
- Kaizen
- Heijunka

MANAGEMENT
- "True North"
- Tools to focus Management Attention
- Go And See
- Problem Solving
- Presentation Skills
- Project Management
- Supportive Culture

PHILOSOPHY/BASIC THINKING
- Customer First
- People Are Most Important Asset
- Kaizen
- Go And See -> Focus On Floor
  - Give Feedback to team members and earn respect
- Efficiency Thinking
  - True (vs. apparent) condition
  - Total (vs. individual) team involvement

TECHNICAL

MANAGEMENT

PEOPLE

PHILOSOPHICAL

Figure 70 The Toyota Production System Triangle

We know all about triangles in Scrumnastics, don't we? Here's another. Recognise it?

* * *

---

[151] Page 176 from "The Toyota Way." I highly recommend you buy this book

Scrumnastics – Start with Scrum and Move Towards Lean

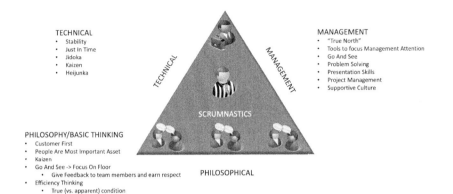

TECHNICAL
- Stability
- Just In Time
- Jidoka
- Kaizen
- Heijunka

MANAGEMENT
- "True North"
- Tools to focus Management Attention
- Go And See
- Problem Solving
- Presentation Skills
- Project Management
- Supportive Culture

PHILOSOPHY/BASIC THINKING
- Customer First
- People Are Most Important Asset
- Kaizen
- Go And See -> Focus On Floor
  - Give Feedback to team members and earn respect
- Efficiency Thinking
  - True (vs. apparent) condition
  - Total (vs. individual) team involvement

Figure 71   The Toyota Production System Triangle With A Scrumnastics Triangle Superimposed On It

And *that's* why I have been banging on throughout the book about why you should do Scrum first, and then borrow bits from the Toyota way.

Scrum is a great Swiss Army knife of tools for leaders and managers. A Swiss Army knife is a really handy tool, but I wouldn't want to build a house or rebuild my car with one.

When the job becomes bigger you need to get a bigger toolkit. There is no bigger toolkit for managers than "The Toyota Way."

The book, "**The Toyota Way,**" by Jeffrey L. Liker, is a really fine and valuable resource and I think is one of *the* management books that all Scrumnasts need to get hold of in order to take their skills to the next level.

Management Books for your library

Right, Scrumnasts. It's time to start developing your wider knowledge of leadership and management, and that means starting your library of management books.

I think it's a lot cheaper and better value to buy a few good books than enrol on an MBA course from Pontllanfraith University, so here we go.

I have spent a small fortune on management books over the years, most of which went into the recycle bin. I still have the ones below.

Best Agile Books

The elephant in the room: unfortunately, many Agile/Scrum books are terrible. I don't know why that is, but they are. The ones below aren't, and I still use all of these. Obviously, you have to make your own mind up, but I reckon you wouldn't actually be wasting your money if you bought these.

The Jeff Sutherland book is well worth the money.

Agile/Scrum Book Title	Author
"Scrum Mastery: From Good To Great Servant-Leadership"	Geoff Watts
"Product Mastery: From Good To Great Servant-Leadership"	Geoff Watts
"Agile Estimating And Planning"	Mike Cohn
"Scrum: The Art Of Doing More In Half The Time"	Jeff Sutherland and J.J. Sutherland

"Agile Kaizen: Managing Continuous Improvement Far Beyond Retrospectives"	Angel Medillina
"Agile Management: Leadership In An Agile Environment"	Angel Medillina

The Best Management Books

Management Books are *definitely* written to a higher standard than the vast majority of Agile books. I have no hesitation in recommending all of the books below. I think every one of them will raise your management game.

Management Book Title	Authors
"The Human Side of Enterprise"	Douglas MacGregor
"The Enthusiastic Employee - How Companies Profit By Giving Workers What They Want"	David Sirota, Louis J. Mishkind, Michael Irwin Meltzer
"In Search of Excellence: Lessons From America's Best-Run Companies"	Tom Peters and Robert H Waterman Jr.
"The Machine That Changed The World - How Lean Production Changed the Car Wars"	James P. Womack, Daniel T. Jones and Daniel Roos
"Lean Thinking - Banish Waste and Create Wealth in Your Corporation"	James P. Womack and Daniel T. Jones
"The Toyota Way"	Jeffrey L. Liker
"Toyota Kata"	Mike Rother
"Managing Flow"	Ikujiro Nonaka, Ryoku Toyama and Toru Hirata

* * *

Of course, if you want free internet resources, may I recommend you search for anything by:

William Edwards Deming

- my favourite management guru of them all - I learned more by reading him than from any other management consultant. A champion of striving for quality, he worked in Japan during the 1950s as a management consultant. Many of the very best Japanese management ideas sprang from him.

Konosuke Matsushita

- Was the founder of the massive Japanese company Matsushita, who are the real power source behind almost all electric cars, electric bicycles, makers of amazing consumer and commercial electronics and, when I worked there were the largest manufacturere of bicycles in the world. They also have a business plan that stretches 250 years into the future.

Matsushita's ideas are where it all really started for me as a management consultant. Up until I got familiar with them all the way back in 1995, I was very sceptical that *any* management philosophy could really make a difference.

Matushita has been renamed the same name as it's biggest brand, which is Panasonic. Panasonic have curated their founder's many management ideas on their own website. I think they are _definitely_ worth a read. They may be free, but they contain gold.

The Toyota Way & The Toyota Production System

Note: these are two completely different websites. The obvious pride that Toyota have in their ways of working stands heads and shoulders above all the others. I am not going to list them here because I would like you to go and read them for yourself. However, I can give no finer praise than to say whenever I have been stumped for an answer to a problem, This is where I have gone to search for an answer _first_, and I have never been disappointed with the result.

Final Wise Words For Scrumnasts -The Finest Project I Never Had To Do…

Preamble:

Not often, but sometimes, just sometimes, you get to do something imaginative that means you can flick a tiny switch over here, and it makes an absolutely immense thing happen over there. It is a little bit like being on the right end of a huge lever. That is, you don't have to put a lot of effort in yourself, but big things happen when you do. These situations don't come along very often, so I thought I would tell you about this one so that you can look out for something similar in your own work. And when that situation turns up you can think, "Ah, yes, I think I know what we should do here…"

Situation: Problems, Problems, Problems…

In 2016, the Department for Education had four problems:

1. As ever, state schools were not exactly awash with money.

2. Newly qualified teachers were finding it even harder to get placements and jobs than they normally did.

3. The traditional education sector newspapers that had carried job adverts for decades were seeing their revenues dry up as people were moving online and employment agencies were moving into the market.

4. Employment agencies were eagerly trying to get teacher training colleges to convince their students that they should sign up with them so that they could sell them onto schools for a considerable fee. Loose phrases like, "an £18 million opportunity every year," were being heard.

* * *

Task: What to do?

Well, the standard response would be for the Department to create some kind of free, official web-based job board. This would be where new teachers and schools could put their jobs and their CVs on, and everybody gets to find a match. Sounds easy enough... Perhaps.

The Pros and the Cons

Pros:

A case of 'problem solved,' just as long as:

1. The marketing of the site is just right, so everyone knows of its existence. That's every teacher/head/admin worker in every different type of school, and every teacher looking for a job.

2. That the site is easy to use and elegant, so people want to use it, and actually works all the time, every time. Also, you need employ the right technical support people to make sure the site keeps working all the time. And a helpdesk. That sounds expensive.

Cons:

1. Government websites tend to be clunky, confusing; they are often hard to use, people don't like using them and so do not have much of a history of success. Oh yes, and people have concerns about government getting even more data about them.

2. Websites and apps written and maintained by the private sector and run for government tend to be much better but are expensive to manage and maintain and are slow to respond to need for change.

3. Squeamishness of government departments at the thought of 'affecting the market,' (taking business away from businesses with well-connected directors).

* * *

Action:

Option 1:

Set up a quick (demonstration grade) jobs and applications website that matched up schools who needed student teachers with student teachers who needed a job. A 'proof-of-concept' app could be written in two to three weeks from scratch and hosted on the cloud so it could be accessed from anywhere. In three weeks, we could have something that people could see and use.

Now, there is a huge difference between 'setting up a demo website' application that can handle ten or twenty applications a minute and rolling out a heavyweight, robust, 24/7, scalable, nationwide application that has to be able to handle potentially hundreds of applications every second at peak times.

The demo app you can easily do in a few weeks, but the the heavyweight application that you actually would roll out requires a *lot* more work. Such as; How many servers? How powerful do they need to be? What software platform and operating system? What database vendor? Which languages will you write it in? How big a team do you need to complete it, and then run it? That means you are into a lot more money and great deal more risk of your project going horribly, badly wrong. And when government projects go wrong, they go *really* wrong, and they get into the newspapers and on television.

Option 2:

Or, if you are really lucky, you could charm someone else to offer to do it for you…

There are some people you bring in to work with you not because of what they do, but because of the outcome of what they can do. It's a bit like a rock band bringing in a star musician: you don't exactly know what they are going to do, but you know that when they sprinkle their pixie dust over whatever you are doing, the result will be magical. Luckily, I knew and had previously worked with a retired and really talented senior civil servant. Like most of these guys, he knew how things _really_ get done. Even better, he had a long list of memberships to some of London best gentlemen's clubs and a very good address book of personal contacts.

So, while I had the very expensive I.T. Team build a great looking demonstration web application that looked great on smartphones, tablets and computers, he and I had a chat or two and then I commissioned him to reach out to some directors of some of the education newspapers and invite them for a bottle or two of something rather special at one of his clubs.

Now most directors of large-ish companies would not return your telephone call, or my telephone call, but what I was buying was the knowledge that they would certainly return _his_ telephone call. His telephone call offered the prospect of tasting a bottle or two of something very nice while sitting in some very well upholstered leather armchairs.

As you can imagine, when they turned up at the club, my 'sound chap' did the pleasantries for a good twenty minutes. Then he sounded out their feelings about employment agencies intruding into their own business model, and also, because the government obviously could not allow schools to be fleeced, whether they had they seen the latest web job application service that the government was thinking of providing as a free service, and did they have any opinions on that?

Then my chap gave them a quick, five-minute demonstration of the app. He showed them how to upload a job, he showed them how to apply for the job, and showed the application details going to the school. He showed them the entire process. When he had finished, he gave them the web address so that they could try it for themselves on their smart phones. He told me they didn't even stay to finish the first bottle of wine.

Two days later, he was phoned up by the very same directors who were wondering that, if they offered their own, free, plain vanilla web application to schools and new teachers as a public service, would the government still feel as though it would have to go to all the 'terrible bother and expense' of offering a fully-fledged web service to the public. Especially with all the bad publicity that would blow up if it all went wrong.

I would love to tell you that this was all my idea, but it obviously wasn't. My idea was to explore whether we had other options. All I really did was tap into the ways and means that things actually get done at that level.

What my 'sound chap,' knew about them was that they had recently been taken over by some vulture fund investors, who were suddenly looking at a total loss in return for their squillion pound investment. What motivated them was that this nice 'sound chap,' was offering them two options:

1. Having their business disappear

2. A completely new business model that leveraged all the newspaper's good will in the market.

I often wonder just how many decisions at the top of business are made because of offers like that? Probably more than you and I will ever know.

Lessons

1. The government was looking at, perhaps, as much as £18 million a year extra expenditure if it did nothing.

2. If they had written an industrial strength web application, by the time you put the support desk and the maintenance on, you were looking at around £2 million to write it and £1 - £1.5 million a year to support it.[152]

---

[152] Yes, I am perfectly well aware that two of your next-door neighbour's kids could probably knock this up in a day, but this is government. I don't make the rules.

* * *

3. All I had to do to make it all go away was pay a one-off fee for a team of four developers for a month's work to make a credible but phoney web application (about £48k). Then about quarter as much again for the time of the retired Sir Humphrey, and his very expensive wine.

4. The best thing about having a demonstration app, is that you can demonstrate it, and not just to the intended audience. That makes it is tool in itself. The second best thing about having a demo tool is that it doesn't necessarily have to become anything more than a demonstration tool.

5. Sometimes it is better to enlist other people's self interest in avoiding potential losses because the prospect of loss will motivate them more than you will ever be.

6. So that's around £60k to make it all go away and, best of all, give the employment agencies[153] a little bit of a kicking at the same time. A good result.

---

[153] I can't stand employment agencies. I think they represent a nasty, grabbing, at-least 20% tax on doing business. It amazes me how business people will grizzle at a 20% VAT rate but think nothing of paying at least that on top of the rate of someone who can actually do something.

Scrumnastics? Where Did You Get That Name From?

Scrumnastics: The Doing Of Scrum

Scrumnastics means the 'doing of Scrum.' A bit like gymnastics is the stuff you do in a gym.

In 2015, a good friend and colleague and I were working as programme managers for one of those huge, American, global consultancies in a huge U.K. government department.

We were both programme managing humungous, multi-million pound programmes and projects with teams of hundreds of people. Then, as the contract wound down, we were given the task of transforming around seventy, hard-bitten, cynical, lazy, reluctant, middle-aged, grumpy project managers into shiny, new, enthusiastic Agile Product Owners and Delivery Managers.

Why did they ask us? Well, for one thing we had a reputation for rescuing projects that had gone bad and always being the last men standing. Besides, another global I.T. Consultancy had already charged an eye-watering fortune and had done a real dog's dinner of retraining the seventy. It had not gone terribly well. They were confused, demoralised and grumpy.

Instead of using people who had a history of delivering projects, they had used a bunch of Agile coaches who were more used to doing the theory than the practice. Unfortunately, that is fairly common. Actually, delivering projects on time and on budget is completely different to coaching people. Unfortunately, these coaches couldn't have delivered a postcard.

Luckily, we were both Certified Scrum Masters and we had also done decades of Agile/Lean projects. We were also qualified old-style

PRINCE2 programme and project managers too. That meant we had credibility in the eyes of the seventy, because we had been in the trenches with them. That matters.

Long story short, we inherited a complete mess. Anyway, there comes a point in some projects after you have chucked out all the experts and you turn to each other and just say "bugger it, we'll just have to redo it all ourselves and start from the beginning."

So that's what we did. We threw out all the crazy, incoherent, mind-numbing PowerPoint slide shows and created a two-day training programme delivered by the two of us. There was no Lego. The point was to convert old-style project managers into shiny, keen, Agile Project managers.

This training course was really intense.   But after they did the course, they not only knew how to do an Agile project, but they also knew why, when, and where to do it. More importantly, also the how, why, when and where not to do it.

We Called The Course "Scrumnastics: The Doing of Scrum."

Fast forward five years, mentor a lot of new, and not so new leaders, train a lot of managers, and run a bunch of completely online, remote teams since 2016, and you get this book.

Later, I was asked to write and deliver a shortened course for some senior civil service managers on the Government Digital Services "Agile Methods," so that they could Sir Humphrey and pretend they knew what Agile was when the particular Secretary of State, or the Minister asked.

One of the things that the Sir Humphreys were most interested in was how to scale Scrum so that you can co-ordinate multiple teams and multiple projects at the same time.

So, I added in a module on how my mate and I scaled up Scrum so you could co-ordinate and deliver much larger projects. How I scale Scrum is not the official way of scaling Scrum. But it works. I know it works because it is still being used today.

Lastly, you should know I am a self-confessed management nut: I am fascinated by the process of transforming a group of individuals into a high functioning team. No matter how many different frameworks I have explored Scrum has always been the one I turn to when the chips are down. In other words, whenever I have inherited a high pressure situation, I bet the farm on Scrum, and if I need anything extra I go and search the Toyota website.

You could do a lot worse…

Staying In Touch

Congratulations!

Wow, we got there! Well done, Scrumnasts. That has certainly been a journey, and now, we are at the end. Or are we?

Well, of this phase, at least. In another sense, we are only at the beginning. My dream for all you fellow Scrumnasts is that you continue to sharpen your leadership and management skills on your path to becoming the finest leaders and managers in the world. Goodness knows, our world needs all of us to be the best.

Please do go and buy the books I recommended to you in the "Best Books On Management" section. But don't buy them all at once. Try buying them on a one-per-month basis at best so that you don't get overwhelmed. I have spent a small fortune on management books over the past thirty years and, unfortunately, most are a waste of money: the ones on the "Best Books" list in the book are ones I use and go back to. I think they are the very best.

If you enjoyed this book and would like to stay in contact and receive tips and tricks on all things to do with leading remote teams and building great businesses, then why not become a proper Scrumnast and join the "Scrumnasts Club" mailing list? The link is on the website which is www.scrumnastics.co.uk.

We also have a Youtube Channel, called Scrumnastics, A Facebook Group, and, just in case I offend the algorithms in the future, various backups on things like Locals.io. Sometimes they called and sometimes they are called NickHewynHolmes.

The mailing list on the scrumnastics.co.uk website is free. I use it to talk about things like tips and tricks on:

Leadership for Agile Business Owners and Agile Managers
* * *

Moving From Scrum to Lean Management

Marketing for Business Owners and Senior Managers and Directors

80:20 (Pareto) analysis on your customers and your products, for Business Owners and Managers

You can join our mailing list by going to www.scrumnastics.co.uk (at the middle and the bottom of the home page). Every email we send will *always* have an unsubscribe option, and no, *we have never, and will not ever, sell your email address*. I have had it done to me and it is a pain, which is why I will not do it to you.

Please note, I will make occasional offers on online courses, etc. Again, if this offends you then please unsubscribe at any time, as I said above, every email will always have that option.

Other Help

Scrumnastics is a consultancy. In the consultancy world there are basically only three different types of consultancy. They are:

1.   Done by you -

Like this book or one of our online courses. You train yourself and you do it yourself. Will it be as good as us doing it? Maybe, maybe not, but it will certainly be better than what 99.99% of your competition are doing.

2.   Done With You -

We have a paid for club subscription. This is where I chair small groups of six (maximum) over Zoom in a 'hot-seat' environment where we share business problems (that includes me,) and we hold ourselves accountable for implementing the business ideas (and that also includes me). For the right people, it is hard work and great fun but it really is NOT for everyone. We also do seminars done by real-life, working managers on things like:

Leadership for Business Owners and Managers

Agile and Lean management for Business Owners and Managers

Moving From Scrum to Lean Management

Marketing for Business Owners and Managers

Pareto analysis on customers and your products, for Business Owners and Managers

3. Done For You - Scrumnastics Elite -

This may sound weird but I am not actually a fan of companies bringing in consultancies and consultants. I think it comes down to the old phrase "Give a man a fish and you feed him for a day. Teach a man a fish and you feed him for life."

We would rather teach, coach and mentor our partners because we think it is a better use of their resources.

We (myself and my fellow Scrum Masters and Product Owners) help you with things like:

1. A mobilisation service for new teams, called "**Sprint -1: Mobilising Your team.**" In the service train your team; we coach you and your team, hold your hands for the first few sprints and then we move to support and mentor you as you need us less and less.

2. A coaching service for established teams to accelarate them to become high performing teams

* * *

3. A mentoring service for mature and experienced Scrum Masters, Product Owners and Agile Coaches.

4. Product and Project Recovery Service: You have big, big problems and you have deep, deep pockets. We find out your problems, prescribe a solution and you are agreeable, help you to overcome them. But the emphasis is on you doing the work. Unlike other consultancies, we won't take any money off you if we can't help you.

5. Leadernomics Elite: A hot seat and accountablility club only open to business owners with real businesses (£250k turnover minimum). There are a maximum of 5 members per club.

Scrumnastics - Join Us?

I am putting this bit in for the last time in this book!

If you would like to see more handy videos, why not join the Scrumnastics mailing list? I post videos regularly on Youtube, FaceBook and the Locals platform.

Who knows what platforms we will all be using next year? If you join the mailing list you can be sure I will email you the latest links to the latest videos on the latest platforms.

You can sign up to the Scrumnastics mailing list at scrumnastics.co.uk (it's at the middle and the bottom of the Scrumnastics home page).

And Finally,

I hope you realise how well equipped you are now to become a great leader and manager. If you do not want to stay in contact, may I take this opportunity to wish you all the very best in all your endeavours. But please stay in touch and never lose hope, there are too many others depending upon us.

The Scrumnastics 250 year business plan:

"Harnessing the unique power of the team to unearth and unleash as yet undreamt-of wealth, technology, products and services for the benefit of all."

I really mean those words. I hope you will come to build something like this too.

I will leave the last words to Field Marshall Montgomery, 1st Viscount of Alamein. If you don't know him he was the man ultimately in charge of the two million men who took part in the Normandy landings in the Second World War. Two million men…

Here he is being interviewed in the 1960s by Lord Stephen Taylor.

Lord Stephen Taylor: "Can you use the same techniques as you used in the Army in civilian life?"

Field Marshall Montgomery: "Yes. The first thing you must do is conquer yourself . If you are going to handle men, and women too (which is much more difficult). If you are to control them, you must first learn to command and control yourself. To conquer yourself. Now I was never told that. If you can't command and control yourself, you will never be able to command other people.

If you are commanding large bodies of men, or even small bodies of men, you've got to get them with you, and feel that their best interests are in your hands, that you want nothing for yourself . You are entirely out to do the best for them. If you can do that, then men, soldiers, will follow you. Of course, all soldiers will follow a successful general, - they like it".

Printed in Great Britain
by Amazon

84807681R00251